Video Shooter
Storytelling with HD Cameras

Video Shooter
Storytelling with HD Cameras

Barry Braverman

AMSTERDAM • BOSTON • HEIDELBERG • LONDON
NEW YORK • OXFORD • PARIS • SAN DIEGO
SAN FRANCISCO • SINGAPORE • SYDNEY • TOKYO

Focal Press is an imprint of Elsevier

ELSEVIER

Focal Press is an imprint of Elsevier
30 Corporate Drive, Suite 400, Burlington, MA 01803, USA
Linacre House, Jordan Hill, Oxford OX2 8DP, UK

Notices
Knowledge and best practice in this field are constantly changing. As new research and experience broaden
our understanding, changes in research methods, professional practices, or medical treatment may become
necessary.

Practitioners and researchers must always rely on their own experience and knowledge in evaluating and
using any information, methods, compounds, or experiments described herein. In using such information or
methods they should be mindful of their own safety and the safety of others, including parties for whom they
have a professional responsibility.

To the fullest extent of the law, neither the Publisher nor the authors, contributors, or editors, assume any
liability for any injury and/or damage to persons or property as a matter of products liability, negligence or
otherwise, or from any use or operation of any methods, products, instructions, or ideas contained in the
material herein.

Library of Congress Cataloging-in-Publication Data
Braverman, Barry.
 Video shooter: storytelling with hd cameras / Barry Braverman.
     p. cm.
 Includes index.
 ISBN 978-0-240-81088-1 (pbk. : alk. paper) 1. Video recordings—Production and direction.
2. Digital cinematography. I. Title.
 PN1992.94.B75 2009
 384.55'8—dc22

                                                                    2009034244

British Library Cataloguing-in-Publication Data

A catalogue record for this book is available from the British Library.

ISBN: 978-0-240-81088-1

For information on all Morgan Kaufmann publications,
visit our Web site at *www.elsevierdirect.com*

Typeset by: diacriTech, Chennai, India

09 10 11 12 13   5 4 3 2 1

Printed in the United States of America

Dedication

To my father, who taught me to see the beauty in technical things

Contents

Acknowledgments

My many students over the years, who have been and continue to be a great source of inspiration and motivation; my friend Wes Anderson, who taught me how to let go of my stodgy old ways; Mira Nair and Musarait Kashmiri at Maisha, who encouraged me to mentor a new generation of African film-makers; Michele Cronin and Elinor Actipis, the disciplinarians at Focal Press who threatened my neck many times with a finely honed battle ax but never quite got around to actually killing me despite my tardiness in delivering this book; Jan Crittenden, Steve Cooperman and Doug Leighton at Panasonic, who provided endless insights and favors; Tom Di Nome at Sony, who supported me more than was perhaps wise or prudent; Jeff Giordano at 16×9, who knows the camera business better than almost anyone and who is also a great person to whine to; Joey Goodsell, Jason Osder and Kerry McLeod, who offered thoughtful suggestions and advice during the review process; Wayne Schulman from Bogen, who bent over backwards to fulfill my oddest requests; Susan Lewis from Lewis Communications and Ali Ahmadi from the Vitec Group, who presumably recognized a kernel of wisdom in all my ramblings; the inimitable Marty Meyer at Birns & Sawyer, who allowed me to run roughshod through her camera inventory for umpteen photos and evaluations; Fujinon's Dave Waddell and Fujifilm's Craig Anderson, who despite being sick to death of me responded to my never-ending questions about lenses and recording media; Lee Bobker at Vision Associates, who gave me my first professional assignment 30 years ago shooting soybean fields; Ira Tiffen, whose vast knowledge, enthusiasm, and love for photography I try to emulate; Sid Platt, my friend and mentor at National Geographic who placed his faith in me as a young inexperienced shooter and sent me to Poland, the Amazon, the North Pole, and other weird places; Ben and Zoe, my fabulous son and daughter, who so graciously posed for dozens of pictures and illustrations; and Debbie, Mary Lou, and my many friends, who've had to put up with me and my difficult ways, and who in their own unique styles and expressions of love encouraged me to write this book.

ONLINE RESOURCES FOR *VIDEO SHOOTER*
Companion Website

Please visit the companion website for *Video Shooter* to find exclusive online resources! You will find:

- EXCLUSIVE chapter on shooting video for DVD, Blu-ray, and the Web
- Video tutorials demonstrating storytelling techniques
- Technical matter, such as a comparison of various filters

The companion website for *Video Shooter* can be found here: *http://booksite. focalpress.com/Braverman.*

Please click on the "Register" link on this page. Please use the following access or pass code to validate your registration: VIDBRAVE2E

Once you have registered successfully, you will be prompted to create your own unique User ID and Password that you may use for all of your subsequent visits to the site. Please retain this information for your records.

Author's Website

Also, please check out Barry Braverman's web material. You'll always find something new and useful at these two sites: tips on cameras, lighting, lenses and accessories, craft lessons for the shooter-storyteller, and more.

www.videoscycles.com (comprehensive video storytelling resource)

www.barrybraverman.com (blog)

Always jaded. Always with an attitude. With no sacred cows.

CHAPTER 1

The Shooter's Point of View

1

Dear Video Shooter:

This is your task. This is your struggle to uniquely and eloquently express your point of view, whatever it is and wherever it takes you. For the shooter storyteller, this exploration can be highly exhilarating and personal. This is what makes your point of view different and enables you to tell visually compelling stories like no other video shooter in the world.

In May 1988, while on assignment for National Geographic in Poland, I learned a profound lesson about the power of personal video. The aging Communist regime had amassed a thousand soldiers and tanks in front of the Gdansk Ship-yards to crush a strike by workers belonging to the banned Solidarity union. I happened to be shooting in Gdansk at the time and despite it not being part of my official assignment, I ventured over to the shipyard anyway in light of the world's attention being focused there and the compelling human drama unfolding inside.

Out of sight of my government "minder," I understood I could've been beaten or rendered *persona non grata*, but I took the chance anyway as I was convinced that history was in the making. The night before, the military had stormed a coal-mine in south Poland and brutally beat many strikers while they were sleeping. Not a single photo or frame of video emerged to tell the horrid tale, but the news of the carnage spread anyway through unofficial channels. The shipyard workers figured that they were in for a similar fate, and I wanted to record a piece of it.

Considering the regime's total control over the press and TV, it was no surprise that the Press Office would deny my Arriflex and me access to the shipyard. But that didn't stop my two friends with less obvious video gear from slipping inside the complex in the back of a delivery van.

Throughout the fall and winter, Piotr and Leszek had been secretly shooting and editing weekly Solidarity newsreels out of a Gdansk church loft. Circumventing the regime's chokehold on the media, the two men distributed the programs through a makeshift network of churches and schools, recruiting daring young grammar school students to ferry the cassettes home in their backpacks.

Piotr and Leszek swore to stay with the strikers to the bitter end to capture the assault and almost certain bloodbath. Piotr's physical well-being didn't matter, he kept telling me. In fact, he looked forward to being beaten, provided, of course, he could get the footage out of the shipyard to me and the watchful world.

But for days, the attack didn't happen, and Piotr and Leszek simply held their ground, capturing the spirit-sapping exhaustion of the strikers as the siege dragged on. In scenes reminiscent of the Alamo, 75 men and women facing almost certain annihilation stood firm against a phalanx of tanks and troops and the provocateurs who would occasionally feign an assault to probe the strikers' defenses.

Amid the tension and long days of the siege, Piotr and Leszek made a startling discovery: their little 8-mm camcorder (Fig. 1.1) could be a potent weapon against the amassed military force. On the night of what was surely to be the final assault, the strikers broadcasted an urgent plea over the shipyard loud-speakers: "Camera to the Gate! Camera to the Gate!" The strikers pleaded for Piotr and Leszek to come with their camera and point it at the soldiers. It was pitch dark at 2 A.M., and the camera couldn't see much. But it didn't matter. When the soldiers saw the camera, they retreated. They were terrified of having their faces recorded!

As weeks rolled by, the strikers' camera became a growing irritant to the Communist regime. Finally in desperation, a government agent posing as a striker grabbed Piotr's camera, ripped it from his arms, and dashed off! The agent ducked into a building housing other agents, not realizing, incredibly, the camera was still running! (Fig. 1.2)

Inside a manager's office, we see what the camera sees: the Sony on a table pointing nowhere in particular dutifully recording the gaggle of nervous agents plotting to smuggle the camera back out of the shipyard. We see the camera then placed inside a brown paper bag and the story continues from this point of view; the screen is completely dark as the camera inside the bag passes from one set of agents' arms to another. And this became the filmmakers' point of view – a black screen with no video at all – conveying a story to the world that would ultimately prove devastating to the totalitarian regime.

FIGURE 1.1
The little camera that could: the Sony model CCD-V110 that changed the world in 1988.

FIGURE 1.2
When a government agent suddenly grabbed Piotr's camera, no one thought about turning the camera off!

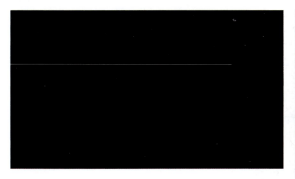

FIGURE 1.3
What's this? A completely black screen? If the context is right, you don't need much to tell a compelling story!

FIGURE 1.5
Conversely, we can force the viewer to focus more intensely on the visual, in this case, on the horrors of the war, by lowering or eliminating the audio entirely. Managing the interplay of picture and sound is the essence of the video shooter's craft!

FIGURE 1.4
In this scene from Orson Welles' "Citizen Kane," we listen to crucial exposition from mostly unseen characters in a dark projection room. Withholding visual content is the key if you want to communicate critical information in dialogue!

FIGURE 1.6
In video stories, 90% of the storytelling is communicated visually. Given the choice viewers always prefer to watch rather than to listen. They cannot effectively do both at the same time!

FIGURE 1.7
This man's eyes are shifty and avoiding eye contact with
the viewer. He may look great on the camera – but do you
believe a word he says?

FIGURE 1.8
Show me, don't tell me! Good storytelling requires strong
visuals to communicate effectively.

STORY, STORY, STORY

This business of developing the shooter's craft is really very simple. As the great
director Sidney Lumet famously observed,[1] story is the conduit through which
all creative and practical decisions flow. And this includes your choice of camera,
lens, recording format, resolution, and a thousand other technical and nontech-
nical things.

Truth is, audiences couldn't care less if you shoot your story on DV, RED Code,
35-mm Cinemascope or Pixelvision.[2] No one walks out of a movie theater and
says, "Great movie but it was shot 4:2:0." So as you read through and hopefully
learn from this book, let's keep this tech talk in perspective. Stories work for
different reasons and often can be quite successful despite a substandard script,
poor lighting, or even, I hate to say, amateur camerawork.

At the same time, we video storytellers have to understand there is a limit to this
notion, as our technical craft really does matter even if audiences cannot readily
recognize these shortcomings. Expressed viewer perceptions can be misleading,
but as with all things technical, we only need to know what we need to know
to support our story. Beyond that is pure geekiness, and geeks in my experience
almost always make lousy storytellers.

THE RIGHT TOOL FOR THE JOB

I'm often asked by new shooters, "Which camera should I buy?" "Which camera
is best?" These questions are rather loaded and are usually laced with fear. Yet
the answer is obvious: It's the camera that best supports the story you've chosen
to tell.

---

[1] Making Movies by Sidney Lumet 1996 Random House, New York
[2] Pixelvision From 1986 to 1989 the toy company Fisher-Price manufactured a primitive black and white
camera that recorded to a standard audiocassette.

There are trade-offs in what gear you choose, and one should be leery of selecting a camera on the basis of a single feature like imager size. Cameras with very high-resolution imagers may, indeed, capture greater picture detail along with more visible lens defects. Many high-definition cameras are also likely to exhibit inferior low-light response, constrained dynamic range, high-power consumption, and a bevy of shuttering artifacts. These shortcomings can impact your storytelling in a dramatically negative way, so the question becomes: Is the highest resolution camera available really what you want?

It may be. It all depends. Of course, the class and price of a camera reflect to a large extent the quality of images it can produce, but it is hardly the only measure when it comes to evaluating a camera. If close-focus capability is crucial to you for a documentary work (Fig. 1.11), then a small handheld camera with servo-controlled focus may be preferable to a full-size camcorder with manual control. High-end broadcast lenses will almost always produce sharper and more professional images, but they cannot (in most models) focus continuously to the front element owing to limitations of their mechanical design.

The physical demands we place on a camera can be intense. Television stations under the stress of a daily grind demand the most rugged, reliable gear they can find; anything less could translate potentially into lost stories and, presumably, lost revenue.

FIGURE 1.9
For National Geographic, I often shot in extreme conditions like this South American coalmine. My camera had to tolerate daily this level of punishment.

There is no perfect camera for every possible application and story. Each manufacturer's offering has its relative strengths and weaknesses, the compromises in each camera being much more evident, of course, at lower price points. If you know your story and know it well, you'll know the right camera for you. Like a carpenter or auto mechanic, the smart shooter understands the relative advantages of his many tools and how they might best serve his storytelling craft. (Fig. 1.12)

FIGURE 1.10
Cameras are all about compromises. For acceptable low-light sensitivity, we must often sacrifice some resolution.

FIGURE 1.11
The correct camera can dramatically increase your story-telling options. Some camcorders can focus literally to the front element of the lens for stunning close-ups!

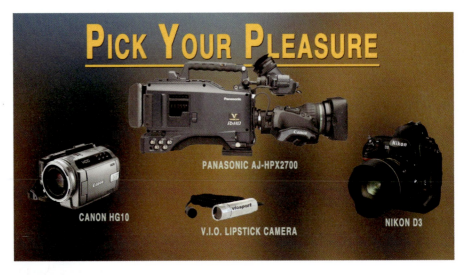

FIGURE 1.12
Are you shooting on a public pier without a permit? A tiny AVCHD camcorder may be ideal. Are you shooting a documentary for The Discovery Channel about the mating habits of the banded mongoose? A full-size camcorder with variable frame rates is perfect. Do you want to secretly capture passenger confessions in the back of a Las Vegas taxi? A lipstick camera fits the bill. Your best choice may not even be a video camera at all: Are you shooting a time-lapse of a cityscape? A DSLR with an intervalometer might be the right tool for the job. When it comes to gear, your story trumps all other considerations!

NO MORE CHASING RAINBOWS

The notion of a shooter as a dedicated professional has been eroding for some time. Now, for several hundred dollars and little or no training, anyone with a Canon HF11 or Panasonic SD100 can produce reasonably decent pictures; which makes for some pretty ugly competition for we professional shooters no matter how talented or inspired we think we are.

For the video shooter and storyteller to prosper in the current environment, he or she must become a twenty-first-century Leonardo DaVinci. Classical paintings, printing presses, and helicopter designs may not be in all of our futures, but the trend is clearly toward craftspeople who can do it all: shooter, writer, editor, producer, and all-around digital troubleshooter. These days, increasingly, we're talking about the same person.

I think of digital video as analogous to life itself. Just as strands of DNA comprise the building blocks of memory and heredity, so do zeros and ones constitute the essence of every digital device and application. Today's video shooter understands the new hyper-converged reality. Whether you're a shooter, actor, sound recordist, graphic artist, or music arranger, it doesn't matter. Fundamentally, it's all the same. We're all manipulating the same zeros and ones.

Twenty-five years ago on the Hawaiian island of Maui, I spent an entire afternoon chasing a rainbow from one end of the island to the other, looking for just the right combination of background and foreground elements to frame the elusive burst of color. It was, in many ways, a typical National Geographic assignment, circa 1985.

Today, I don't think many producers for National Geographic or anyone else would care to pay my day rate for a wild rainbow chase. Why? Because producers versed in today's digital tools are more likely to buy a stock shot of the Hawaii landscape (or create their own in *Bryce 3D*) and then add a custom rainbow in *Adobe After Effects*.

These folks, like the rest of us, are learning to harness the digital beast, layering sometimes dozens of elements to assemble their scenes. Whereas shooters were responsible for creating finished frames in the camera, today's image makers are much more likely to furnish the raw elements inside the frame to be rearranged, relit, or eliminated entirely by a multitude of downstream creative types including control-freak directors. After completion of principal photography for *The Phantom Menace*, George Lucas is said to have digitally recomposed landscapes and rearranged his actors in scenes, even removed unwanted eye blinks from his stars' performances! Alas! No one is safe in this digital-run-amok world! Not even the actors!

In my camera and lighting classes at film schools and universities, I recognize that my students are receiving digital arts training at a feverish pace. And what are they learning? To create backgrounds that never existed, to shift the color and mood of scenes, and to crop, diffuse, and manipulate objects in three-dimensional (3D) space. In short, they are learning the job of a shooter and an entire production company!

WEARING MANY HATS NOW

In August 2006, director Wes Anderson (*Rushmore, The Royal Tenenbaums, Life Aquatic*) asked me to shoot the behind-the-scenes show for *The Darjeeling Limited*, which he planned to shoot in India the following winter. Owing to the director's style and sensibilities, Anderson didn't just want a typical BTS show. Instead, he suggested a more personal approach in which my presence as a shooter and *interlocateur* would figure prominently.

Wes Anderson and I had worked together before, on the original *Bottle Rocket* in 1992, and we were actively collaborating again on a documentary in the summer of 2006. Now, Anderson wondered whether I could capture the essence of his latest project, the story of three brothers aboard an Indian Railways train chattering across the Rajasthan Desert.

Apparently, my proposed four-month stint in India posed a challenge to the studio. To support my modest budget, Fox Searchlight drew on the resources of multiple divisions – publicity, home video, marketing, and Web. That's how I came to wear many hats beyond shooting second unit; I was also editing and producing a one-hour HBO special, a thirty-minute featurette for DVD, sixteen podcasts for the studio Web site, and six EPK (Electronic Press Kit) interviews for news stations featuring the director and members of the cast. I obviously was no longer just a shooter but an ersatz producer, editor, DVD author and Web content specialist!

FROM THE SET OF THE DARJEELING LIMITED

FIGURE 1.14
A versatile go-anywhere camera expands your visual storytelling palette.

FIGURE 1.13
Prowling the streets of Jodhpur India. The performance of a full-size camcorder is indispensable for shooting high-detail city scenes and landscapes.

FIGURE 1.15
The smart shooter uses the right tool for the job. Here, the Panasonic HVX200 shares the ceiling dolly with a 35-mm Panaflex aboard the Darjeeling Limited.

FIGURE 1.16
Here, I double for Bill Murray inside a taxi racing to the Jodhpur train station. The HVX200 beside me captures the scene for the behind the scenes show!

'दार्जिलिंग लिमिटेड' ऑन रेलवे स्टेशन

वे प्लेटफार्म नंबर एक पर गुरुवार की दोपहर टोपी पहने एक विदेशी दोनों हाथों में सूटकेस लिए चीखते हुए दौड़ रहा था, 'हे... स्टॉप आर्थ एम कमिंग लवे स्टेशन पर सुबह से ही खुसरो फिल्म्स की कू ने डेरा जमा लिया था। यहां गुरुवार सुबह से हॉलीवुड मूवी 'द दार्जिलिंग लिमिटेड' की शूटिंग शुरू ई। दिन भर चली शूटिंग में स्टेशन के बाहर टैक्सी रुकने, टिकट खरीदने और हड़बड़ाहट में ट्रेन पकड़ने के सीन फिल्माए गए। बैकग्राउंड में ग्रामीण मों का ग्रुप ट्रेन के इंतजार में बैठा दिखाई दिया वहीं स्टेशन पर आम दिन जैसा ही माहौल दिखा। ट्रेन का इंतजार कर रहे पैसेंजर्स भी शूटिंग देखने स्त रहे। शूटिंग को देखते हुए कुछ ट्रेनों को दूसरे प्लेटफार्म पर लिया गया। वेस्ट एंडरसन निर्देशित 'द दार्जिलिंग लिमिटेड' की शूटिंग शुक्रवार को रेलवे स्टेशन पर होगी। इसके लिए पिछले दिनों ट्रेन के चार डिब्बे स्पेशल डिजाइन किए गए हैं जो सुबह प्लेटफार्म पर पहुंचेंगे। एक यूनिट जहां रेलवे स्टेशन पर शूट कर रही थी वहीं दूसरी यूनिट ने शहर में टैक्सी पासिंग के शॉट फिल्माए। — भास्कर

FIGURE 1.17
A visually compelling story lies at the heart of everything we do!

LEARNING THE DISCIPLINE

HD cameras have greatly expanded our storytelling capabilities. Even relatively modest cameras are capable of producing superb images, which begs the issue: *It's no longer a matter of who owns the tools; It's who owns the craft.*

And therein lies the challenge to today's video shooter: to acquire the discipline and skills necessary to realize his storytelling goals. It's not about a camera's imager size, "native" resolution, or which manufacturer's nameplate appears on the side. Exercising good craft requires a lifetime of learning and relearning, a task made even more difficult these days by the rush of new technology coming at us at warp speed.

Things were simpler for shooters in the 1970s. We lived in a mostly mechanical world then, which meant when our machines failed, we could look inside and figure out how they worked. We were more apt to troubleshoot and remedy a problem without having a theoretical understanding of bits and bytes or the inside track to someone at MakeItWork.com.

The mechanical nature of film cameras facilitated development of good craft because it imposed a fundamental discipline in the shooter. From manual loading of a magazine to setting of the shutter, lens iris, and focus, we could see and understand how the camera worked – and just making it function at all required some expertise. (Fig. 1.20)

Today, an entry-level camera runs on autopilot, is relatively foolproof, and offers better than decent

FIGURE 1.18
My 1966 VW. When it didn't start, you pushed it. No understanding of Firewire or USB required.

FIGURE 1.19
San Francisco cable car. The ultimate expression of the mechanical world we knew and loved.

FIGURE 1.20
My spring-wind Bolex propelled a perforated band of photosensitized acetate through a series of sprockets and gears. It was an easy process to see, study, and absorb.

performance, as evidenced in the clean images possible in relatively modest AVCHD camcorders. The dizzying pace of new technology has been disconcerting but also amazing, and the fact that camera manufacturers have made these advances with such economy is even more remarkable. If we consider the DV revolution that began in 1995, we can see the democratization of the medium and the empowerment of the masses in venues like YouTube and Facebook. We've seen the incarnation of a new generation of shooter storytellers from whom we can cite a litany of work, including feature films captured in whole or in part with inexpensive handheld camcorders: *Supersize Me* (2004), *Once* (2006), and *The Class* (2008) to name a few.

However, low-cost easy-access video has a dark side as well, and it has nothing to do with high compression, reduced color gamut, or shoddily manufactured hardware. No, my disdain for inexpensive video stems from one dispiriting realization that cheap technology enables – no, indeed encourages! – an appalling lack of discipline in the shooter. Given the low or no cost of shooting video today, there is an insufficient financial penalty for exercising a bad craft.

FIGURE 1.21
The film camera imposed a discipline and love of craft not easily gained in today's low-cost, auto-everything video cameras.

It used to be if a shooter knew the five Cs of Cinematography – camera angles, continuity, cutting, close-ups, and composition – that would be enough to assure a reasonably successful career in the film and television industry. For decades, shooters pawed over Joseph Mascelli's masterwork, which described in exhaustive detail the five components that comprise the shooter's craft.

When shooting film was our only option, the stock and laboratory costs were significant, and so the discipline of when to start-and-stop the camera was critical. Shooters and directors had to consider their storytelling options before rolling the camera or they would face severe, even crippling, financial pain.

I can remember in 1976 trying to line up the resources to shoot a PBS documentary on 16 mm. After an arduous struggle, I landed a grant for a few thousand dollars and can still recall the anxiety of running actual film through the camera. Every foot (about a second and a half) meant 42 cents out of my pocket, a figure forever etched into my consciousness. And as if to reinforce the sound of dissipating wealth, my spring-wound Bolex would fittingly sound a mindful chime every second en route to its maximum 16 1/2-foot run.

Thus the camera imposed a discipline and the notion of limitations. By necessity, every shot had to tell a story, with a beginning, middle, and end. Every choice of framing, lens focal length, actors' eyeline, and background had to be duly considered. A skilled cameraman able to manage the technology and craft of shooting motion pictures was somebody to be respected and appropriately remunerated.

Oh, God. I was such a special person then!

FIGURE 1.22
Shooting film required an essential understanding of f-stops and shutter angles, A-wind versus B-wind emulsions, and incident versus reflected light meter readings. There was a basic expertise required to shoot anything.

FIGURE 1.23
Sony's DCR-VX1000 introduced in 1995 transformed the kinds of video stories that could be told and by whom.

EVERYBODY IS A SHOOTER NOW

So what happened since those halcyon days of yore? The five Cs of Cinematography are of course still relevant – now more than ever. But look at who is exercising the hallowed cinematographic principles now. It's not just shooters. It's anybody with a hand in the filmmaking continuum: editors, directors, 3D artists, DVD menu designers, anyone with a newer Macintosh or fast PC, and that covers just about everyone.

So if everyone can afford a camera capable of producing high-quality images, the question is: do we still need the shooter specialist at all? Increasingly, it seems many producers are wondering the same thing, acquiring inexpensive cameras to shoot their own projects. And if you're an editor, you're in no better shape as your potential employers have access to the same low-cost editing tools that you do. It is the same for the beleaguered musician in this godless revolution where desktop samplers can produce results almost as good as having a 26-piece orchestra at your disposal.

So no craftsman is safe-not shooters, not editors, not anyone else. Several years ago, I was asked to shoot a few episodes for The History Channel's *Sworn To Secrecy* series. My assignment on the first show was straightforward: to fly with a "crew" to Spokane to interview Air Force pilots undergoing wilderness survival training. I was warned in the usual way that "the producers didn't have much money" – a refrain I hear on most projects, documentary and otherwise, these days.

Of course, shooting for a notable TV series, I assumed that the quality of audio was critical. Thus, on the plane out of Los Angeles, I couldn't help but notice that my "crew" was rather small, consisting in fact of only myself and the 22-year-old director. Not knowing any better I expressed astonishment to my boyish colleague who thought for a moment and then broke into a broad smile.

"I don't know why you're so happy," I said. "We're doing hours of interviews and we've got no soundman!"

"Yes," he said, his eyes shining brightly. "But I've got a cameraman!"

It was then that the depth of this depraved revolution really sank in. This newbie director, fresh out of film school, was hired to write, direct, shoot, and edit a one-hour show for a respectable cable TV series. And what was he receiving as compensation for this most onerous ordeal of ordeals? $150 per day!

Oh, God. I'm feeling ill as I write this. Maybe I'll just commit hara-kiri and be done with it. But first, let me pass along a valuable tip. In this brave, new world of low- and no-cost video, you cannot compete on price. As a shooter, whatever rate you quote no matter how low, someone will always offer to do the job for less. If you say you'll shoot a project for $100 per day, someone else with the same latest and greatest camera will bid $50. And if you bid $50, someone will almost certainly offer to do it for $25, and so forth until some poor loser *grateful* for the opportunity will offer to do the project for "credit"!

So forget about undercutting the competition. It's hopeless. We're all shooters now, and we have to deal with it.

STILL A PENALTY FOR BEING A ROTTEN SHOOTER

Of course craft matters – always has, always will! In the days when film cameras were all we had, the penalty for inefficiency and lack of storytelling skills was severe, so the "posers" lurking among us were quickly weeded out and returned to their day jobs.

Today, no thanks to the technology, such weeding out seldom occurs in any kind of predictable way. The posers with their thousand-dollar Sonys or JVCs simply blast away, cassette after cassette, memory card after memory card, until fatigue or boredom finally cuts them down.

And does it matter if they're not getting anything interesting or useful? Of course not. They keep rolling and rolling. Tape or hard drive space is cheap, they'll tell you, as if that's the issue. OMG!

Fact is, there's still a major penalty for a shooter's lack of discipline. Burning through a truckload of tape or flash memory cards will not save you if you're not providing what the editor needs to tell a compelling story. This means in most cases, providing adequate *coverage*, that is, the range of shots necessary to assemble a coherent and efficient finished production. In the cable documentary genre, you simply don't have time for the novice's shotgun approach. The successful shooter is consciously editing as he is rolling, watching (and listening) for cut points that will make or break the show in post.

Consider also the effect of returning to your Final Cut Pro or Avid workstation with tens or hundreds of hours of unnecessary material. Somebody (maybe you!) has to go through this onslaught of footage, log it, and capture it. This can be a costly and colossal waste of time and effort, truly God's payback for not learning good camera craft in the first place.

YOU HAVE THE POWER

Thanks to technology, today's shooter has enormous storytelling potential. You can use this potential for nefarious or unsavory ends as some storytellers have done, or you can use your camera to transform the world and create works of lasting beauty for the betterment of mankind.

It all depends on your point of view and the stories you wish to tell. The camera gives you the power. Now, the question is how to use that power wisely, creatively, and effectively.

CHAPTER 2

The Video Storyteller

Today is a great time to be a shooter. Owing to the proliferation of Web opportunities, cable outlets, and DVD, the demand for video storytellers is enormous, with experienced shooters regularly pursuing an array of interesting and engaging projects. Given the reality of today's fragmented marketplace, however, the video shooter must do a lot with relatively little and that's the focus of this chapter.

Today's low- (or nonexistent)-production budgets mean that shooters must adopt a highly-disciplined approach to the craft, and because modern video's perceived low cost tends to work against such discipline, the effective shooter must impose the discipline on himself – a major challenge for many of us for the same reasons we tend not to eat right, get enough sleep, or go to the gym.

MY FIRST TASTE

I got my first taste of DV in 1999 while working on a documentary series for The Discovery Channel. The inaugural show, focusing on the world's largest shopping mall in Edmonton, Alberta, was part of the series, *On the Inside*, which examined a range of lifestyle subjects. Until this time, my documentary work had been for the major networks or National Geographic, for whom I shot many educational films and TV specials on 16-mm film. This time, the exotic "wildlife" wasn't the usual gnus and bald eagles, but obstreperous mallrats, overzealous security guards, and flaked-out shoppers who haunt the sprawling mall's corridors and food courts.

CHANGING TIMES AND BUDGETS

In the not too distant past, the budget for a one-hour nonfiction program might have been half a million dollars or more and would have been almost certainly shot on BetacamSP or 16 mm. The shooter lucky enough to land such a project would have been treated like royalty, assigned anything and everything he could possibly want

FIGURE 2.1
The low-cost
DV format unleashed
a huge demand
for documentary
programs that could
be produced quickly
and cheaply. Today,
the appetite for
human-interest shows
appears insatiable.

to make the production run smoothly, including an affable soundman, lighting crew, and a five-ton grip truck.

Today, many shooters operate alone, and with the advent of cable and umpteen Web outlets, hard-pressed producers are targeting much smaller audiences and cranking out programs for a tenth of what they used to. For camera specialists with years of experience, the changes have been especially vexing, as programmers have turned increasingly to low-cost prosumer cameras to capture primary content.

The trick for shooters now is maintaining a professional look in a medium and business that has gone decidedly downscale. Indeed, for all the scrimping and cutting of corners, most viewers still demand broadcast-quality glitz regardless of whether they're watching *American Idol, The Situation Room with Wolf Blitzer,* or a neighbor's bar mitzvah. Of course, as a shooter who likes to work and work a lot, I feel obligated to meet that expectation regardless of monetary and other considerations.

Craft is and will always be the crucial factor in your success, not which camera you use, which flavor of flash media you employ, or which recording format you ultimately decide on. Craft is the most intangible of commodities, that elusive quality that places your head and tripod above the next guy who just happens to have the same mass-produced camera with all the same bells and whistles and useless digital effects.

FIGURE 2.2
The antithesis of small-format video. Great American photographer and a documentary filmmaker Willard Van Dyke prepares to shoot with an 8 × 10-view camera in 1979. To the great shooters of the past, every shot had to count. Composition, lighting, camera angle — it all had to work and work well in service to the story. Once upon a time, the economics of the medium demanded solid craft and clear, uncluttered storytelling.

TELLING A GOOD STORY

As a high-school sophomore competing in the New York City Science Fair, I constructed a Rube Goldberg-type device that garnered considerable media attention. Concocted from an old tube radio, a recycled coffee can, a photocell, and a hodgepodge of home-ground lenses and prisms, the motley assemblage dubbed *The Sound of Color* aimed to associate wavelengths of light with specific squeals, whines, and whistles. In the era of Apollo and men walking, driving, and playing golf on the moon, my crackpot creation purporting to hear colors did not seem *that* out of this world. Certainly, the concept made eyes roll for the hard-core physicists and engineers in the crowd, but despite this, *The Sound of Color* was a success (Fig. 2.3), eventually taking top honors at the fair and a commendation from the U.S. Army.

Of course, the Army knew that one could not *really* hear color. But it didn't seem to matter. The storytelling was so engaging that folks couldn't look away; isn't that what great filmmaking and winning

FIGURE 2.3
The melding of art and science. Your audience just wants to be told a good story!

science fair projects are all about? Telling a good story? Just as in any good book or piece of folklore, there must be compelling characters; in my case, I had the discarded junk: the Chase & Sanborn coffee tin turned makeshift heat sink, the pitched squeal of a 1950s tube amplifier, and the romance and thrill of a universe populated by fringe patterns and amorphous splashes of color. To most folks, including the Army brass, *The Sound of Color* seemed plausible and relatable – the two criteria that also happen to lie at the heart of every good screenplay, movie, or television show.

GO AHEAD! YOU CAN EXCEED 108%

In stories that are otherwise riveting, the shooter need not be overly concerned with technical anomalies, such as the occasional artifact or hue shift, as such (usually) subtle defects are not likely to threaten the integrity of the underlying storytelling. Four decades ago, I suspect the Army recognized *The Sound of Color* not for its engineering prowess (which was dubious) but for its engaging storytelling. The judges were responding to a *feeling*. And if the U.S. Army can respond in such a manner, there must be hope for the most technically obsessed among us.

Engineers will tell us that only 108% of a video signal can be recorded before *clipping* and loss of highlight detail occurs. But what does this mean in the context of telling compelling visual stories? Do we not shoot a gripping emotional scene because the waveform is peaking at 110%? Is someone going to track us down like rabid beasts and clobber us over the head with our panhandles?

In the ideal world, engineers provide the tools and not the rules for video storytellers. I can recall many an engineer over the years complaining bitterly about what they saw as my flagrant disregard for sacred technical scripture. But isn't that what a true artist does? Push the envelope and then push it some more, failing most of the time but also succeeding once in a while, by defying convention, exceeding 108% and pushing one's craft to the brink?

And so dear shooter, there's your challenge to wed your knowledge of the technology with the demands of your story; Yes, you need the proper tools at your disposal – the camera, the tripod, the lighting, and the rest – and you should have a decent technical understanding of all of them. But let's not forget that the real goal here is to connect with your audience and tell the most compelling *visual* story you can.

While breaking the "rules" should be a part of every shooter's playbook, my intent is not to transform you into a trogladyte or launch a pogrom against guileless engineers. Rather, I simply wish to offer the shooter craftsman a bit of insight into the technical universe that is inherently full of compromises. Of course, the competent shooter must be knowledgeable of the engineer's world, but the shooter must also recognize that the engineer's mission is not necessarily his own. The skilled video shooter knows that compelling stories do not begin and end with the shifting amorphous blobs of the waveform.

So go ahead, exceed 108%. Blow past it with alacrity. You may lose a touch of detail in the highlights, but where's the harm if you move your audience to laugh or cry, smile or grimace? Only make sure that those pesky engineers don't see what you're doing. After all, we don't want them having a coronary. We still need them to build our next-generation camera with a 60-megapixel imager and built-in 100TB Solid-State Drive.

PUT A FRAME AROUND THE WORLD

Go ahead. Try it. What do you see?

In the 1970s, in lieu of a social life, I used to run around the Dartmouth campus flaunting a white index card with a small rectangle cut out of it. (Fig. 2.4a,b) Holding it to my eye, I'd frame the world around me: there's a bunch of maple trees, there's an overflowing dumpster, there are my friends streaking naked through Thayer dining hall in 1972. It sounds silly in retrospect, but this simple exercise with a two-cent index card forced me to think about visually compelling stories, and oddly, it had little to do with the subject itself.

Indeed, I found that almost any subject could be interesting given the proper framing and point of view. Paradoxically, what mattered most, I discovered, was not what I included in the frame but what I *left* out. To a young shooter developing awareness in the art of the camera, this was a major revelation!

If you like the index card idea, you can go all out by placing a second similar card behind it. Holding the two cards to your eye and altering the distance between them simulates the variable field of view of a zoom lens. Expensive gear manufacturers might not appreciate this (almost) no-cost gimmick, but it can be invaluable to the new shooter developing his eye and storytelling prowess.

(a)

(b)

FIGURE 2.4
Go ahead, put a frame throughout the world. The world is a mighty chaotic place.

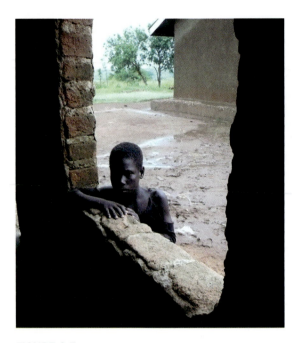

FIGURE 2.5
You can help contain the world's chaos by placing a frame inside the frame, for example, by shooting through a doorway or window.

FIGURE 2.6
The shooter's most valuable skill is the ability to exclude from the frame what is not helpful or essential to the visual story. The shooter storyteller must rigorously control the frame's boundaries, like the Old Masters and photographers of old.

EXCLUDE, EXCLUDE, EXCLUDE

This is the motivating force behind every great shooter: every element in a composition is there for a reason. Like every light has a function, every movement of the camera must advance the story.

As we go about our daily lives, we subconsciously exclude the irrelevant story elements, as the human eye is quite adept at framing the world and focusing on only what is integral. In our minds, we frame an establishing scene every time we enter a new locale. We enter a coffee shop (Fig. 2.7) and our eye is drawn to a friend seated at a table, and as we move closer, we seek (in close-up) the *relevant* story details in her face – maybe a tear, a runny nose, or bloody lip. We see these details and try to decipher their meaning, but we don't notice the distracting elements behind, around, and in front of her. The processor in our brains works constantly to reframe and maintain proper focus. And so without realizing it, we are creating a movie in our mind, composing, exposing, and placing in sharp focus only those elements that are essential to the "story."

The brain as an excluding machine is very efficient, but it can be overloaded. Feel blessed you're not the great comic book artist Robert Crumb, who was reportedly so tormented by the visual clutter in the world that it eventually drove him mad. Indeed, most of us living in large cities are only able to do so because we've learned to exclude the visual and aural chaos around us. Just as we don't notice after a while the roar of a nearby freeway, we also come to ignore the morass of hideous utility lines criss-crossing the urban sky. The camera placed in front of our eye interrupts this natural filtering process, the unintelligent image-gathering device having no automatic ability to exclude, exclude, exclude!

FIGURE 2.7
The movie in our mind. Without giving it a thought, our eye frames the scene at right, excluding what is irrelevant to the story. Your camera has no such built-in capability.

(a)   (b)

FIGURE 2.8
Like the roar of a subway, visual noise can be just as deafening. In framing a scene, the shooter must first identify then exclude the clutter that can undermine clear and efficient storytelling.

BACKGROUNDS TELL THE REAL STORY

It may come as a revelation that backgrounds often communicate more than foregrounds or even the subject itself. This is because audiences by nature are suspicious, constantly scanning the edges of the frame for story cues. An audience wonders: Is it supposed to laugh or cry? Feel sympathy or antipathy?

Poor control of background elements may undermine your story and communicate the opposite of what you intend. I recall a radical soundman friend who invested every dollar he earned in pro-Soviet propaganda films. His latest *chef d'oeuvre* sought to equate 1970s America with Nazi Germany, and so he hoped to

FIGURE 2.9
Don't get stabbed in the back! The rigorous control of background elements is critical! In every scene, ask yourself whether the background is working for or against you. i.e., is it serving the story you intend to tell.

open up the minds of Westerners to the *enlightened* Soviet system. The world has of course changed since then, and few folks would make this kind of movie today, but at the time, intellectuals ate this stuff up.

Now, you have to remember that this guy was a *soundman*, so it was understandable that he should focus primarily on the audio. Indeed, the film was little more than a series of talking heads, consisting mostly of out-of-touch university professors and fellow radicals. I recall one memorable scene in front of an auto plant in the Midwest. The union foreman was railing against his low wages: *"Capitalism is all about f---ing the working man!,"* he ranted.

Not surprisingly, the message and film played well in the Soviet Union where officials were eager to broadcast it on state television. When it finally aired, the show drew a large appreciative audience much to the delight of government apparatchiks and the film-maker, but not for the reason they imagined.

In the scene featuring the union foreman, the labor leader came across as compelling. His remarks *sounded* sincere. But Soviet audiences were focused on something else. Something *visual*.

In the background by the entrance to the plant, viewers could catch a glimpse of the parking lot where the workers' cars were parked. This was unfathomable at the time that workers at a car plant could actually own the cars they assembled. To Russian audiences, the parking lot in the background full of late-model vehicles told the real story; that brief glimpse and fragment of the frame completely undercut what the union foreman was so eloquently articulating.

So the lesson is this: the most innocuous background, if not duly considered, can have a devastating effect on the story you're trying to tell. *When you take control of your frame, you take control of your story!*

BOX-GIRDER BRIDGES ANYONE?

Compelling compositions can play a pivotal role in communicating the correct visual message. Considering the Great Pyramids and box-girder bridges, the triangle can be the source of great strength, lying at the heart of our most engaging and seductive frames.

The essence of developing a shooter's eye is learning to see the triangles in the world around us. These triangles serve our storytelling needs by helping direct the viewer's eye appropriately inside the frame. In prosumer cameras with excessive depth of field,[1] the relative inability to focus in clearly defined planes means we must rely more on composition and less on selective focus to highlight

---

[1]See the full discussion of depth of field later this chapter.

(a)

(b)

FIGURE 2.10
The triangle as a source of compositional strength was widely exploited by the Old Masters, as in *The Geographer* (1668) by Vermeer.

(c)

(d)

FIGURE 2.11
Like the steel-girder bridge, strong compositions often rely on the triangle for maximum strength. Whether realized or not, seeing the world as a series of triangles is a core capability of every competent shooter storyteller.

important picture elements. The video shooter, like a builder of steel-girder bridges, can derive great strength and storytelling prowess from compositions built on the power of the triangle. (Figs. 2.10, 2.11a–d)

THE LAW OF THIRDS

For centuries, the power of the triangle has been recognized by artists and engineers who've attempted to codify the overriding compositional principle. The Law of Thirds roughly divides the frame into three horizontal

FIGURE 2.12
The Old Masters seldom placed the center of interest in the middle of the canvas. As an artist, you too can take advantage of the Law of Thirds to achieve powerful compositions.

(a)   (b)   (c)   (d)

FIGURE 2.13
(a) The columns of the Pantheon dwarf the figures at the lower third of frame. TV's horizontal perspective generally precludes such vertically oriented compositions. (b) The eye is drawn naturally to the laundry lines and departing couple trisecting this Venice alley. (c) The kissing couple in front of La Comédie Française occupies a favored position at the right third of the frame. (d) A salt gatherer in northern Colombia. The empty two-thirds of the frame above increases the subject's apparent isolation in the desert expanse.

and vertical parts, the artist typically placing the center of interest at the intersection of one of the boundaries. A composition built on the Law of Thirds is the *de facto* approach for many shooters, a starting point for further exploration.

THE GOLDEN RECTANGLE

Centuries ago, the School of Athens recognized the power of the widescreen canvas to woo audiences. Today, HD shooters have inherently the same capability, as cameras with imagers as small as 1/5 inch are originally 16:9. Many camcorders now no longer shoot 4:3 in any flavor, shape, or form!

EVOKING PAIN

In general we want to connect with our audience and form an intimate bond. We exploit our craft to make viewers feel comfortable and welcome. But suppose our story requires just the opposite. Tilting the camera at a *Dutch angle* suggests a character's emotional instability or disorientation. Cropping the head off someone makes that person seem less human. Running the frame line through a subject's knees or elbows is fraught with pain and induces the same in the viewer. Maybe this is what you want. Maybe it isn't.

Proper composition and framing is not about following a prescribed set of rules but rather communicating a clear point of view. As a shooter storyteller, we have the obligation to infuse a point of view in every shot, and just as each scene in a screenplay must propel the story forward, so must every shot in a sequence accomplish the same goal. The story as it unfolds must never stop. We can abbreviate action to speed it up or milk a scene to slow it down by, but the story itself must never completely stop. *Ever.*

The point of view you embrace may be the one you're paid to present, but it is your point of view nonetheless – and it is your story, at least visually. So go ahead. Express your view of the world. Express it with gusto. Make Jean-Paul Sartre proud!

FIGURE 2.14
The Golden Rectangle can be highly seductive! There's a reason credit card companies chose 16:9!

FIGURE 2.15
In a true 16:9 camera, the imager is originally configured for widescreen, the 4:3 framing crops a bit from each side.

FIGURE 2.16
Ouch! Cropping through sensitive areas of the body can evoke pain in your viewer. *You dig?*

FIGURE 2.17
When shooting close-ups, the upper third of frame normally passes through the subject's eyes. Most viewers comfortably accept this composition as correct.

FIGURE 2.18
Respecting cinematic conventions can make your storytelling more efficient. Here, Air Force One is flying eastward from Los Angeles to New York.

(a)

(b)

FIGURE 2.19
(a) A compelling visual story has no rules! These "poorly" composed scenes for National Geographic recreated the rocking and rolling earthquake that devastated Mexico City in 1985. (b) The Dutch angle helps tell the story.

EMBRACE THE THEORY

Effective storytelling in whatever medium requires an understanding of point of view. Point of view determines everything in a scene from camera placement and choice of lens to the level of the horizon and the steadiness of a moving camera. After more than a hundred years, the conventions of cinema are well established. Today's video shooter would be wise to understand them.

Following is cinema's basic conceit (Fig. 2.20):

1. We see the protagonist.
2. We see what the protagonist sees.
3. We see the protagonist react.

That's it. This triptych is then repeated over and over until the movie concludes some two hours later.

Some filmmakers, like French avant-garde director Jean-Luc Godard, may pursue various detours along the way, but most cinema (especially *American* cinema) are constructed on this simple premise. Indeed, one reason why Hollywood stars command such huge fees is because audiences are conditioned to experience the film story through their points of view. This intimacy with the mass audience fostered over many decades of cinematic tradition has contributed mightily to the market value of a relatively few stars.

Expressing a clear point of view is the hallmark of a great shooter and director. In the classic, *Citizen Kane*, Orson Welles uses point of view masterfully to drive the story. When the scene opens at a political rally (Fig. 2.21a), the camera drifts in slowly towards the stage and assumes an extremely low angle of the candidate in front of a towering campaign poster of himself. It is soon revealed that this low perspective belongs to Kane's son who (literally) looks up to his dad. As the scene progresses, the POV shifts subtly so we are looking *down* on the candidate, his stature dramatically reduced from a high overhead perspective. This turns out to be the point of view of Kane's political rival who must now go off and expose the scandal that will ruin the candidate.

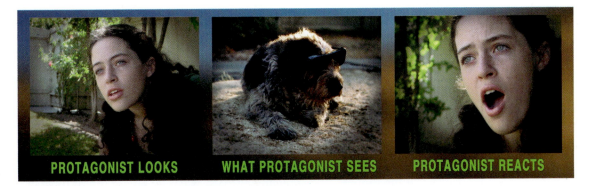

PROTAGONIST LOOKS   WHAT PROTAGONIST SEES   PROTAGONIST REACTS

FIGURE 2.20
The cinema distilled to its essence: Entering the protagonist's point of view as quickly as possible helps build intimacy with the viewer. Stories and characters in which the viewer feels a strong connection need not be technically flawless.

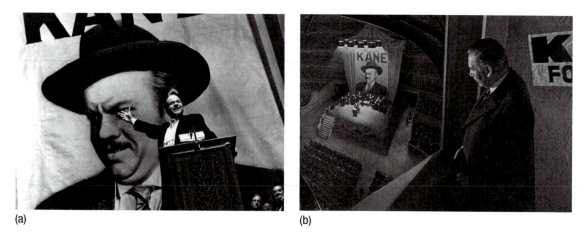

(a) (b)

FIGURE 2.21
(a) From his son's point of view, Kane appears larger than life. (b) Kane is looked down upon by his political nemesis. This shift in point of view propels the scene and story forward.

OVERSHOOTING AS AN OCCUPATIONAL HAZARD

While shooting I am constantly watching and listening for the cut points that will make for a unified and coherent show. It's really a matter of knowing what you want, which also implies knowing what you don't want and therefore don't have to shoot.

The temptation to overshoot is an occupational hazard for the video shooter. One reason is the low price usually associated with video recording that fails to sufficiently penalize a shooter's lacking of discipline. But there's another reason – insecure shooters and directors who lacking a clear notion demand the camera keep rolling no matter what. These folks figure that they must be getting *something* if the shooter is blowing through cases of videotapes or boundless gigabytes of data from a camera's internal memory cards.

In the days when craft meant everything and the recording medium (film) was expensive, shooters might barely shoot two 8-minute 35 mm magazines for a 30-second commercial. This happened to me on a health club spot in 1980. If I had shot more, I'd risk being seen as wasteful or incompetent. Now, on some assignments, if I don't shoot a case of cassettes per day or fill a 1-TB hard drive, I risk being accused of dogging it. "What am I paying you for?" I heard one producer bitterly complain on a recent cable shoot.

C'mon, what are we talking about? Certainly, bits of data stored in whatever form are relatively cheap. But that's not the whole story. Consider the poor devil (maybe you!) who has to review, log, and capture the umpteen hours of pointless drivel. Regardless of how cheap it may have seemed to roll the camera without much forethought, the shotgun approach is hardly a wise use of time and money. As a shooter and ersatz plumber, you must provide the range of shots and fittings to form a complete working system.

In 1987, I was on assignment in Lourdes, one of the most visited tourist destinations in the world. Each year, millions of visitors flock to the grotto in the south of France where the young Bernadette was said to have conversed with the Virgin Mary in 1858. To the faithful legions, the water in the grotto offers the promise of a miracle, and indeed, many pilgrims in various states of failing health come seeking exactly that.

From a shooter's perspective, the intensity etched into each pilgrim's face tells the story, and if there were ever a reason for close-ups, this would be it. I figured I would need two wide shots, the first to establish the geography of the grotto and streams of pilgrims and the second to reveal the crutches abandoned at the grotto exit, presumably by pilgrims who had been miraculously cured.

In practical terms, I usually work my subjects from the outside in (Fig. 2.22a), meaning I do my establishing shots first, and then move in, exploring interesting

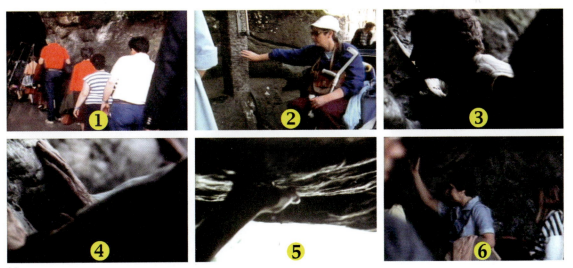

(a)

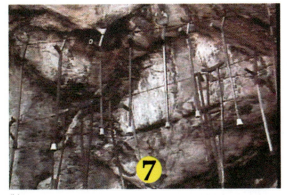

(b)

FIGURE 2.22
(a) The grotto scene from the 1987 Lourdes documentary illustrates good coverage. In the opening shot, we establish the grotto. We reverse and work closer in shot 2. Close-up shots 3, 4, and 5 do most of the storytelling in the scene. The pilgrims crossing in shot 6 provide the transition to a tilt up to the crutches (7) abandoned by pilgrims. (2.22b)
(b) The abandoned crutches of presumed miraculously cured pilgrims.

angles along the way. Thus, the viewer shares in my exploration, as I uncover compelling details in tighter and tighter close-ups.

This exploration can be exhilarating for an audience. In the grotto, the close-ups told a gripping and emotional story: the outstretched hands rubbing across the rock, a pilgrim woman in semi-silhouette kissing the grotto wall, and the hands of believers clutching a well-worn crucifix or rosary.

CLOSE-UPS TELL THE STORY!

Any shooter worth his lens cap understands that close-ups do most of the heavy lifting in video storytelling. That close-ups play such a key role should not be surprising as television owing to its traditional small screen is by nature a medium of close-ups. With the Web and computer screens becoming a principal display environment for much of our work, the fundamentals haven't changed; the smart shooter knows that effective video stories still rely principally on close-ups to properly focus and engage the viewer.

(a)

(b)

(c)

(d)

FIGURE 2.23
(a) A tear running down a cheek. This is a sad story. (b) Getting married. This is the story of a happy couple. (c) A girl and her dog. Love is a furry friend. (d) Gears and cables. This is the story of a precision machine!

I often describe my job as analogous to a plumber. To assemble a working system, I need a range of fittings – a way in, a way out – plus the runs of longer pipe, i.e., the close-ups that do most of the work and ensure functionality and efficiency. Shooting a boatload of tape, discs, or flash memory cards will not save you if you're not providing the range of shots necessary to tell a visually compelling story.

It's not about how much footage you shoot. It's the coverage you provide.

ATTACK CLOSE-UPS OBLIQUELY

Just as a tiger doesn't attack his prey in a straight line, so should you not approach your subject too directly. Sometimes a lazy cameraman will simply push in with the zoom to grab a close-up, as in Fig. 2.24b. This lazy close-up should be avoided, however, as the intended point of view is unclear, and the story's natural flow and shot progression are disrupted. Better that the camera comes around and unmistakably enters one or the other character's perspective. (Fig. 2.24c)

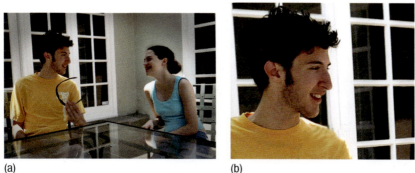

(a)   (b)

(c)   (d)

FIGURE 2.24
(a) Moving in at an oblique angle enables the viewer to see slightly around your subject, thus heightening the three-dimensional (3D) illusion. Don't just zoom in! Come around! (b) The "lazy" close-up. (c) Correct. When dollying into a close-up, the size and position of the talent in frame may be subtly adjusted. Focus and exposure may also be seamlessly tweaked with the repositioning camera. (d) A shooter crouches uncomfortably to achieve the proper eyeline.

THE POWER OF EYELINE

As noted in the campaign rally scene from *Citzen Kane* (Fig. 2.21a), an eyeline captured from below can impart power and stature to a subject, while an eyeline looking down diminishes the subject, as might be appropriate in an interrogation. With multiple actors, the eyeline helps orient the audience to the geography of a scene and the relative positions of the players. When shooting interviews or working with talent, we generally place the camera slightly below eye level. This imparts an air of respect and authority without it appearing heavy-handedly so.

SHOOTING THE LESS THAN PERFECT

The appropriate eyeline can de-emphasize shortcomings in an actor's face. A double chin or large nostrils, for example, are less noticeable with the camera set slightly above eye level. Conversely, a man self-conscious about his baldness might appreciate a lower angle eyeline that reduces the visibility of his naked pate.

Following are a few tips to handle potentially delicate issues:

- Are you shooting someone with an unusually long nose? Consider orienting him more frontally.
- Are you shooting someone with a broad, flat nose? Consider more of a profile.
- Are you shooting someone with a facial scar or disfigurement? Turn the imperfection away from camera. If this is not possible or in the case of a bad complexion overall, reduce camera detail level, use a supplemental diffusion filter, and/or light flatly to reduce texture and visibility.

UH UH. NOT FLATTERING   MORE FLATTERING

FIGURE 2.25
Study closely your subject's features to determine a flattering perspective. This is excellent career advice!

A MATTER OF PERSPECTIVE

Whether working in traditional fine arts or video, the visual storyteller fights a constant struggle to represent the 3D world in a two-dimensional (2D) space. There are two principal ways to accomplish this goal – through use of perspective and texture. Usually, we want to maximize both.

The lonely highway converging to a point on the horizon is a classic example of linear perspective. Linear perspective helps guide the viewer's eye to essential story elements inside the frame. (Fig. 2.26)

Aerial perspective is gained from looking through multiple layers of atmosphere in distant landscapes. Owing to the high contrast and fine detail in such scenes, the use of aerial perspective is not practical for many shooters with prosumer cameras that lack dynamic range and are thus unable to satisfactorily capture the subtleties. (Fig. 2.27)

Besides linear and aerial perspectives to convey a heightened sense of 3Ds, the skilled shooter also usually strives to maximize texture in his subjects. This can often be achieved through supplemental lighting to produce a raking effect, or as in Fig. 2.28, by exploiting the natural quality and direction of the sun and shadows.

FIGURE 2.26
In most cases, the shooter seeks to maximize the illusion of a third dimension. This scene, photographed by the author while bicycling across the United States in 1971, conveys the story of a journey and highway that seem to have no end.

FIGURE 2.28
This backlit scene with prominent shadows strongly communicates a 3D world.

FIGURE 2.27
Aerial perspective seen through increasing layers of atmosphere is seldom used to advantage in low-cost video but is common in classical art and still photography.

FIGURE 2.29
The receding cobble-stones in this Roman Street help lift my daughter from the 2D canvas.

FIGURE 2.30
Reducing texture in the skin is usually desirable when shooting close-ups of your favorite star. This can be achieved by soft lighting, appropriate lens diffusion, and/or enabling the reduced skin-detail feature in your camera [see Chapter 5].

WE ARE ALL LIARS AND CHEATS

As honest and scrupulous as we try to be, the successful video storyteller is frequently required to misrepresent reality. Skateboard shooters do this all the time, relying on the extreme wide-angle lens to increase the apparent height and speed of their subjects' leaps and tail grinds.

Years ago, I recall shooting (what was supposed to be) a hyperactive trading floor at a commodities exchange in Portugal. I've shot such locales before with traders clambering on their desks, shrieking quotes at the top of their lungs. This was definitely not the case in Lisbon where I found seven very sedate traders sitting around, sipping espressos, and discussing a recent soccer match.

Yet a paid assignment is a paid assignment, and I was obligated to tell the client's story, which included capturing in all its glory the wild excitement of what was supposed to be Europe's most vibrant trading floor.

So this is what I was thinking: first, I would forget wide coverage. Such a perspective would have only made the trading floor appear more deserted and devoid of activity. Clearly this was for a narrow field of view to compress the floor area and take best advantage of the few inert bodies I had at my disposal.

FIGURE 2.31
As a cheater-storyteller, the video shooter is often required to misrepresent reality. Through a combination of tight framing, use of a long lens, and abundant close-ups, this nearly deserted trading floor appears full of life.

Stacking one trader behind the other, I instantly created the impression (albeit a false one) that the hall was teaming with brokers. (Fig. 2.31) Of course, I still had to compel my laid-back cadre to wave their arms and bark a few orders, but that was easy. The main thing was framing the close-ups to the point of busting; these tight shots jammed with activity suggesting an unimaginable frenzy of buying and selling *outside* the frame. The viewer assumed from the hyperactive close-ups that the entire floor must be packed with riotous traders when of course quite the reverse was true. What a cheat! What a lie!

So there it is again: what is excluded from the frame is often more helpful to the story than what is actually in frame! *Exclude, exclude, exclude!*

SHOOTING THE ROTUND

Question: My boss thinks he looks fat on camera. Do you have any tried and true ways to make him look and feel thinner on camera? I can't shoot him above the waist or behind a desk all the time.

Barry B
One suggestion: Light in limbo. The less you show, the less you know! You can use a strong sidelight to hide half his shape. Keep it soft to de-emphasize any wrinkles and rolls. You can also add a slight vertical squeeze in your editing program. A few points in the right direction will often work wonders!

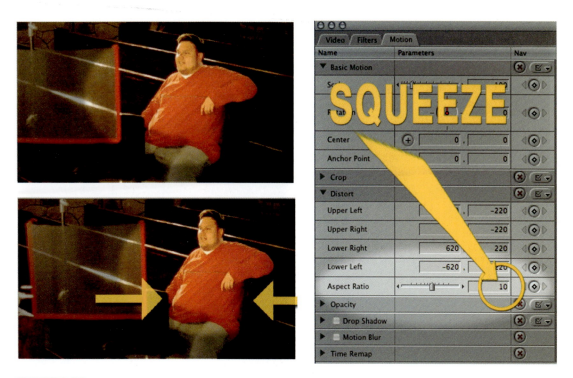

FIGURE 2.32
Shooting the rotund. Applying the squeeze. Hey, it's a lot quicker than Jenny Craig!

MAKE 'EM SUFFER

Like in any intimate relationship, it's a good idea to consider your loved one's needs. What does your viewer really want when seeing your images flicker across the screen? Most of all, he wants to be shown the world in a way he has not seen before and he is willing to work hard – very hard – to achieve it.

I recall interviewing the great photographer curmudgeon Ralph Steiner at his home in Vermont in 1973. Ralph was one of the twentieth century's great shooter storytellers, and his photographs, like his manner of speaking, were anything but boring. One afternoon, he clued me in to his secret:

"If you're just going to photograph a tree and do nothing more than walk outside, raise the camera to your eye and press the shutter, what's the point of photographing the tree? You'd be better off just telling me to go out and look at the tree!"

"Acquiring a unique perspective on the world is not easy. It's painful!" Ralph would bellow, his voice shaking with passion. "You have to *suffer*! Running around with a camera can be fun once in a while, but mostly it's just a lot of suffering."

FIGURE 2.33
Avoid like the plague medium shots at eye level! Such shots are boring and no wonder. They're what we normally see every day as we stroll down the street past the 7-Eleven or DMV office.

FIGURE 2.34
Interesting angles help build intimacy by drawing the viewer into your visual story.

FIGURE 2.35
"Curves Ahead" (Photo of Gypsy Rose Lee by Ralph Steiner).

FIGURE 2.36
A bird's eye view can offer a unique perspective. This view is of Venice's San Marco Square.

FIGURE 2.37
A shooter sometimes has to lie low—

FIGURE 2.38
—or get in the face of a recalcitrant subject and bear her wrath!

OBSCURE, HIDE, CONCEAL

This suffering notion is worth exploring because I truly believe the viewer wants to share our suffering. It's a noble thought, and it also happens to be true.

If you look at great cinematographers' work, you'll notice that they like to shoot through and around foreground objects. This helps direct the viewer's eye inside the frame and heighten the 3D illusion.

But what are we really doing by obscuring or completely concealing our subject at times, then revealing it, then maybe hiding it again? We're making the viewer *suffer*. We're skillfully, deliciously, *teasing* the viewer, defying him to figure out what the heck we're up to. Yes, point your viewer in the right direction. Yes, give him clear visual clues. But make it a point to obscure what you have in mind. Smoke, shadow, clever placement of foreground objects can all work, but however you do it, the key is not to make your viewer's job too easy. Make him wonder what you're up to and make him *suffer*, and he'll love you and your story for it.

FIGURE 2.39
Shooting through and around foreground objects can add a strong 3D sense and a touch of mystery to your compositions.

FIGURE 2.40
The nineteenth-century impressionists didn't make it easy for viewers and were greatly revered for it. Viewing a Van Gogh is an adventure! Try to instill a comparable challenge in your compositions.

JUST NOT TOO MUCH

While making viewers suffer is a noble and worthwhile goal, too much suffering can be counterproductive. Some shooters may express cerebral delight at alienating their audiences but most of us can ill afford such a result given the demands of earning a living and the nature of clients we are normally required to serve.

The successful shooter seeks to build intimacy with the viewer, while challenging him at the same time. We accomplish this primarily through close-ups, and by (1) placing less important objects out of focus, (2) cropping distracting elements out of frame, (3) attenuating the light falling on an object, or (4) de-emphasizing the offending object compositionally.

FIGURE 2.42
The cropping of distracting elements excludes what isn't helpful to your story.

FIGURE 2.41
Selective focus isolates what is important in the frame and helps to pull the viewer's eye into the scene.

FIGURE 2.43
The adept use of color and contrast can be integral to your visual story.

FIGURE 2.44
Strong compositions de-emphasize what is not essential. Here, my son's pointing finger gains weight in the frame while his mom (partially obscured) is compositionally reduced in importance.

Exclude, exclude, exclude! Like a screenwriter culls and trims his scenes. Like a soundman identifies and removes distracting noise. Like a shooter crops and frames, lights and focuses – in service to telling a more concise and compelling story.

KNOW YOUR GENRE AND MAKE SURE YOUR AUDIENCE KNOWS!

You're sashaying down the aisle of your local Blockbuster. What shelf is your latest epic on? Is it in Comedy? Horror? Suspense? Identifying your story's genre is the first step towards being an effective storyteller and ultimately reaching your intended audience.

My philosophy is simple: if your story is a comedy, your audience should ideally be laughing most of the time. Conversely, if your story is a drama about starving children in Africa, your audience probably shouldn't be rolling in the aisles. Of course, your comedy may have serious moments and your drama may be quite funny at times, but the genre or tone of your story should be clear from the first frame and evident in every scene, in the feel of the images, and in how they're framed, lit, and represented.

The effective shooter storyteller understands that genre and story inform every creative decision from camera and format selection to lens choice, framing and placement of lights. When considering a close-up, how close should it be? A loose framing is usually consistent with comedy. (Fig. 2.45a) Tighter choker close-ups are more associated with dramas. (Fig. 2.45b) The use of

(a)

(b)

(c)

FIGURE 2.45

The shooter provides visual cues to properly predispose an audience to the story. A loose close-up (a) may be right for a romantic comedy, while a tighter close-up (b) is more appropriate for a drama. (c) Thinking about your story and genre: How close should the close-ups be?

close-ups exclusively while withholding the greater context is suggestive of horror. Story and genre are one of the same. To properly prepare your audience to laugh or cry and respond appropriately, you must establish your story's genre from the outset.

WHAT'S YOUR POSTER LOOK LIKE?

Hollywood execs pose this question all the time in story meetings to evaluate writers' pitches. Previsualizing the poster for a production can be useful in helping distill the story to its essence. The story could be a corporate or music video, commercial spot or sweeping epic, but the requirement of a well-tuned story is the same: the ability to capture its appeal and uniqueness in a single snapshot.

FIGURE 2.46
Go ahead. Create a poster for your next production. Is the log line compelling? Do the characters grab you? Would you plunk down $10 to see the movie suggested in your poster?

KNOW YOUR LOG LINE

In the same way, as a poster coalesces your story into a single image, so does the log line help focus and communicate the story's theme. Ideally, this bit of verbal shorthand should convey both genre and tone, so the shooter and production team can make appropriate creative decisions.

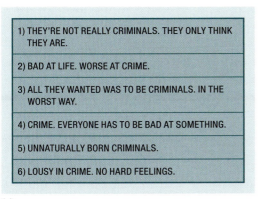

1) THEY'RE NOT REALLY CRIMINALS. THEY ONLY THINK THEY ARE.

2) BAD AT LIFE. WORSE AT CRIME.

3) ALL THEY WANTED WAS TO BE CRIMINALS. IN THE WORST WAY.

4) CRIME. EVERYONE HAS TO BE BAD AT SOMETHING.

5) UNNATURALLY BORN CRIMINALS.

6) LOUSY IN CRIME. NO HARD FEELINGS.

(a)

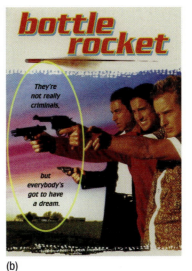

(b)

FIGURE 2.47

Acknowledging the power of the log line, Studio marketing departments consider and reconsider a movie's tag phrase ad nauseam (a). For Bottle Rocket (1996), Columbia Pictures pawed over dozens of potential log lines before making its choice (b).

EMBRACING YOUR LIMITATIONS

Whether bound by a tiny budget, sub-standard equipment, or too few crew, the limitations imposed on a project can be a positive force in your storytelling. Consider the eloquence of Vittorio DeSica's *The Bicycle Thief*. In postwar Italy amid the devastation of the Second World War, the filmmaker had barely scraps of film to capture his story. There were no studios so the filmmaker shot in the streets. There wasn't a budget for regular actors so nonprofessionals were cast. Most importantly, the story was stripped down to the essentials with few setups, focusing on the struggle of father and son, their survival and relationship, which is after all what audiences really care about anyway.

FIGURE 2.48

DeSica's *The Bicycle Thief* (1948). Storytelling stripped to its essence.

With today's cameras and digital tools, you don't need many materials to accomplish your goals. In fact, I bet you have everything you need to shoot your dream project right now: if you don't have a camera, borrow one. If you don't have a computer, use one at the public library. And if you still don't think you have the resources to pull it off then, well, focus more on story!

Story, story, story. It's what it's all about. It's all it's ever been about.

FOR DIFFERENT REASONS

Several years ago, I attended the premiere of *Titanic* at the Mann Chinese Theatre. The studio executives in attendance were clearly anxious as the $200 million epic unspooled in front of hundreds of underenthused industry insiders, including Bill Maher whose moans of protracted agony I can still vividly recall.

And who could blame him? The movie's trite dialog and banal love subplot were hardly the makings of great motion picture. Indeed, the polite applause at the film's end only served to underscore one inescapable fact: this movie was going to sink and sink badly.

Of course, things didn't work out that way, and the movie went on to become the top-grossing film of all time. This only confirms William Goldman's often cited observation about Hollywood that no one knows anything. But to me, there was a more critical lesson to be learned: *Movies work for different reasons*.

Titanic captivated young audiences who responded overwhelmingly to the tale of the doomed ocean liner. Cinematic elements – the well-staged action scenes, scope, and compelling score – appealed to teen-age viewers who never questioned the plausibility of Kate Winslet in a sleeveless dress perched atop the ship's bow in the frigid North Atlantic. Audiences worldwide accepted the story and film-hook, line, and sinker.

For the modest shooter, the lesson is clear: your stories, whether shot on DV, HD, 35 mm, or Fisher-Price Pixelvision,[2] can be hugely successful if audiences connect with them on some level. Of course, it would be foolish to tell a story with the scope of *Titanic* on DV. On the other hand, a smaller more intimate tale might work just as well or better. So when it comes to shooting a feature, documentary, or other project on low-cost video, it is really a matter of recognizing the entertainment value in your story and then focusing the bulk of your energy there.

YOUR COMPARATIVE ADVANTAGE

Every shooter storyteller needs to recognize his comparative advantage. That advantage might be personal in the type of stories you choose to tell. When you speak with passion, insight, and authenticity, audiences listen and respond. Only you see the world like you do. Only you have the stories and point of view that you do.

Prosumer video offers remarkable flexibility and economy. The trick is to recognize the strengths afforded by the low-cost medium and then exploit the hell out of them.

---

[2] Pixelvision's cryptic images continue to attract a following today, as evidenced by the annual PXL THIS Film Festival in Venice, California.

Such was the case for two Irish street musicians who adapted their personal experiences and artistic genius into a low-budget HDV feature that was eventually acquired by Fox Searchlight. The scrappy, heart-on-its-sleeve love story *Once* (2007) was hardly well shot; indeed much of it is out of focus! Nevertheless, the movie connected with a large and appreciative international audience who flocked to theaters and record stores to buy the soundtrack album.

We may never compete directly with the great moviemaker titans' *Spiderman* or *Batman Returns* but that doesn't mean we can't compete. We certainly can!

LIMIT YOUR CANVAS

Owing to their tiny imagers and relatively unsophisticated processing, inexpensive HD, HDV, and AVCHD cameras typically exhibit very deep shadows with little subtlety in the highlights. For this reason, shooters may want to limit the visual scope of their projects, with an eye to minimizing such scenes as expansive landscapes with very high detail and contrast. In general, character pieces work best when working with low-cost video; the camera and lens system perform best when high detail and a broad dynamic range are not demanded of it.

FIGURE 2.49
The modest HD shooter must be mindful of scenes with extreme contrast or detail.

RESPECT YOUR CAMERA'S DYNAMIC RANGE

Even the most modest prosumer camera is capable of producing superb images if you don't push it too far. The dynamic range of your camera is defined as its ability to capture a range of tones from light to dark. In low-cost models, the number of steps inside the gradient is typically less than seven stops, with the brightest areas in high-contrast scenes potentially appearing blown out and the darkest areas appearing as solid black devoid of detail. Respecting as much as feasible your camera's limited dynamic range will help retain detail at both ends of the spectrum, this being the single best thing you can do to improve the perceived performance of your modest SD or HD camera.

FIGURE 2.50
The modest images attainable from most prosumer cameras were never intended for large-screen projection.

FIGURE 2.51
It's the major reason why amateur video looks "amateur":
the loss of detail due to the clipping of highlights or fringing along high-contrast edges. Deep-punishing shadows
can also communicate to your audience an amateur feel.

FIGURE 2.53
Venice, California, beach at Magic Hour.

SHOOT THE MAGIC HOUR

Shooting just before dawn or after dusk has been
a favorite strategy of artists for years. At National
Geographic, my shooting day would typically
begin one hour before sunrise and not end until
long after sunset. In summers, this would result
in very long days, but it was necessary to take
advantage of the Magic Hour – that exquisite time
of day after sunset (or before sunrise) when the
landscape is softly illuminated only by skylight.
Like the Old Masters, the modest video shooter
should relish this time of day, the shooter being
able to produce remarkable results with even the
most basic camcorder. With the camera iris wide
open and error correction[3] off high alert, shooting
at Magic Hour is where your modest HD camera
really shines! (Fig. 2.53)

FIGURE 2.52
The Old Masters took advantage of this magical light for
centuries. Today's shooter storyteller should likewise take
advantage. Pictured here is *Les Glaneuses* by Millet.

---

[3] Robust error correction is fundamental to every digital recorder and playback device. See Chapter 3
"The Processor In Your Mind".

WATCH THE FRAME SIZE

Recognizing that close-ups sustain the shooter in matters of video storytelling, the true craftsman understands the importance of maintaining a consistent frame size. In narrative projects less professional camera gear can be a challenge in this regard particularly in dialog sequences.

When shooting a group of actors, the ideal shot progression quickly serves up a series of alternating *single shots* of each actor and his respective POV. If the players on screen are not consistently sized, the viewer may become disoriented as the storytelling reflected in each character's POV is less clear. Owing to many cameras' weak controls for zoom and focus, the maintaining of proper frame size can be difficult to achieve. (Figs. 2.54a,b)

(a)

(b)

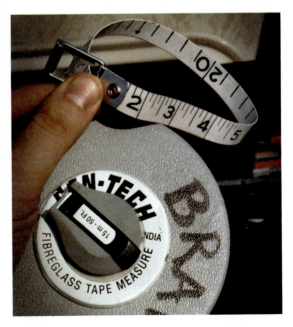

FIGURE 2.54
Many amateur productions exhibit an inconsistent frame size when alternating between actors' close-ups. The problem is exacerbated in cameras that lack clear witness marks for zoom and focus. To ensure proper continuity in dramatic productions, make a note of the lens focal length and distance for each setup, using a tape measure for accurate placement of the talent in reverse and reaction shots.

FIGURE 2.55
Most cameras with integrated lenses measure focus from the front element, not the imager plane!

YOU SHOOT, THEREFORE YOU ARE

Don't read this section if you are the self-absorbed type who believes that shooting is all about you. You relish your fanciful gyrations, dips, and swoons to call attention to your genius. In fact, you couldn't give a rip about the appropriateness of your shenanigans – the inverted camera, pointless zooms, and weird framings – you just want a vehicle to show off your talents as an *artiste*. Look, it's the same reason you don't pay your parking tickets, put money in the toll machine on the Dallas Tollway, or treat people you don't need very well. You shoot for a living so that makes you a special person, someone to be admired, fawned over, and treated like aristocracy. *You shoot, therefore you are.*

Problem is if you're one of these "special" types, someone has to clean up your mess, whether it's a poorly covered scene or an entire sequence in which the camera won't sit still. If you're a director who has been so victimized, the first order of business is to fire *Monsieur Artiste*. But what about his sickly footage?

Before opting for a costly reshoot, you should know there may be ways to remedy the diseased footage in software. In some cases, the unstable scenes may not have been intentional – for example, when shooting on a wave-tossed sea. I've used the tracker in Adobe After Effects

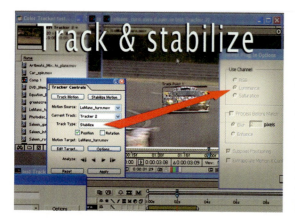

FIGURE 2.56
Many shooters are finding increased use for compositing tools like Adobe After Affects to stabilize a footage shot with a long lens, level a bobbing camera at sea, or remove the annoying breathing in footage captured with autoexposure.

FIGURE 2.57
The Smooth Cam feature in Final Cut Pro can compensate for an unsteady camera up to a point. The tool works best when applied to footage with unwanted movement along a single axis.

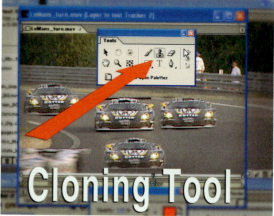

FIGURE 2.58
If you're shooting a racing movie and are short of cars, you can easily paint in a few more with AE's cloning tool. Same for crowds. You don't have to hire thousands of extras to fill a grandstand. The cloning tool in AE can do it for you.

(Fig. 2.56) to minimize the rocking effect with excellent results. Of course, it is always preferable to capture such scenes properly in the first place, as the process later can often be time-consuming and not particularly effective.

NO SHOPPING!

It's frustrating to work with directors who don't know what they want, and unfortunately, low- and no-cost production tends to attract them in droves. The low cost of capturing images with inexpensive cameras is surely one reason as newbie directors think it's somehow okay not to do their homework when the financial stakes are low. The experienced shooter can help these shopper-types choose a direction by helping frame the visual story well before the first day of shooting. The poster and log line exercises I described earlier can help!

FIGURE 2.59

No shopping allowed! If you're the director, do your homework, know what you want, and communicate that to your crew. To tell a compelling story, the shooter needs clear direction!

WORKING WITH THE EGO-CRAZED AND OTHER DIFFICULT PEOPLE

This may be your greatest challenge and perhaps the most critical aspect of your craft: how you manage and survive difficult personalities. It is critical as it will largely determine whether you succeed in the business of the video shooter. In whatever niche you find yourself, you're going to encounter egomaniacal types – maybe you're one yourself! – so it stands to reason that difficult-people-management is a skill worth pursuing.

I should know: I was one of these difficult people. I took myself and my craft way too seriously. Certainly, I was good at what I did and was recognized for it. But I was also a jerk. And it cost me in terms of relationships, more and better work opportunities, and even the perfecting and evolution of my craft. Bad. Bad. Bad.

It's no secret that relationships lie at the center of our success. After all, this is a business where freelancers rule the roost, and most of us work from project to project, producer to producer, client to client. We rely wholly on the strength of those relationships for our livelihood as well as our financial and creative well-being.

In my own career spanning over 30 years, I've never had a staff job or worked for one company exclusively. The freelance existence can be very exciting; one phone call can change your life and whisk you off to some exotic land. But the life of a freelancer can also be highly unpredictable. Fundamentally, our lives are insecure and fearful.

FIGURE 2.60
The occasional argument with a collaborator is part and parcel of the creative process. How you handle these inevitable conflicts is pivotal to your success as a shooter and human being.

The realization of complex video stories requires collaboration and a suspension of personal ego in service to the common cause. It's important to separate your emotions from the real artist in you, that artist being someone highly skilled in the craft but also who can listen and respond constructively to a director, even when disagreeing to your core with his or her seemingly unreasonable dictates.

It was only when I adopted this awareness, I was able to grow as an artist and human being. In fact, many of my collaborators' suggestions that I thought asinine at the time, I now consider strokes of genius and have since integrated them into my craft and into this book! I am a better shooter for it.

CHAPTER 3
The Storyteller's Box

We discussed how story is the conduit through which all creative and technical decisions flow. While *story, story, story* is our mantra, it isn't the whole story. Not by a long shot. Just as a painter needs an understanding of his brushes and paints, the video shooter needs an understanding of his camera, lens, and accessories. You don't have to go nuts in the technical arena. You just need to know what you need to know.

It should be reassuring that craft can compensate for most, if not all, of low-cost video's shortcomings. After all, when audiences are engaged, they don't care if you have shot your movie with a 100-man crew on 35 mm or single-handedly on MiniDV. It's your ability to tell a compelling *visual* story that matters, not which camera has a larger imager, more pixels, or better signal-to-noise ratio. The goal of this chapter is to address the technical issues that impact the quality of your images but only so much as they influence the effectiveness of your storytelling.

Consider for a moment *The Blair Witch Project* shot on a hodgepodge of film and video formats, including DV. Given the movie's success, it is clear that audiences will tolerate a cornucopia of technical shortcomings in stories that truly captivate. But present a story that is offensive, boring, or otherwise uninvolving, you better watch out! Every poorly lit scene, bit of video noise, or picture defect will be duly noted and mercilessly criticized.

FIGURE 3.1
The success of *The Blair Witch Project* underlies the power and potential of no-budget filmmakers with a strong sense of craft. The movie's ragged images were made a part of the story, a lesson to shooters looking to take advantage of low-cost video's flexibility.

FIGURE 3.2
Overexposed. Out of focus. Poor color. Maybe this is your story!

WHEN THE TECHNICAL MATTERS

The savvy shooter understands that viewers have a breaking point when it comes to technical shortcomings. Often this point is hard to recognize as viewers cannot usually articulate technical flaws or craft discrepancies in a scene, like an actor's face illogically draped in shadow beside a clearly defined candle. (Fig. 3.3)

However, this doesn't mean that audiences aren't negatively impacted. They certainly are! Illogical lighting, poor framing, and unmotivated camera gyrations all take their toll – the audience *feeling* every technical and craft-related fault you throw at it. The issue is whether these glitches in total are enough to propel the viewer out of the story.

FIGURE 3.3
Illogical lighting and technical flaws can undermine your storytelling.

THE TECHNICAL NATURE OF THE WORLD

Sometimes, while sitting in the endless snarl of Los Angeles' 405 freeway, I ponder the true nature of the world: Is this an analog mess we live in or a digital one?

There seems to be plenty of evidence to support the analog perspective. After all, here I am on the 405 aware of the sun rising and setting, the sky brightening and darkening in a smooth, continuous way. That seems pretty analog, and 99% of folks I've asked agree that the natural world we know and love is fundamentally an analog place.

Gazing over a sea of stopped vehicles, I suddenly recall my ninth-grade science class and remember how the eye works. My freeway experience is coming at me at 15 snapshots per second[1] flashing *upside down* on the back of my retina. So why am I not seeing all these cars with their road-raging drivers poking along, inverted, with an obvious stutter?

THE PROCESSOR IN YOUR MIND

Our brain is a *digital processor* that flips the image and smoothes out the motion by filling in the "missing" samples through a process of *interpolation*. In science class, we called this phenomenon *persistence of vision*. In video, we call it *error correction*. However you describe it, the world may only seem like an analog place. It could be a digital mess after all – or maybe it's a combination.

FIGURE 3.4
Is this an analog or digital mess?

FIGURE 3.5
Each day, the sun breaks the horizon and the sky brightens in a seemingly continuous manner. Yup. The world seems like an analog place to me.

LET'S HAVE AN ANALOG EXPERIENCE

Attach a dimmer to an ordinary incandescent table lamp. Over the course of a second raise and lower the light's intensity from 0% to 100% to 0%. In Fig. 3.6, this profound experience has been plotted on a graph.

FIGURE 3.6
The output of an incandescent lamp appears smooth, continuous-analog. The ideal digital recording approximates the analog curve as closely as possible, which is how we through years of conditioning perceive the world.

---

[1] While many scientists acknowledge the sample rate of the eye at 15 fps, some engineers consider the interpolated frame rate of about 60 fps as potentially more relevant.

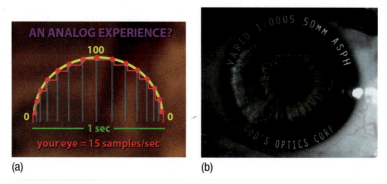

(a)   (b)

FIGURE 3.7
(a) Sampling the world at 15 "snapshots" per second, we need a lot of error correction to get through our day! (b) Our eye: Autofocus. Autoexposure. Good low-light sensitivity. Subject to aging artifacts.

CAN YOU READ THIS?

Olny ralley srmat poelpe can. Cdonuolt blveiee that I cluod aulaclty uesdnatnrd what I was rdanieg! The phaonmneal pweor of the human bairn! Aoccdrinig to rscheearch at Cmabrigde Uinervtisy, it deosn't mttaer in what order the ltteers in a wrod are, the only iprmoatnt tihng is that the frist and lsat ltteer be in the rghit pclae. Yuor bairn lkie any daigtil plyabcak dvecie msut alppy erorr crorceoitn bcesaue smalpes can asusme an inrcorcet vulae, bcemoe unrdaelbae, or mghit smilpy be msisnig due to a rdeutcoin in flie szie aka 'cmopsresoin'. If you can raed this, you got a good porcesosr on yuor souhdlers!

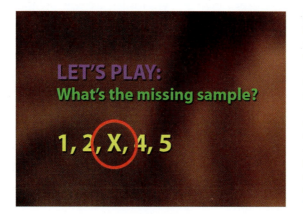

FIGURE 3.8
Let's play "Guess the missing sample!" If you say "3," you'll receive credit on your IQ test and be deemed "intelligent." But must "3" be the correct response? The "x" can be any value but "3" seems most correct because we assume the world is an analog place that acts in an uninterrupted way. So the brain applying "error correction" draws a smooth curve from 2 to 4 through the missing sample "3."

IMPROVING OUR DIGITAL RECORDINGS

The brain's processor interpolates missing samples based on certain assumptions about the world. This guesswork is prone to inaccuracies and may often lead to obvious artifacts and obvious defects in video and sound. To reduce the amount of guesswork and more accurately approximate the original analog curve, we can increase the *sample rate*.

A BIT OF KNOWLEDGE

A second way to improve the quality of digital recordings is to increase the *bit-depth* sampling. While adding samples reduces the step size and produces a smoother digital representation, a greater bit depth more accurately *places* each sample vis-à-vis the original analog curve.

When I'm in a mischievous mood I often ask my students "What is the most common element on Earth?" I usually receive a range of responses. Someone will typically suggest "iron," which would be correct if we lived on Mars; somebody else will often say "water," which isn't an

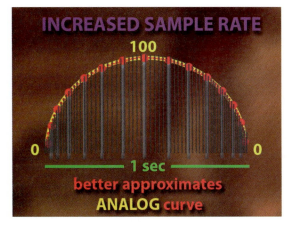

FIGURE 3.9
Increasing the number of samples produces a more accurate representation of the analog source and a better digital recording.

element but a compound; and some other folks may volunteer "carbon," "hydrogen," "carbon dioxide," or any number of other possibilities.

The correct answer is silicon which is the most abundant element on earth and essentially free, given the fact it is the principal component of sand. Alternately exhibiting the properties of a metal or a nonmetal, silicon belongs to a group of elements known as *semiconductors* because they might or might not conduct electricity depending on the presence of an electron bond.[2] If the bond is present, silicon assumes the qualities of a conductor like any other metal, but if the bond is not present – i.e., the electrons have gone off to do some work, say, light a bulb or charge a battery – the silicon that's left is essentially a nonmetal, a nonconductor.

The two states of silicon form the basis of all computers and digital devices. Engineers assign a value of "1" to a silicon bit that is conductive, or "0" if it is not. Your favorite electronic device executes untold complex calculations according to the conductive states of trillions of these silicon bits.

Like your brain, the traditional Charge-Coupled Device (CCD)[3] processor is an analog-to-digital converter (ADC). Its job is to sample every so often the analog stream of electrons emanating from the sensor. If the processor in your camera were comprised of only a single silicon bit, it would be rather ineffective given

---

[2]Yeah, I know it's more complicated than this, and we should really be talking about N- and P-type silicon, multi-electron impurities, and covalent bonding. See http://www.playhookey.com/semiconductors/basic_structure.html for a more in-depth discussion of semiconductor theory.
[3]Charge-Coupled Devices are fundamentally analog devices. Complementary Metal Oxide Semiconductor sensors perform the analog-to-digital conversion on the imager surface itself.

that only two possible values – conductor or nonconductor, "0" or "1" – can be assigned to each sample. Obviously, the world is more complex and exhibits a range of gray tones that can't be adequately represented by a 1-bit processor that knows only black or white.

Adding a second bit dramatically improves the digital representation as the processor may now assign one of four possible values: 0–0, 0–1, 1–0, and 1–1.

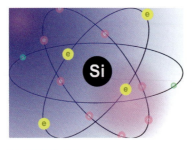

FIGURE 3.10
A silicon "bit" assumes one of two states: conductor or nonconductor, "0" or "1," black or white. You get the idea.

FIGURE 3.11
A 1-bit processor can assign only one of two possible values to each sample: pure black or pure white.

FIGURE 3.12
A 2-bit processor increases to four times the number of assignable values to each sample. The result is a dramatic improvement in the captured image.

FIGURE 3.13
An 8-bit NTSC/PAL television system produces a near-continuous gray scale and color gamut. Most HD formats – HDV, XDCAM EX/HD, DVCPRO HD, and Blu-ray – are 8-bit systems. Panasonic's AVC-Intra is a 10-bit recording format that produces very smooth gradients and exceptional color fidelity.

FIGURE 3.14
The Pixelvision PXL 2000 introduced in 1986 featured a crude 2-bit processor and recorded to a standard audiocassette.

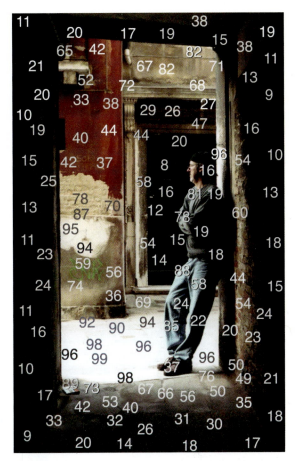

FIGURE 3.15
The world's passageways feature a delicate interplay of light and shadow. To capture the nuances, the video shooter requires an understanding of analog and digital principles. The analog luminance values in this Venice doorway are indicated on a scale from 7.5 to 100 (NTSC).

In other words, both the bits could be conductive, neither bit could be conductive, one or the other could be conductive, and vice versa. In 1986, Fisher-Price introduced the *Pixelvision* camera, a children's toy utilizing a 2-bit processor that recorded to a common audiocassette. The camera captured crude surreal images that have since inspired a cult following, including a popular festival each year in Venice, California.[4]

Most current CCD cameras utilize a 14-bit ADC. Because a greater bit depth enables more accurate sampling, a camera employing a 14-bit ADC produces markedly better, more detailed images than an older generation 8- or 10-bit model. The Panasonic HPX170 with a 14-bit ADC can select from a staggering 16,384 possible values for every sample, compared with only one of 256 discrete values in a 1990s-era 8-bit Canon XL1. Given the range of values available at 14 bits, it's very likely that one of those values will be an accurate representation of reality!

OVERSAMPLING: WHAT'S THE POINT?

Some shooters may question the wisdom of 14-bit sampling if the end result must be squeezed into an 8-bit format like DV, HDV, XDCAM, DVCPRO HD, or Blu-ray.

---

[4]The PXL THIS festival has been held each year in Venice, California, since 1991.

FIGURE 3.16
When shooting bright saturated objects, the strongest highlights may not be compressed evenly leading to a shift in hue. In some cameras, the orange in this basket may appear more like a lemon due to greater attenuation in the red channel.

Suffice it to say it's a favorite strategy among engineers to over-sample by 300–400% to preserve detail in an image's brightest highlights; the additional data is then folded down into the *knee* section of the camera's 8-bit recorded signal. Digital devices typically limit their playback output to about 108% of the video signal; so, some compression of highlights is inevitable to (partially) accommodate the huge amount of extra information. The highlight squeeze is helpful to preserve detail in what would otherwise be blown-out areas of the frame.

This squeeze, however, may produce undesirable hue shifts in some cameras due to uneven compression of highlights. (Fig. 3.16) The problem arises in saturated scenes when one (or more) of the color channels maxes out and is then compressed in a disproportionate way. In DV models such as the Sony DSR-PD150, the red hue shift in the highlights was especially apparent, and even though less of a concern today, some effort should still be made to avoid brightly saturated scenes when shooting with low-cost camcorders.

HUE SHIFTS IN SHADOWS

In low light, especially at HD resolution, hue shifts may become more evident in skin tones as the green channel is substantially more attenuated than red at minimum light levels (Fig. 3.17), leading to the excessively red faces and flesh tones.

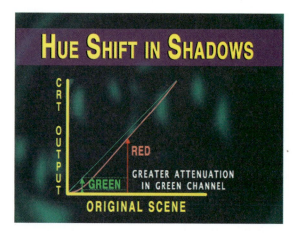

FIGURE 3.17
In low light, green is attenuated more than red; so shadow areas acquire a warm cast in some cameras. Monochromatic objects with little or no color do not display a hue shift because their RGB values are inherently equal.

FIGURE 3.18
Hue shifts are more likely to occur in Caucasian skin due to the predominant red tones.

FIGURE 3.19
Compression anomalies, including contour artifacts, are more noticeable in the shadows, so the shooter should look there first for trouble. (Illustrative images courtesy of JVC)

When evaluating a new camera, the shooter should pay particular attention to facial shadows. Cameras that display a noticeable hue shift, blocking, or other distracting artifacts should be rejected.

COMPRESSION: WHY IS IT NECESSARY?

Earlier, we established how more samples per second produce a smoother more accurate representation of the analog curve that defines our experience on Earth (as we perceive it to be). Of course, if we all had our druthers we'd shoot and record our programs with as many bits as possible. And why not? Uncompressed recordings, i.e., with no deleted samples, mean much less guesswork and error correction during playback. By eliminating encoding and decoding, we avert much of the noise and picture anomalies that come inevitably with the compression process.

In our daily jobs, we work commonly with uncompressed audio, and indeed, most cameras record two to eight channels of 48 kHz 16-bit PCM.[5] An

---

[5]Pulse code modulation (PCM) is frequently listed in camera specs to denote uncompressed audio recording capability. Many HDV and low-cost HD camcorders record compressed (MPEG, Dolby Digital, or AAC) audio.

uncompressed audio file is easy to identify by its telltale extension: *.pcm*, *.wav* (windows audio video), or *.aif* (audio interchange file format). If you're on a PC, you're probably working with *.wav* files and if you're on a Mac, you're probably handling *.aif* files. Practically speaking, there isn't much difference. It's mostly just a matter of how the samples are arranged and described in the data stream.

Keep in mind that uncompressed audio and video do not equate necessarily with a superior recording. At a low sample rate and shallow bit depth, a telephone recording may be uncompressed but it can hardly be considered "good" audio.

Chart: Uncompressed Audio Sample Rates
Telephone (typical) ≤ 11,025 samples per second
Web (typical)/AM Radio = 22,050 samples per second
FM Radio/some DV/HDV audio = 32,000 samples per second
CD audio = 44,100 samples per second
Digital video/DV/DVD = 48,000 samples per second
DVD-Audio/SACD = 96,000 samples per second

FOR PRACTICAL REASONS

Let's say we want to release the 92-minute masterpiece, *Romy and Michele's High School Reunion*, uncompressed on single-sided single-layer DVD. The capacity of the disc is 4.7 GB. Assuming a single uncompressed stereo track,[6] the audio alone would consume about one-fourth of the disc, approximately 1.1 GB. It's a big file but doable – theoretically, at least.

Let's now look at the video. Uncompressed standard definition (SD) requires 270 Mbps. At that rate, given the movie's running time of 5,520 seconds, we would fit less than 135 seconds of this glorious work on a single DVD. So right away, you're talking about a boxed set of 41 discs! That's borderline insane.

Going one step further, consider the same movie transferred to DVD as uncompressed HD. At the staggering rate of almost 1,600 Mbps, each disc would run a little over 22 seconds and the size of the collector's boxed set would swell to a whopping 250 discs! Loading and unloading that many discs in your DVD player is tantamount to serious calisthenics, and while cranking through the stacks of discs may be technologically feasible, it is

---

[6]PCM 48 kHz 16-bit stereo audio at 1.6 Mbps.

hardly practical, and so the need for compression to reduce the movie file size to something a bit more manageable and marketable.

REDUNDANCY, REDUNDANCY

What do compressors want? What are they looking for? The goal of every compressor is to reduce the size of a file in such a way that the viewer is unaware that samples (indeed most samples, 97% or more in many cases) have been deleted.

Compressors look for *redundancy*. A veteran shooter can probably recall holding up a strip of film to check for a scratch or read an edge number (Fig. 3.20). He may have noticed over any given stretch of frames that one frame seemed hardly different from the next. In other words, there seemed to be a lot of redundancy from frame to frame.

Engineers also recognized substantial redundancy *within* the frame. Consider a winter landscape in New England, a group of kids playing beside a snowman in the snow, and the sky is a typical overcast – a solid, slate gray. Your HD camcorder framing the scene divides the idyllic tableau into 4 × 4 pixel blocks, the camera compressor evaluating the blocks across the sky sensing little difference from block to block.

So the data from one block is retained, the bits from the "redundant" blocks are deleted, and a message is placed in the descriptor text file for the frame, instructing the playback device to repeat the information from the first block in the subsequent blocks when the frame is decoded and reconstructed. As a shooter, this gimmickry can be dismaying since I know the sky is not really uniform but actually contains subtle variations in color and texture. What happened to my detail?

FIGURE 3.20
In this strip of 35-mm film, one frame appears hardly different from the next or previous frames. Compressors take advantage of this apparent redundancy to reduce file size.

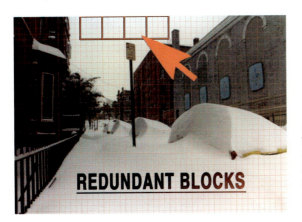

REDUNDANT BLOCKS

FIGURE 3.21
The HD camera divides the frame into a series of blocks down to 4 × 4 pixels. The blocks across the gray sky appear identical and so are deemed "redundant" and replaced with a mathematical expression instructing the player to utilize the values from one block in the subsequent "redundant" blocks when reconstructing the frame.

IT'S IRRELEVANT?

Based on decades-old assumptions, many engineers believe that humans lack an inherent capability to discern detail in dark shadows. Because we can't readily see the detail anyway, these engineers say, the detail is *irrelevant* and

(a)

(b)

FIGURE 3.22
Compression can be ruthless! The samples inside each block of the original are subject to "quantization," a profiling process (Fig. 3.22c) by which pixels of roughly the same value are rounded off, declared "redundant," and then discarded. Such shenanigans inevitably lead to the loss of detail and resolution in compressed files.

(c)

Intrablock matrix:								Nonintrablock matrix:							
8	16	19	22	26	27	29	34	16	16	16	16	16	16	16	16
16	16	22	24	27	29	34	37	16	16	16	16	16	16	16	16
19	22	26	27	29	34	34	38	16	16	16	16	16	16	16	16
22	22	26	27	29	34	37	40	16	16	16	16	16	16	16	16
22	26	27	29	32	35	40	48	16	16	16	16	16	16	16	16
26	27	29	32	35	40	48	58	16	16	16	16	16	16	16	16
26	27	29	34	38	46	56	69	16	16	16	16	16	16	16	16
27	29	35	38	46	56	69	83	16	16	16	16	16	16	16	16

can be discarded. Thus engineers look to the shadow detail in particular to achieve their compression goals. It is also why deep impenetrable blacks can be such a nagging problem, especially in lower-cost camcorders.

The assault on shadow detail can seriously impact our craft since we as shooters are often judged by the depth and character of our images' dark tones. Aren't shadows the essence of the Great Masters' brilliance and the principal ingredient of effective visual storytelling?

YOU DON'T MISS WHAT YOU CAN'T SEE

The mandate to reduce file size leads engineers to search for other presumed irrelevant picture elements, most notably in the realm of color space as it pertains to the limits of human perception.

Citing again my ninth-grade science class curriculum, the eye contains a collection of *rods and cones*. The rods measure the brightness of objects and the cones measure the color of objects. We have twice as many rods as cones, so unsurprisingly, when we enter a dark room, we can discern an intruder looming with a knife but not the color of his Evan Picone jacket.

In the video world, compression engineers adopted an analogous approach, mimicking the ratio of rods and cones in the human eye. Accordingly, your camera shooting 4:2:2[7] samples a pixel's brightness (indicated by the "4") at twice the rate of the red and blue components. Other recording formats, including DV's 4:1:1 and XDCAM's 4:2:0, further reduce red and blue sampling to achieve a greater reduction in file size.

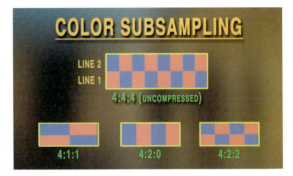

FIGURE 3.23
Owing to the eye's reduced sensitivity to red and blue wavelengths and the imperative to reduce file size, most cameras do not sample all three color channels at full resolution. While the green or luminance component is invariably sampled at full resolution, the blue and red channels are typically sampled at only one-half (4:2:2) resolution. XDCAM HD, EX, and HDV cameras utilize 4:2:0 color with reduced vertical resolution; every other vertical line is sampled alternately in the red and blue color channels.

INTERFRAME VERSUS INTRAFRAME COMPRESSION

In most professional applications and formats, such as DVCPRO HD, HDCAM, AVC-Intra, compression is applied *intraframe*, that is, within the frame. This makes practical sense since discrete frames are consistent with our workflow downstream that requires editing and processing, including color correction, at the frame level.

---

[7]The "4" in 4:2:2 indicates "full" resolution, i.e., the green channel or luminance value of a pixel sampled four times per cycle, 13.5 million times per second in SD, 74.25 millions times per second in HD.

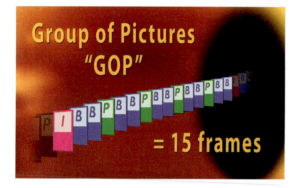

FIGURE 3.24
While the frame is the minimum decodable unit for most professional video, the GOP is the basic unit for HDV, XDCAM HD, and XDCAM EX cameras, which utilize inter-frame compression to achieve a smaller file size. A GOP size of 15 frames is typical.

However, in the further attempt to reduce file size, recording formats like XDCAM HD, EX, and HDV utilize *interframe* compression as well. In this case, the minimum decodable unit is not the frame but the *group of frames or pictures* (GOP), comprised usually of 15 frames, but reduced by hook and by crook to only one complete frame, the "missing" frames in each "GOP" being mathematically derived from the initial *intra* or I-frame. Within the GOP, the fields, frames, and fragments of frames deemed to be redundant or irrelevant are discarded and no data is written. In their place, a message is left in the GOP *header* instructing the playback device how to resurrect the missing frames or bits of frames based on the embedded cues.

Bidirectional B and predictive P frames enable long-GOP formats to anticipate action inside the GOP. The scheme seeks to identify and fill in completed action, referencing the previous I-frame, each B frame looking ahead and back in conjunction with a forward-looking P frame to precisely track changes inside the GOP interval.

H.264, also known as AVC,[8] utilizes a system of bidirectional prediction that looks ahead or back over the extended video stream, substantially increasing the codec's processing and decoding times. H.264 may be either long-GOP as implemented in AVCHD cameras or intraframe as used in Panasonic AVC-Intra models.

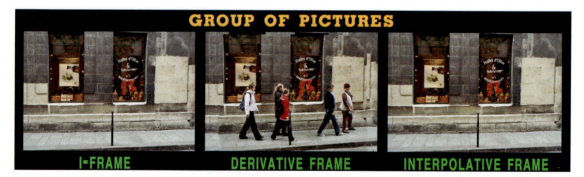

FIGURE 3.25
As pedestrians enter and leave the GOP, the background of the building is revealed and must be interpolated. Clues recorded during compression enable the playback device to reconstruct the missing portions of the frames by referencing the initial I-frame — the only complete frame in the (usual) 15-frame GOP. AVCHD cameras utilizing long-GOP H.264 compression consider the extended video stream for optimal file-size reduction.

---

[8]Advanced Video Codec (AVC) is one of several popular HD compression schemes in use today. A COmpressor/DECompressor ("codec") is a strategy for encoding and decoding a digital stream.

THE MINIMUM DECODABLE UNIT

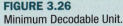

FIGURE 3.26
Minimum Decodable Unit.

In a computer, the minimum decodable unit is the byte, the 8-bit sequence that defines each stroke and key on a 256-character keyboard. In video, the minimum decodable unit is usually the frame, although in XDCAM HD/EX, HDV, and DVD-Video, the GOP is the minimum unit. Most nonlinear editors (NLEs) must decompress the long-GOP formats in real time to enable editing at the frame level. A fast computer is imperative.

THE IMAGER AND YOU

For years, the traditional three-chip camera has been a virtual imperative for the serious shooter. Single-chip models without the internal optics or processing were cheaper to manufacture and therefore sold for less, sometimes much less, but there's more to the story. Single-sensor cameras were at a disadvantage: the red, green, and blue sensors had to be merged into a supersensor with an overlying filter for achieving the required color separation. It's an imperfect process that applies with some variation to virtually all single-chip cameras.

The three-chip camera, on the other hand, utilizes a beam splitter or prism behind the lens to divert the green, red, and blue image components to the respective sensors. The result is discrete color channels that can be precisely manipulated according to the whim and vigor of the camera maker, compression engineer, and the shooter storyteller.

However, the three-imager approach has its own set of compromises. At some point, someone realized that the eye could be fooled into seeing thousands of colors when in fact it is only seeing three. Because of differences in the energy levels of red, green, and blue light, the component waves navigate the dense prism glass at different rates. The camera processor must then compensate and recombine the beams as if they had never been split – an imprecise process of considerable complexity. (Fig. 3.28)

FIGURE 3.27
Single-chip cameras without the intervening optics and compensating algorithms are inherently less complex than competing three-chip models.

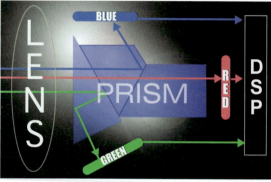

FIGURE 3.28
Three-chip cameras employ a prism behind the lens to achieve color separation. The strategy allows maximum creative control of each color channel.

FIGURE 3.29
Given their performance and ability to shoot under a wide range of conditions, three-chip camcorders have dominated the professional world for years.

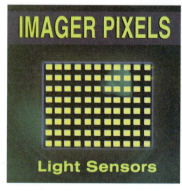

FIGURE 3.30
Organized pixel arrangement in rows.

PIXELS IN A GRID

We've all heard the endless discussion of *film* versus *video* "looks." Fundamentally, a video sensor resolves focus and edge contrast much differently than film. Film allows for a smooth transition of an object in to out of focus; this is due mostly to the randomness of the film grain and the more complete coverage that allows. By comparison, the regular pixel pattern of a sensor is interspersed with gaps (Fig. 3.30); so, the transition between sharp and soft is abrupt and thus appears more like "video" in the displayed image.

THE SPATIAL OFFSET RUSE

Engineers have long recognized the negative impact of a discontinuous grid pattern. The pixels arranged in neat rows made the manufacturing process easier, but it also inhibited the satisfactory recording of fine detail falling between the rows. This relative inability to capture high-frequency detail can produce a range of objectionable artifacts, most notably a pronounced chiseled effect through sharply defined vertical lines.

To suppress these artifacts, engineers adopted a strategy in some cameras of *spatial offset* (Fig. 3.31) whereby the green sensor in a three-chip configuration is offset one-half pixel with respect to the red and blue. To veteran shooters who recall not too fondly the finicky tube-type cameras of decades past, the notion of increasing resolution by deliberately moving the green sensor out of register seems illogical, but suppressing the most egregious sharpness and contrast-robbing artifacts seems to have precisely this effect.

The spatial offset ruse is not without its drawbacks. As a National Geographic shooter, I recall shooting many high-detail landscapes that contained mostly green tones. Given the spatial offset, a large portion of such images as a grassy meadow or lush rainforest would not be offset and thus subject to substantial artifacts and loss of image quality (Fig. 3.32a).[9]

Shooters with a penchant for high-detail landscapes may want to investigate the spatial offset, if any, in their camera. Most CCD models utilize some spatial offset. While the amount is fixed at the time of manufacture, some mitigation of artifacts caused by too much or too little offset may be possible by adjusting the camera detail level or adding a physical diffusion filter – the slight blurring actually improving resolution and contrast in scenes where fine details may fall inside the imager grid structure.

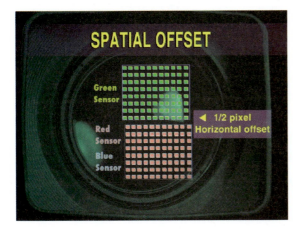

FIGURE 3.31
Applying spatial offset, the green sensor is moved one-half pixel out of alignment with respect to the blue and red targets. The strategy is intended to capture detail that would otherwise fall inside the grid, i.e., between the regularly spaced pixels.

---

[9] Conversely, the same can also be said for images containing very little green, as such scenes would also not be offset and thus subject to a loss of resolution.

(a)

(b)

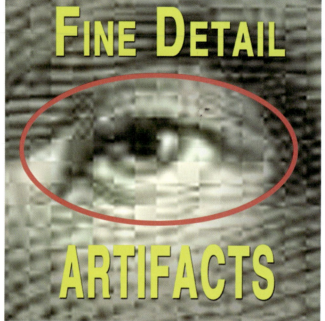

FIGURE 3.32
In complex scenes that contain mostly green tones (as well as in scenes that contain no green at all), a large portion of the image is not offset, increasing the likelihood of artifacts in high-detail areas of the frame.

FIGURE 3.33
CMOS-type cameras with full-raster[10] 1920 × 1080 imagers do not utilize spatial offset.

[10]The TV raster is a rectangular pattern comprising progressive or interlaced scan lines. Full-raster HD may be either 1920 × 1080 or 1280 × 720 pixel configurations.

CCD VERSUS CMOS/ANALOG VERSUS DIGITAL

It's a basic difference between CCD and complementary metal-oxide semiconductor (CMOS) imagers; the CCD is an analog device whose entire surface is exposed in the same instant, the more light that strikes the CCD the more silicon electrons that are displaced, sampled, and processed in the digital sphere. The instantaneous charging of the CCD mimics the exposure of photographic emulsion,[11] this *global shutter* system being very familiar to the traditional shooter storyteller as a means of image capture.

FIGURE 3.34
The rolling shutter in CMOS type cameras may produce an objectionable skewed effect when tracking or panning across scenes with pronounced vertical elements. Most CCD-type cameras do not exhibit such artifacts.

With cameras now equipped with CMOS imagers, shooters are facing a new, potentially disruptive impediment to the visual story. CMOS sensors are digital devices comprising rows of pixels that are scanned (progressively or interlaced) in a rolling fashion pixel by pixel. The scanning of a surface containing millions of pixels can take a while, and so we may see in some panning or tracking scenes a highly disconcerting skewed or "rubbery" effect.

Virtually all CMOS cameras regardless of manufacturer are subject to *rolling shutter* artifacts, the skewing exacerbated when shooting zoomed in owing to the increased magnification.

The temporal displacement inherent to a rolling shutter can produce truly bizarre effects, for example, in a photographer's flashing strobe light (Fig. 3.35).

FIGURE 3.37
This DSLR features a 21-megapixel (5616 × 3744) CMOS sensor – the equivalent of almost 6 K in video parlance. Note that still cameras describe imager resolution in total pixels while video cameras refer to horizontal resolution only. This better accommodates the various frame heights associated with film and video – 2.35:1, 1.85:1, 16:9. 4:3, etc.

FIGURE 3.35
Due to the scanning nature of CMOS-type cameras a discharging strobe light may be captured in only a portion of the frame. The banded effect can be highly unnatural. Later model CMOS cameras like the Panasonic HPX300 are beginning to address this issue.

FIGURE 3.36
A high-resolution CMOS sensor consumes only 20% of the power of a comparable size CCD.

---

[11]Back to the future! One can argue that film is the only true digital technology. A grain of silver is either exposed or not exposed, like a bit that is either a conductor or not a conductor, a 0 or a 1. The binary nature of film emulsion seems as digital as digital can be!

FIGURE 3.38
CMOS sensors eliminate CCD's vertical smear often seen in urban night scenes.

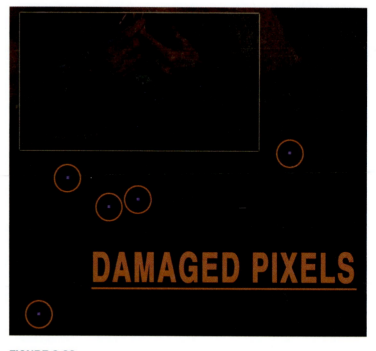

DAMAGED PIXELS

FIGURE 3.39
CCD pixels damaged by cosmic rays are seen as immovable white or violet dots on screen. In many cameras, this damage can be masked by black balancing the camera. (See Chapter 5 Balancing.) CMOS sensors are impervious to the pixel-killing cosmic rays encountered on long, international flights.

FIGURE 3.40
Sony F35. Most top-end digital cinema and broadcast cameras utilize CCD type imagers owing to fewer shuttering artifacts, better low-light response, and lower noise.

A portion of the frame may contain the discharging flash while another section above or below may not.[12] Who knows? In the future, viewers may be more accepting of such anomalies.

Not all shooters will experience or even recognize the rolling shutter issue in their CMOS camera. It really depends on the nature of your stories. You'll likely never see the vertical skewing, for instance, in a static interview with the CEO or in the still life of a fruit bowl on the camera maker's set at NAB. But the risk is real when shooting action sports or aerial shots from an unstable helicopter – and so the shooter must be aware.

By comparison, CCD cameras are free of rolling shuttering issues, are lower in noise, respond better in low light, and provide what many shooters perceive to

---

[12]If you've encountered this partial frame effect in your own work, it is possible to replace the truncated frame in post by substituting an adjacent frame. Desperate times call for desperate measures!

be a more organic look. Superior performance (even at the price of slightly lower resolution compared to CMOS) is the reason why CCDs continue to dominate cameras in high-end markets. Pro shooters must have the versatility and confidence to work successfully under a wide range of conditions – without fear of potentially disturbing skewing or other artifacts appearing on screen.

SIZE MATTERS – SORT OF

In stories that captivate the size of a camera's sensor is hardly an audience concern. Still, imager size can be important as it influences the professional look and feel of our images. A larger imager with a greater surface area allows larger pixels at a given resolution, which translates (usually) into greater dynamic range[13] and better low-light sensitivity, the two attributes most critical to our storytelling prowess, beyond merely higher definition.

A larger diameter imager exhibits a more favorable depth of field owing to the longer focal length lens required to cover the greater surface area. Long lenses intrinsically make it easier to establish a clearly defined focal plane, which can be pivotal to communicating an effective visual story.

While a larger imager is usually desirable, the trade offs may not always be worth it, owing to a camera's increased size and weight, greater compression

FIGURE 3.41
Audiences don't study resolution charts and neither should you! The shooter storyteller must bear in mind the number of pixels in an imager is not synonymous with a camera's performance. In fact, the opposite is usually true!

---

[13] Dynamic range describes the ability of a camera system to record detail in the brightest and darkest areas of a scene.

requirements from the higher pixel load, and the cost of the chipset itself, which constitutes a major part of the overall investment in a professional video camera.

Today's cameras feature imagers ranging in size from ⅙ to 1⅜ inches (35 mm) or larger. Like most everything in this business, the numbers are not what they seem. When referring to a ⅔-inches imager, its actual diameter is only 11 mm, less than half an inch, while a ½-inch sensor has a diagonal of 8 mm, less than a third of an inch. The reason for the discrepancy goes back to the era of tube cameras, when the outside diameter of ⅔-inches imager inclusive of its mount did measure ⅔ of an inch.

THE RESOLUTION RUSE

For many shooters, the illogical numbers game rules the roost, as cameras are judged and sold not on performance or suitability for a project but by simply which offers the largest imager with the most pixels.

FIGURE 3.43
Just as fine grain film sacrifices some low-light response for increased resolution, HD imagers with diminished pixel size also tend to suffer under minimal illumination. There is no free lunch. Imagers of 4- and 6-K resolution may sound appealing but do they really make sense for the stories you intend to tell?

FIGURE 3.42
The converging lines suggest how resolution and contrast work together. With improved contrast, the converging lines appear more distinct, and thus seeming of higher "resolution."

FIGURE 3.44
Clipping, compression anomalies, lens defects. In HD, the viewer sees it all – the good, the bad, and the ugly!

It goes without saying that feature films and other programs intended for big screen projection must display enough picture detail to fill the large canvas; soft focus lackluster images with poor dynamic range and contrast serve only to distance the viewer and convey an amateur sensibility. Remember your implied message as a shooter storyteller: if you don't value your story enough to deliver compelling images, then why should your audience value your story enough to invest its time and attention?

Viewers' perception of resolution is determined by many factors, of which the native resolution of the camera sensor is only one. Just as important and perhaps even more so is the exercise of your good craft, especially in how well you maintain satisfactory contrast in the captured image. High-end lenses low in flare and chromatic aberration[14] produce dramatically better images regardless of the camera, sensor, or native pixel count.

So, too, is the proper use of key accessories like a matte box or sunshade to prevent off-axis light from striking the front of the lens too obliquely and thus inducing flare and lowering contrast. Simple strategies like using a polarizing filter when shooting exteriors can also dramatically improve contrast and the apparent resolution of daylight images.

Perceived resolution is a complex issue influenced by many factors like the amount of compression, the character and direction of the light, even atmospheric haze. Ultimately, there's more to be gained from the proper application of good craft than focusing too narrowly on the pixel count of the imager.

---

[14]See Chapter 8 for a discussion of lens flare and chromatic aberration issues.

CHAPTER 4
The World in High Definition

It's sickening, really–all the new formats and great, new cameras to demand our love and attention and financial resources. If we're to survive this tumult and tell compelling stories with our new P2/XDCAM/EX/AVC/HDV/MPEG4/HD camera, we must accept to some degree the technological onslaught descending upon us. If we've chosen this medium for our livelihood (or serious avocation), we ought to bear in mind that the business of storytelling with a camera should be fun even in the face of the unrelenting madness. At times, I feel the bomb bay doors are opening and we're like Slim Pickens in *Dr. Strangelove* cackling atop the A-bomb hurtling to earth (Fig. 4.1). At least we should enjoy the ride crashing down to our mutually assured destruction!

TOO MANY CHOICES?

The California restaurant chain In-N-Out Burger is enormously successful despite the fact (or due to the fact) that its posted menu features only three options: you get a plain hamburger with a medium soda and fries, a cheeseburger with a medium soda and fries, a double hamburger with a medium soda and fries. That's it. (Fig. 4.2) No anguished equivocation, no soul-sapping handwringing, no paralysis at the drive-up window. Despotism has its advantages.[1]

Now compare the autocratic In-N-Out Burger experience with the mayhem that is HD! At last count, there are at least 32 different flavors of high-definition (HD) video at various frame rates and resolutions. Throw in a dozen or more compression types and scan modes with or without pull-down, segmented frames, MXF, QuickTime "wrappers", and umpteen aspect ratios, and pretty soon we're talking about some real choices. Yikes! When I think about it I should have included a motion discomfort bag with this book (Fig. 4.3)!

---

[1]I'm told it's possible to order off the menu at In-N-Out Burger, but you need to know a secret handshake or code word or something. It's worth investigating.

FIGURE 4.1
Slim Pickens whooping it up in *Dr. Strangelove*. Given the capabilities of today's HD cameras, you should feel no less power and exhilaration beneath you!

Nevertheless, we can safely say one thing about the technology that "newer is usually better." This means in a given class of camera, we can assume that a Sony HDCAM camera introduced in 1997, is not going to perform as well or as efficiently as Panasonic AVC-Intra model introduced in 2006. Similarly, in the prosumer class of camcorders, we see better performance in the latest AVCHD cameras than in the older HDV models grappling with the rigors of MPEG-2.[2]

FIGURE 4.2
You know it and I know it: human beings are happiest with fewer choices.

FIGURE 4.3
HD motion discomfort bag. Nauseating. Really.

[2] AVCHD using H.264 compression is much more efficient than MPEG-2 (HDV) at roughly the same bitrate 21–24 Mbps.

Of course many factors apply when assessing a camera's storytelling capabilities: the quality of optics, mechanical precision, and appropriateness for a given task. But in the end, audiences don't care which format or HD camera you use to record your epic so long as the tale you tell is engaging and the technical snafus not too egregious.

THE HELICAL SCAN ON THE WALL

After three decades of false starts and promises, HD in some shape, form, or group of pictures (GOP) is finally here. But why has it taken so long? Clearly, one problem has been defining what HD really is. Is it 720p, 1080i, or 1080p? Is it 16:9, 15:9, or even 4:3? Many viewers with wide-screen TVs simply assume they are watching HD. This appears to be especially true for folks experiencing the brilliance of plasma displays for the first time. If it looks like HD, it must be HD, right?

FIGURE 4.4
The short viewing distance in most electronic stores help sell the superior resolution of HDTV. Viewers at home at a more "typical" viewing distance can usually perceive little improvement in definition until they buy a much bigger TV or move closer to the screen!

VIVA LA RESOLUTION!

Can you read this? Sure you can. Now move this page 10 ft. away. The text on the page is still very high-resolution 300 dpi or more, but now the print is too small and too far away to be readable.

FIGURE 4.5
There is a practical upper limit to resolution and how much is actually useful and discernible and worthwhile. Do we need the increased detail of HD? Yes, yes! But how much resolution is ideal, how much resolution is enough?

Truth is, most viewers are hard-pressed to tell the difference between standard definition (SD) and HD images at a "normal" viewing distance. In a typical U.S. home, for example, the viewing distance to the screen is approximately 10 feet. At this range according to studies,[3] the average HD viewer would require a minimum 8-foot display (fixed pixel plasma or LCD) before he can reliably perceive an increase in resolution over SD. In Japan where the living rooms are much smaller, HDTV's higher resolution is more readily apparent, and thus, unsurprisingly, HD gained faster acceptance there.

---

[3]Source: Videography, August 2004. "HDTV: Myths and Math" by Mark Schubin.

Uncompressed HD	10.0
Sony HDCAM SR	9.5
Panasonic D-5	9.3
Panasonic AVC-Intra 100	9.2
Sony XDCAM HD 422	8.6
Panasonic DVCPRO HD	8.3
Panasonic AVC-Intra 50	8.2
Sony XDCAM EX	7.9
Sony XDCAM HD 420	7.5
Blu-ray (H.264)	7.2
Sony DigiBeta	6.4
DVCPRO 50	5.8
JVC Digital-S	5.5
Sony XDCAM	5.3
Sony Betacam SP	4.6
HDV (multiple manufacturers)	4.3
Sony Betacam	4.0
Panasonic DVCPRO 25	3.8
Sony DVCAM	3.8
DV (multiple manufacturers)	3.6
DVD-Video	2.9
MPEG-1 Video	1.2
VHS	1.0
Fisher-Price Pixelvision	0.05
Hand shadows on wall	0.00001

FIGURE 4.6
This chart assesses the relative quality of various SD and HD formats on a scale of 1–10, uncompressed HD = 10, rough and ready VHS = 1. You may want to take these rankings with a grain of oxide or cobalt binder – to go with your In-N-Out burger.

FRAMING THE ARGUMENT

Clearly, the shooter has many options: in HD, at 1080p, 1080i, or 720p; and in SD, 480i NTSC[4] or 576i PAL. Reflecting industry practice, we specify in video the vertical frame dimension, so 1920 × 1080 or 1440 × 1080 is referred to as "1080," whereas 1280 × 720 or 960 × 720 is referred to as "720."

A TRUISM ABOUT STANDARDS

The "standard" is what everyone ignores.

What everyone actually observes is called industry "practice."

Images can be captured progressively in a continuous fashion at a rate of one complete scan per frame, or in an *interlaced* fashion by scanning every frame twice, the combined odd and even fields merging to produce an entire frame.

---

[4]NTSC is the acronym for the National Television Standards Committee, which first met in 1941 to establish the frame rate and resolution for broadcast television. Although the 525 line/60 field standard was ultimately adopted, at least one committee member Philco championed an 800-line standard at 24 fps. To industry professionals, NTSC is often pejoratively referred to as "Never Twice the Same Color."

FIGURE 4.7
Although 1080i has more lines and therefore higher "resolution," the absence of aliasing artifacts in progressive mode may contribute to 720p's sharper look. Note that error correction applied to the deinterlaced frame (as seen in a progressive-scan home TV) produces an inaccurate result. Illustrative images courtesy of NASA.

There are advantages to each approach. Progressively scanned frames eliminate the temporal (1/50 or 1/60 s) artifacts that can occur between fields, the suppression of this *aliasing* being a significant factor in improving the real and perceived resolution at 24p.[5] Indeed, many professionals citing their own experience and the *Kell* factor[6] insist that progressive scan imagers at 720 deliver higher *actual* resolution than interlaced 1080 imagers, owing to the absence of aliasing artifacts.

There are other advantages as well to progressive capture: the ability to shoot at true variable frame rates and the enhanced ability to perform frame-based operations such as keying and color correction in postproduction. We must also consider the inherent compatibility with progressive playback devices such as DVD and Blu-ray players, which owing to the demands of Hollywood feature films are native 24p devices.

Progressive frames don't always make better images, however. When shooting sports or panning swiftly an interlaced frame may provide a smoother, more faithful representation of the action than the same scene recorded at 24p or even 30p.

Problem is, just as in film, progressive frames captured at 24 fps may be subjected to *strobing*, a phenomenon whereby viewers perceive the individual frame "samples" instead of continuous motion. During interlaced frame capture, there is often an inherent blur between the two fields displaced in time (Fig. 4.8). In progressive mode, the shooter finds no such comfort, and the motion blur must be added in some other way to reduce the strobing risk. For this reason when

---

[5]When describing *progressive* frame rates, we reference the fps followed by the letter "p"; when referring to *interlaced* frame rates, we specify *fields* per second followed by the letter "i." So "24p" refers to 24 progressive fps, whereas "60i" refers to 30 interlaced frames per second.
[6]The Kell factor specifies a 30% reduction in resolution for interlaced frames due to blurring between fields when compared to progressive frames.

shooting 720p, it is usually advisable to record at a higher frame rate and/or greater shutter angle, say, increasing the angle from 180° to 210°. The "wider" angle, i.e., longer shutter time, increases the motion blur inside the progressive frame, thereby reducing the strobing risk at the expense of some sharpness and resolution. The longer shutter time also improves a camera's low-light capability by approximately 20%.[7]

SAFE TRACKING AND PANNING SPEEDS

At 24 fps, strobing may occur in consecutive frames, when the displacement of a scene is more than half of its width. High-contrast subjects with strong vertical elements such as a picket fence or spinning wagon wheel tend to strobe more severely. As a remedy it helps to shoot at a higher frame rate and keep that higher rate through postproduction, for example, shoot 30 fps for a 30-fps workflow.

FIGURE 4.8
When panning across an interlaced frame, the telephone pole is displaced 1/60th of a second, leading to a "combing" artifact when the odd and even fields are merged. Shooting in progressive mode eliminates the aliasing seen commonly in interlaced images.

---

[7]Variable shutter may be expressed in fractions of a second or in degrees of shutter opening, just as in a traditional film camera. The default in most cameras is 180° or 1/48th of a second at 24 fps.

In many cases, the resolution and scan mode are dictated by a client or network. If you're shooting HD for ESPN or ABC you'll likely be shooting 720p, which is the standard for these networks. On the other hand, if you're shooting HD for CBS or HDnet, you'll probably be shooting 1080i. Keep in mind that deriving 1080i from 720p is easy and straightforward, but the reverse is not the case. In other words, if you're shooting 720p, you can *uprez* to 1080i with little if any detrimental effect, but *downrezzing* from 1080i to 720p is another matter with substantial risk for image degradation.

So, when shooting 1080 advantageous? If you need the larger frame for output to film or if your program is primarily intended for digital cinema, then 1080

FIGURE 4.10
Cartoon speed lines are used to convey a sense of motion inside progressively scanned film frames. These fake artifacts mimic the aliasing associated with interlaced images.

FIGURE 4.9
Interlaced images usually convey a better representation of fast-moving objects owing to the natural blurring between fields. Progressive frames comprised of a single field must rely on motion blur inside the frame to convey smooth motion.

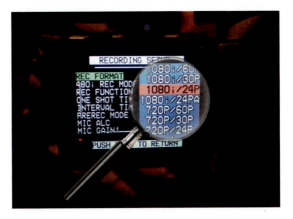

FIGURE 4.11
Solid-state progressive-scan cameras like the Sony PMW-EX1 and Panasonic HPX170 offer many recording options, including 1080p resolution at 24 fps. The setting is ideal for output to film or digital cinema.

(preferably 1080p) makes sense because it contains 2.25 times more lines than 720. Many cameras are now able to shoot 1080p24, which is ideal for narrative projects destined for the big screen or Blu-ray distribution. On the other hand, if you're shooting a documentary or nonfiction show where ease of workflow and variable-frame capability are critical, then 720p is the best choice, offering an easy upconversion later, if necessary, to 1080i.

Most cameras perform best at the frame size closest to the native resolution of its imager. Thus, the Panasonic HPX2000 with a 1280 × 720 3-CCD sensor will likely perform better at 720 than 1080. On the other hand, the Sony PMW-EX3 with a native resolution of 1920 × 1080 will almost certainly perform better in 1080 mode.

As in all matters, creative, technical, or otherwise, the story you choose will dictate the appropriate resolution for you; and, oh yes, your client's needs and desires may play a small role as well.

HMM: WHAT'S THIS?

1080i24p?? How can a format be both interlaced and progressive? The first reference "1080i" is the system setting and refers to the output to a monitor, i.e., what a monitor "sees" when plugged into the camera. The second number is the frame rate and scan mode of the imager; in this case, 24 fps progressive (24p).

SELECTING A FRAME RATE

Beyond the requirements of a particular network or client, the choice of frame rate is a function of one's storytelling goals. For sports and news operations, 60 fps makes sense because the higher frame rate ensures more reliable capture and smoother motion in the unpredictable ENG (*electronic news gathering*) world of street protests and endless police chases. Sixty frames per second also provides excellent compatibility with SD and HD broadcast environments, conveying to viewers a hyperreal present-tense look consistent with the news "story" imperative.

For Web and SD broadcasts, 30 fps is the logical option. This frame rate in progressive or interlaced modes is supported in current television environments and can adapt easily for the Web where 15-fps video is *de rigueur*. Thirty frames per second progressive images also suggest a nonfiction story unfolding in real-time, the frame rate not exhibiting quite the same hypersmooth look characteristic of 60-fps capture. The 30-fps "story" is ideal for reality TV, corporate, and documentary-type programming where a clean, elegant, contemporary feel is appropriate.

For production and most dramatic applications, 24p offers the shooter storyteller a filmic, more lyrical look rooted in the past tense. Reflected in the actors' slightly truncated movements, 24p communicates the sense of a classic story-teller sitting by a campfire late at night engaging his audience, "Oh, let me tell you a story…"

Beyond the feel and story implications 24p provides optimal compatibility with downstream display vehicles such as DVD and Blu-ray. Given the near-universal support for 24p in postproduction, the shooter storyteller can capture, edit, and output entirely in 24p, without incurring the wrath of NTSC (or PAL) interlacing artifacts or the encoding snafus stemming from the redundant frames and fields inserted in the *2:3 pull-down*.[8]

WHY THE GOOFY FRAME RATES, OR WHY 24p ISN'T 24p

In video, as in much of the modern world, there seems to be a paucity of honesty. So when we say "30p," we really mean 29.97 progressive fps; when we say "24p," we usually mean 23.98 progressive fps, and when we say "60i," we usually mean 59.94 fields per second. This odd frame rate business is an unfortunate legacy of the 1950s NTSC standard, which instituted a 29.97 frame rate and not a more cogent and logical 30 fps.

You may recall how we faded a light up and down for 1 second and we all shared and appreciated that (seeming) analog experience. We understood our eye was actually witnessing the event as a series of 15 or so snapshots, but our brain as a digital signal processor applied *error correction* and interpolated the "missing" frames, thus producing the perception of smooth, continuous motion.

This error correction is evident when thumbing through a child's flipbook. Flip through too slowly and we see the individual snapshots. But flip through just a little faster and suddenly our brains are able to fuse the motion by fabricating the "missing" samples.

In the early days of cinema in the nickelodeons of 1900, silent films were normally projected at 16–18 fps, above the threshold for folks to see continuous motion, but not quite fast enough to completely eliminate the *flicker*, a residual perception of the individual frames. Audiences even then found the effect apparently so distracting that moviegoers a century later still unknowingly refer to this past trauma as going to see a "flick."

So engineers had to devise a solution. They could have increased the frame rate of the camera and projector and, thereby, delivered more samples per second to the viewer. But this would have entailed more film and expense;

---

[8]The term *pull-down* comes from the mechanical process of "pulling" film down through a projector. A *2:3 pull-down* pattern enables playback of 24p video at 30 fps on a conventional television. The blending of frames and fields, however, introduces complexity inside the frame and may lead to a loss of sharpness when encoding to DVD and Blu-ray.

the increase in frame rate to 24 fps did not occur until the advent of sound in 1928, when the increased frame rate was necessary to provide better audio fidelity.

When film runs through a projector, each frame is drawn into the gate and stops. The spinning shutter opens and the frame is projected onto the screen. The shutter continues around and closes, and a new frame is pulled down. The process is repeated in rapid succession, which the processor in our brains fuses into continuous motion. To reduce flicker, engineers doubled the speed of the *shutter,* so each frame was effectively projected twice. This meant that viewers of 16-fps movies actually experienced the visual story at 32 samples per second; viewers of modern movies at 24 fps typically see 48 samples per second projected onto the screen.

The imperative to reduce flicker continued into the television era. Given the mains frequency in North America of 60 Hz and the need for studios, cameras, and receivers for synchronization, it would have been logical for a 60-fps television standard except for the need to sample every frame twice to reduce flicker.[9]

So engineers divided the frame into odd and even fields producing an interlaced pattern of 60 fields or the equivalent of 30 fps. A total of 30 fps is a nice round number. But then what happened?

With the advent of color in the 1950s, engineers wanted to maintain compatibility with the exploding number of black-and-white TVs coming to market. Interweaving the color information in the black-and-white signal, they noted a disturbing audio interference with the color *subcarrier,* which could only be remediated, after much debate, by a slight slowing of the video frame rate to 29.97 fps.

Today, this seemingly insignificant adjustment in video frame rate is the on going cause of enormous angst and at least 90% of our technical woes. When things go wrong, as they are apt to – synchronization issues, dropped frames, inability to input a file into the DVD encoder – your first impulse should always be to suspect a frame rate or timecode issue related to the 29.97/30-fps quagmire. Even as we march headlong into HD, owing to the need to downconvert to SD, we still must deal with the legacy of NTSC's goofy frame rate, particularly as it pertains to timecode. We'll further discuss the implications of timecode snafus in Chapter 5.

The bottom line is this: if we want our 24p programs to be broadly compatible with existing SD broadcast channels that use 29.976 fps, it is far more practical and easier to compute mathematically if we actually shoot 24p at 23.976, the

---

[9]In audio, the dual-sample requirement is known as *Nyquist's Law.* When CD-Audio was first contemplated in the 1970s, engineers looked to a toddler with optimal hearing. Determining a maximum frequency of 22,050 Hz that the child could perceive, engineers doubled that value to reduce "flicker" and thereby established the 44,100 Hz sample rate for CD-Audio.

simple six-frame conversion to SD being a straightforward operation without elaborate algorithms or undue shenanigans and loss of picture quality.

THE MANY FLAVORS OF 24p

For shooters with aspirations in feature films and dramatic productions, the advent of 24p represented a significant milestone with improved resolution and a more cinematic look. Before 2002, DV filmmakers engaged in various skullduggery, like shooting 25-fps PAL,[10] to achieve the desired 24p feel. All of that changed with the introduction of the Panasonic AG-DVX100 that offered 24p capability for the first time in an economical camcorder recording to standard DV tape.

SHOOTING 24p FOR DVD AND BLU-RAY

Since DVD's introduction in 1996, the Hollywood studios originating on film have logically encoded their movies at 24 fps for native playback on a DVD player. Relying on the player to perform the required "pull-down" and interlacing, the savvy shooter can pursue an all-24p workflow, and thus avert most NTSC shortcomings while *also* reducing the size of the encoded program by 20% – not an insignificant amount in an era when producers are jamming everything and the kitchen sink on a DVD or Blu-ray disc.

FIGURE 4.12
Every DVD and Blu-ray player is inherently a 24p device, which may be the best reason of all for the video storyteller to originate in 24p.

---

[10]PAL, an NTSC derived television system, was adopted in Europe in the 1970s and later in much of the 50 Hz world. PAL operates at exactly 25,000 fps, thus averting NTSC's criminal frame rate intrigue. Some folks point to PAL's superior 625-line vertical resolution compared with NTSC's 525-lines, but NTSC has more fields and frames per second. Some industry professionals pejoratively refer to PAL as "Pay A Lot."

Today with 24p firmly entrenched in a wide range of production, there is a compelling need for the shooter to understand the frame rate, its implications, and the many permutations.

SO YOU'RE SHOOTING 24p?

Over the last decade, camera manufacturers have used various schemes to record 24 fps to videotape. The Panasonic DVX100 offered three progressive recording modes: at 30p, the camera captured standard rate 29.97 fps but without NTSC interlacing. This was an option which appealed to Web video producers and news organizations for whom 24p had little relevance given the 60i protocol in the United States, Japan, and other 60-Hz countries.

The DVX100 also offered *two* 24p recording modes (Fig. 4.16), which continue to be relevant in current Panasonic P2 models: in *standard* mode, images are captured progressively at 24 fps (actually 23.976), then converted to 60 interlaced fields (actually 59.94) using a conventional 2:3 pulldown. After recording to tape or flash memory and capturing into the NLE, the editing process proceeds on a traditional 30 fps (29.97 fps) timeline. Thus, the benefit of shooting 24p over 60i standard mode; we can retain the look and feel of 24 fps while keeping the familiar 60i postproduction workflow.

In 24pA *advanced* mode, a 24p workflow is maintained from image capture through ingestion into the NLE and output to DVD, Blu-ray, or hard drive. The camera still scans progressively at 24 fps, but the 60i conversion to tape (or flash memory) is handled differently. In this case, the 24p cadence is restored in the NLE by weeding out the extra frames inserted temporarily for playback in standard definition NTSC or at 1080i60 HD.

For shooters reviewing takes with their directors, it is important to note that playback of 24pA footage from tape displays an obvious stutter due to the inserted redundant frames. This is completely normal and is not to be construed as just another cameraman screw up!

FIGURE 4.13
The camera that ignited a revolution in digital video: the Panasonic DVX100 24p camcorder.

FIGURE 4.14
Freed from the shackles of videotape and frailties of a mechanical transport, solid-state camcorders are able to shoot multiple formats at variable frame rates.

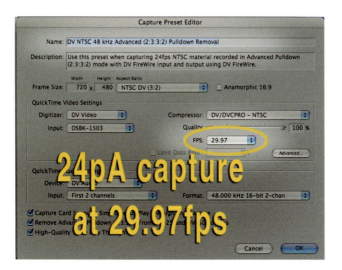

FIGURE 4.15
Current NLE software, including Apple Final Cut Pro, supports 24p capture in standard, advanced, P2 and XDCAM "native" modes. Note that 24pA only applies to interlaced formats at 480 and 1080 resolutions.

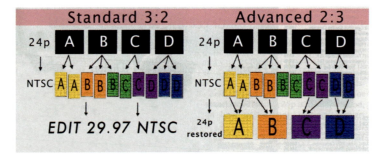

FIGURE 4.16

In 24p standard mode, progressive images are captured at 24 fps (23.97p) then converted to 29.97 fps (60i) by adding 2:3 pull-down. The process merges every second or third field and contributes to 24p's noted film look. Footage recorded in 24p standard mode is treated like any other 60i asset in your NLE timeline. Images captured in advanced mode are also scanned progressively at 24 fps, but in this case, complete frames are added to make up the 29.97 time differential; these extra frames being then subsequently removed during capture into the NLE. The shooter can thus maintain a 24p workflow throughout a production and avert interlacing artifacts in postproduction and encoding to DVD and Blu-ray.

FIGURE 4.17

Every camera manufacturer handles 24p differently. Canon's inscrutable "24F" format derives a progressive scan from an interlaced imager – not an easy task! Some Sony 24p cameras output "24PsF," a display format comprised of two identical (segmented) fields per frame. For the shooter storyteller, it's important to note that 24PsF (actually 23.98PsF) is generally used for monitoring, not for image capture.

FIGURE 4.18
For film shooters, the latest solid-state camcorders have a familiar feel as many can record native frames just like a film camera. Mechanical tape and disc-based camcorders invariably record "24 over 60 frames" per second, meaning they shoot 24p with "filler" frames to fill out a 60-frame sequence. Recording only native frames reduces by up to 60% the required storage when recording to flash memory.

FIGURE 4.19
SD still rules the roost in some commercial and cable markets, especially overseas. With the advance of HD, superior SD cameras are becoming increasingly available and inexpensive.

IF SD STILL LIVES WITHIN YOU

It doesn't make you a bad person. Maybe HD just isn't your thing yet. Or maybe you're leery of HDV's 40:1 compression or long-GOP construction that can instill convulsions in your NLE timeline. Maybe the newfangled tapeless workflow seems too daunting or recording to flash memory with no backup original strikes you as too risky.

Then there is also the matter of performance. Perhaps you're shooting a cop show late at night and you need the low light capability that only your old SD camcorder can deliver – about two stops better sensitivity on average than a comparable-class HD or HDV model.

FIGURE 4.20
Shooting SD for HD output to Blu-ray? Magic Bullet's Instant HD "plug-in" enables high-quality upconversion of SD footage inside the NLE.

FIGURE 4.21
DV is DV. Apart from the size and shape of the physical cassette and relative robustness, there is no inherent difference in image quality between MiniDV, DVCAM, and DVCPRO.

ATTENTION LAGGARDS!

A quick primer if you're still shooting DV or one of its many variants: there isn't much difference among the competing formats. Consumer MiniDV, DVCAM, and DVCPRO all share the same compressor with all the relative strengths and weaknesses that implies.

THE HD TO SD STORYTELLER

Just as originating in 35 mm yields a more professional result when outputting to VHS than shooting VHS in the first place, so does shooting HD yield a more polished look when outputting to SD or SD DVD.

For shooters on the cusp of taking the HD plunge, it may be the most compelling reason of all: HD makes our SD images look better! The additional fineness infused into the SD image is evident in the increased contrast at the 720 horizontal pixel cutoff seen in Fig. 4.22.

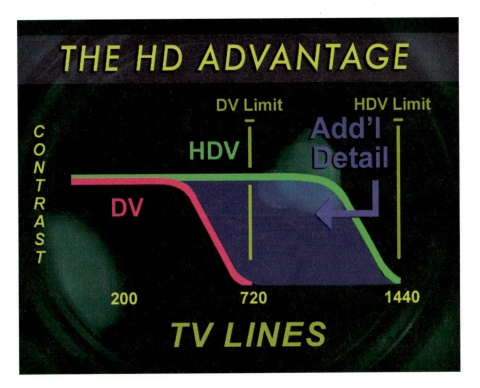

FIGURE 4.22
Two bell-shaped curves plot the relative contrast ratios of DV and HDV against detail fineness. At 1440 resolution, HDV fine detail is maximized, but the lowering of contrast at this resolution reduces perceived sharpness. HD's advantage becomes more apparent to viewers when viewed in SD owing to the higher contrast retained at the 720 cutoff.

FORMAT	Resolution	Data Rate	Raster Size	Aspect Ratio	Audio
DV	720 × 480	25 Mbps	720 × 480	4:3/16:9	PCM
	720 × 576	25 Mbps	720 × 576	4:3/16:9	
HDV	720p/24/25/30/60	19.2 Mbps	1440 × 1080	16:9	MPEG-1 L2 PCM
	1080i/50/60	25 Mbps	1280 × 720		MPEG-1 Level 2
	1080p/24/25/30	25 Mbps			MPEG-1 Level 2
AVCHD	720 × 480 NTSC	<24 Mbps	1440 × 1080	4:3/16:9	1–7.1 PCM
	720 × 576 PAL		1920 × 1080	4:3/16:9	1–7.1 PCM
	720p/24/50/60			16:9	1–5.1-channel AC3
	1080i/24/50/60			16:9	1–5.1-channel AC3
DVCPRO HD	1280 × 720	40–100 Mbps	960 × 720	16:9	1–4-channel PCM
	1080i/50		1440 × 1080		
	1080i/60		1280 × 1080		
XDCAM HD	1080i/50/59.94	<35 Mbps	1440 × 1080	16:9	1–4-channel PCM
	1080p/23.98/25/29.97				
XDCAM EX	720p/23.98/25/29.97/50/59.94	<35 Mbps	1280 × 720	16:9	1–2-channel PCM
	1080i/50/59.94		1440 × 1080		
	1080i/50/59.94		1920 × 1080 (effective)		
	1080p/23.98/25/29.97		1920 × 1080 (effective)		
DVD-VIDEO	720 × 480	<9.8 Mbps		4:3/16:9	PCM/AC3/DTS
	720 × 576				
BLU-RAY	720 × 480 NTSC	<36 Mbps	720 × 480	4:3/16:9	PCM/AC3/DTS
	720 × 576 PAL		720 × 576	4:3/16:9	
	720p/23.976/24/50/59.94		1280 × 720	16:9	
	1080/23.976/24/50/59.94		1440 × 1080	16:9	
			1920 × 1080	16:9	

FIGURE 4.23
The most popular SD/HD formats at a glance.

CHAPTER 5
Command and Control

It stands to reason: When we take control of our camera we take control of our storytelling. If we're a singer, we modulate the tone and timbre of our voice. If we're a writer, we temper our choice of words and phrases, and if we're a shooter, we control our images' look and feel.

For shooters with consumer camcorders, this chapter may seem moot, as most models lack rudimentary setup options. The cameras' key imaging parameters – white balance, color saturation, and detail level – are controlled automatically according to the preordained dictates of omniscient engineers located in far-off lands.

The demands imposed by video's mass market have had a profound effect on the storytelling capabilities of today's cameras. In generations past, Kodak was said to have designed its Kodachrome films assuming mindless vacationers would leave the undeveloped film in their car's hot glove box. This expectation of less-than-intelligent behavior played a central role in the product's engineering, and the same can be said for many consumer video cameras. Most models are designed to require as little user brainpower as possible.

It's almost as if some shooters want the technology to do the storytelling for them! Autofocus, autoexposure, autowhite balance – these aren't so much "features" as sales gimmicks, and relegating such critical decisions to an automated process does not a gifted storyteller make!

Camera manufacturers transcending this autoeverything predisposition have enabled increased manual control of focus, white balance, exposure, and audio levels. Some cameras go further, allowing shooters to tweak gamma, master detail, and the color matrix. For the video storyteller coming to grips with one of the newer generation cameras, the creative options can be overwhelming.

FIGURE 5.1
Which way to go? Too many choices can be paralyzing.

AUTOEVERYTHING: WHO NEEDS IT?

Autofocus, autoexposure, autowhite balance – yikes! What silly notions! How is any camera supposed to know inherently what part of the frame should be in focus, what "normal" exposure is supposed to look like, or how much red is really in a scene?

Savvy shooters understand that mastery of the camera's imaging functions is imperative for telling visually compelling stories. While new shooters

FIGURE 5.2
Effective storytelling with a camera requires rigorous control of its imaging capabilities.

FIGURE 5.3
Taking control of your camera can be frustrating. This menu selection button may have saved the camera manufacturer a few pennies, but its skittishness will drive you nuts.

FIGURE 5.4
The autoeverything switch on the side of your camera is there for a reason – to be switched off!

may be attracted initially to a camera with few manual functions the benefit of increased control becomes quickly apparent with the first significant project.

DOWN WITH AUTOEXPOSURE

Proper exposure is the key to establishing a desired mood, but what constitutes "proper" exposure in the context of your story? Clearly, this is a creative matter because deliberate underexposure can add drama and mystery to a scene. So can intentional *overexposure*; although usually inadvisable due to the loss of highlight detail, it, too, can support the appropriate context, maybe a sci-fi romance piece taking place on the surface of Venus or a desperate traveler dying of thirst in the middle of a desert. Unfortunately, the autoexposure "feature" in your camera often precludes such creative treatments, and unless your story happens to demand a uniform gray look, the autoexposure function should be disabled. If you need additional convincing, consider the most horrible of amateur effects – the telltale breathing of a camera's auto iris constantly adjusting and readjusting mid-scene.

The latest and greatest camera may seem intelligent in many ways, but in this respect, it certainly is not. When set to autoexposure, it will interpret the world and everything in it as 18% gray. A solid white wall will be captured as gray even though it clearly is not. A solid black wall will likewise register as gray even though it most surely is not. C'mon, camera engineers, get with the program! The world is a rich and vibrant place full of color and nuance. (Fig. 5.7) It is not all 18% gray!

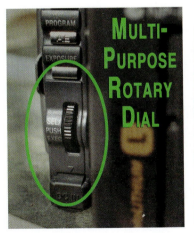

FIGURE 5.5
Engaging manual exposure may require pushing a button at the back or side of the camera. This multifunction rotary dial controls aperture, white balance, and audio record levels.

FIGURE 5.6
The external controls on the Canon XL H1S are readily accessible, obviating the need to drill down through a multitude of cryptic menu options.

FIGURE 5.7

The world is full of color, but your camera's autoexposure assumes all things are a uniform grey. Many shooters record a gray scale at the beginning of every scene. The practice can provide a valuable reference for color correction later.

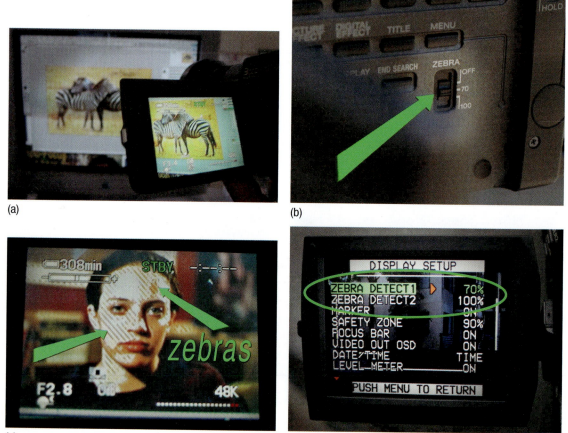

(a)

(b)

(c)

(d)

FIGURE 5.8

Go ahead! Earn your stripes! Your camera's zebras can help determine proper exposure. When set to 70% (Fig. 5.8b), some stripes should normally be visible in your subject's brightest skin tones (Fig. 5.8c). Some cameras feature two zebra sets with the ability to input custom values for each (Fig. 5.8d).

(a)   (b)   (c)

FIGURE 5.9
(a) Overexposure produces washed-out blacks and loss of detail in the brightest image areas. (b) Underexposure deepens shadows and may reduce detail visible in the darkest tones. (c) For the shooter storyteller, "correct" exposure is a creative judgment as deliberate underexposure can often add drama to mundane scenes.

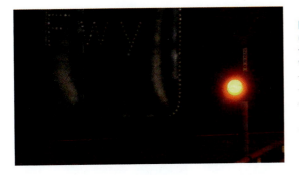

FIGURE 5.10
Our eye is drawn naturally to the brightest object in a frame. When shooting in low light, try to frame in a strong source like this freeway caution light to distract the viewer from any noise in the underlit shadows. It's a great way to improve the apparent sensitivity of your camera in very low light scenes.

YOUR CAMERA'S ISO

A shooter may want to rate a camera's low-light capability and ascertain its ISO.[1] This can be challenging because a camera's performance in low light is largely dependent on the individual's tolerance for noise. Like film grain, some shadow noise may be acceptable in one context but not another, and so a camera's ISO must necessarily be subjective. It's also worth noting that some cameras apply noise reduction better than others, which might lead shooters to assess a higher ISO rating in these models.

Some HD camcorders seem to exhibit a high ISO because they are tweaked for capturing maximum shadow detail. As a general rule of thumb, most cameras may be rated at approximately ISO 320, although some cameras with larger imagers relative to their resolution (like the Panasonic HPX500) may be rated higher. Standard definition camcorders with larger pixels generally exhibit lower noise and thus a higher ISO – about two stops better on average in terms of low-light sensitivity.

Ultimately, a camera's ISO is an arbitrary assessment based in large part on user-settable values like *gamma* and *gain*[2] that impact a scene's gray scale. The ISO rating simply suggests the camera's relative ability to produce a comparable image on film given the same exposure parameters.

---

[1] *International Organization for Standardization*. ISO is not an acronym; it is derived from the Greek word *iso*, which means "equal." The ISO rating reflects a film or video camera's relative sensitivity to light.
[2] See Chapter 6 for a discussion of gamma and to gain setup parameters.

THE CHINA GIRL

For years, the China Girl – who knows who she was or is, whether she's married or single, or even if she's actually more than one person – provided visual storytellers with a common printing reference for Caucasian skin. The fact that

FIGURE 5.11
This girl may not technically be from the Far East, but for decades, the flesh tones of an Asian woman served as a visual guide for filmmakers and laboratory technicians.

FIGURE 5.12
The Caucasian flesh tone reference presumed by camera engineers fails to consider the range of skin colors apparent in diverse populations.

FIGURE 5.13
The white ethnocentric globe of a professional cinematographer's exposure meter.

FIGURE 5.14
Note to humanity: in truth, we are all the same color with common flesh tones regardless of race or ethnicity. However, the brightness or *luminance* of our skin tones can vary considerably.

a large part of the world's population is not Caucasian apparently eluded the designers of most motion-picture films. The same seems true for video camera engineers today who, like their film brethren, mostly live and work in countries located in the northern latitudes, where the facial tones of the China Girl are the norm.

I'm not about to dwell on the political correctness of film emulsions, CCD or CMOS imagers, or a camera designer's proclivities. Suffice it to say that your camera's autoexposure is trying its hardest to render every face as though we all shared the flesh tones of that China Girl.[3]

RIDING THE WAVEFORM

It used to be that a waveform monitor could only be found in top-tier production and broadcast control rooms. Today, shooters with certain model cameras, LCD monitors, and software for their laptops have easy and cheap access to a waveform, this tool being extremely useful to gauge overall exposure and minimize the clipping risk. The waveform can also be useful for

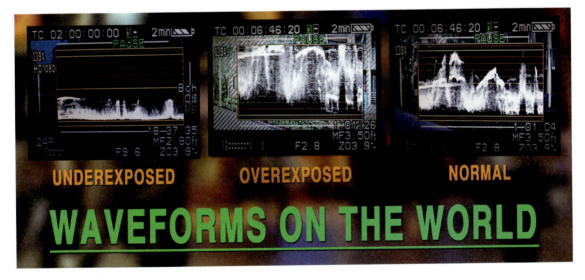

FIGURE 5.15
Some cameras feature a built-in waveform that enables greater control of images, for green screen, color correction, and matching multiple cameras in the field. At left, a dark scene (possibly underexposed); at center, a hot "clipped" scene (possibly overexposed); at right, a "normal" scene with wide dynamic range (possibly what you want). Any of these waveforms may be correct for the story you intend to tell!

---

[3]In British television, the girl widely used as a reference was reportedly the daughter of BBC's head of video engineering. She still appears on the U.K. test card though she may well have grown up, married, and had children of her own.

shooting green screen to ensure an even illumination of the panel surface. (See Chapter 9 for tips on shooting green screen.)

I SHUTTER TO THINK ABOUT IT

The camera's shutter can impact your storytelling in profound ways. At slower than normal speed (<1/48 or 1/60 s), the increased motion blur may add a surreal look to your images. At higher shutter speeds (>1/60 s), individual frames may appear sharper but with an increased risk of stutter or strobing from frame to frame. Varying the camera shutter may have dramatic implications for your visual story!

FIGURE 5.16
Adobe's OnLocation recreates in software the utility of a waveform monitor, vectorscope, and other tools on a Mac or PC laptop.

FIGURE 5.18
A faster shutter freezes action inside the frame, but the reduced motion blur can produce choppiness between frames, especially at 24p. In this scene, the frozen shoots of water add emphasis to the large splash swallowing a speeding vehicle.

FIGURE 5.19
Certain scenes are inherently problematic. To avoid strobing when panning or tracking across a white picket fence, shoot at an oblique angle and use a slightly slower shutter speed, especially at 24p.

FIGURE 5.17
A slower shutter with increased motion blur helps capture the frenzy and hyperactivity of this New York City street scene.

THE SYNCHRONIZED SHUTTER

Your camera's precision *synchro scan* shutter, also referred to as *clear scan*, enables the capture of out-of-sync computer monitors without the rolling bars or distracting convulsions. When shooting overseas, the camera's main shutter (Fig. 5.20) is potentially more useful, however, to eliminate the flicker often seen in television screens, fluorescent light banks, neon signs, and other discontinuous light sources. The itinerant shooter should be mindful of this risk, particularly in supermarkets, train stations, and other commercial locations, as the noxious defect is not normally apparent in a camera's tiny LCD screen. For North American shooters operating in Europe and in 50Hz countries in general, a slight adjustment of the camera's main shutter from 1/48 or 1/60 second to 1/100 second may be all that is required to eliminate the flicker risk.

FIGURE 5.20
Some cameras express shutter "angle" in degrees, a reference understood by shooters accustomed to the mechanical shutter of a traditional film camera.

FIGURE 5.21
Your camera's *synchro scan* shutter can help reduce or eliminate the undesirable rolling when shooting out-of-sync computer monitors.

FIGURE 5.22
Setting the camera's coarse shutter to 1/100 second will often eliminate the flicker from fluorescent sources when shooting in 50Hz countries.

FRAME RATES AND YOUR STORY

We don't normally think of frame rate as a key storytelling tool but it certainly is! Frame rate and story go hand in hand, the tempo of our images parading before the viewer varying in cadence, faster or slower, to add emphasis, drama or humor. Second only to focus in the shooter's bag of tricks, the ability to

FIGURE 5.23
Shooting with a long telephoto lens at high magnification, this flamingo would appear to move unnaturally fast if shot at "normal" speed. Capturing the scene at 60 fps (for 24-fps playback) produces a much more natural look.

vary frame rate is critical to one's visual storytelling. On many shoots, I vary the frame rate on nearly every shot, tweaking a scene by one or two frames per second (fps) for maximum emotional impact. This level of control isn't possible in all cameras and doesn't apply as much to dialog scenes, but even there, in a character's reaction, I may alter the frame rate slightly to add weight to an actor's performance.

After determining resolution (1080, 720, 480, etc.), the shooter's next order of business is selecting an appropriate frame rate. In general, your thinking should go something like this: if you're shooting a feature or narrative-type production intended for the big screen, DVD, Blu-ray, or digital cinema, then 24p may be your best choice. The 24p frame rate imparts a filmic look while offering greater efficiency in workflow from image capture, through output to film, hard drive, D-5 tape, or optical disc. On the other hand, if news or sports is your application with a parallel focus on the Web, then 30p or 60p capture makes more sense, given the Web's typical 15-fps frame rate and the relative ease of downconverting material from HD captured at an even multiple of that frame rate.

Currently, 60p image capture is limited to 720-resolution; there is no video standard for 1080p60 acquisition, although most Blu-ray players and HDTV displays support it. If shooting progressively at 1080, the options are limited in most cameras to 24 or 30 fps.

Beyond tweaking actors' performances, I regularly use a range of *cranking* speeds in subtle ways, for example, when shooting a car chase, I will *undercrank* by 2 or 3 fps to increase the speed and peril of the pursuit (Fig. 5.24). Conversely, if shooting a mood piece, I will *overcrank* slightly to impart a faint dreamlike quality (Fig. 5.25). In either case, the effect is restrained, and the viewer is quite unaware of the manipulation.

FIGURE 5.24
We can increase the drama in a chase scene by slightly *undercranking* the camera. Shooting at 20 or 22 fps accelerates the action just enough to add peril while not making the scene appear artificially treated or comical when played back at 24 fps.

FIGURE 5.26
Dramatic undercranking can be used subtly or for more dramatic effect. In low light or at night, a frame rate of 4–6 fps can be effective for capturing stunning cityscapes.

FIGURE 5.25
I often *overcrank* slightly to add a dreamlike quality to a scene. This scene of my daughter at Mauna Loa was shot at 30 fps for 24-fps playback.

FOCUSING ON WHAT'S IMPORTANT

It would be easy to rant about the pointlessness of autofocus – it's idiotic, intended for amateurs, it's the scourge of mankind – and all these statements would be true. In general, autofocus should be avoided like a Neil Diamond TV special on Christmas Eve. Indeed, the very notion of "autofocus" from a storytelling perspective is dubious because there is no way your camera can inherently know your story and what element or elements ought to be in focus. For the shooter, the appropriate guiding of the viewer's eye within the frame is a vital storytelling function. Why would you give this power to some nameless engineer who just happened to design the autofocus system in your camera?

THESE GUYS ARE NOT ARTISTS

Consider autofocus more intently. For some unbeknownst reason engineers believe that whatever is at the center of the frame should always be in focus. Never mind the insights of the Old Masters and the Law of Thirds. In most cameras, the shooter is stuck with this illogical center-focus conceit, with no ability to target an alternative section of the frame.

The ability to assign focus is fundamental to our craft. When we move the camera switch from AUTO to MANUAL, we are making a statement about who we are as

FIGURE 5.27
Your camera's proclivity to maintain focus at center-frame runs counter to most artists' notion of good visual storytelling. Normally, we direct viewer's attention inside the frame by assigning relative importance to in or out-of-focus objects. Only we, the inspired shooters of the world, can make this determination!

FIGURE 5.28
In normal operation, the camera should be switched to manual to prevent the irritating search for focus mid-scene. To focus manually, many cameras feature a momentary push-auto button on the side of the lens or camera body.

craftsmen and human beings. We must never hand our craft off to a machine or the whimsy of artless number crunchers. Not now! Not ever! To focus manually, we zoom in and bring our image into sharp, glorious focus, then pull back to frame our shot. We do this even in cameras without a mechanical focus ring, in which case we momentarily depress the AUTO button – and that's OK. We can live with that. But we always re-frame afterwards in a manner consistent with our humanity and our storytelling goals.

HD FOCUS CAN BE TOUGH!

When it comes to shooting movies, the Society of Operating Cameramen has a long-time slogan *"We see it first!"* With the advent of HD cameras and their miniscule viewfinders, at least one frustrated shooter has suggested a new more appropriate motto: *"We see it worst!"*

For those of us in the HD trenches, we know too well the frustration of trying to focus on a tiny 3/4-inch viewfinder or low-resolution LCD. After all, audiences will likely be seeing the same image on a big screen several feet across or projected in a theater at high magnification. It is truly troubling to think that our audiences have a clearer view of our work – focus, color, and everything else – than we do!

As a shooter and craftsman, it's a noble thought to see what we're actually doing. One would think this should be a given in a business where seeing is everything, but it clearly isn't the case. Heck, we discuss to no end the relative merits of shooting 2-, 4-, or even 6-K resolution cameras, but ask about something practical like the size and quality of a camera's viewfinder and our eyes grow dim. Often, it seems the *fantasy* of capturing great images is more appealing than *actually* being able to capture great images.

Things have improved recently with the introduction of new swing-out high-resolution LCDs and *liquid crystal on silicon* (LCoS)[4] viewfinders, but even these latest displays are too small for achieving consistent critical focus. Manufacturers have long been aware of the focusing issues facing HD shooters and have tried various assist strategies.

One system favored by Panasonic is a 2X viewfinder magnification scheme (Fig. 5.29a). Some of us may have used an analogous system years ago in a traditional photographic darkroom, employing a microscope over the projected enlarged image to precisely focus on the film grain.

HD camcorders may also utilize a focus bar or *histogram* as a graphical focus assist (Fig. 5.29b). This strategy associates sharper focus with an increase in detail frequency. Both the graphical and 2X magnification approaches share the same disadvantage: they are awkward or impossible to use while shooting, especially in documentary and reality TV applications.

Shooting impromptu behind the scenes on feature films, I use a simple zone system for setting focus employing the rangefinder readout in a camera's swing-out finder (Fig. 5.30a). Supporting the camera in one hand, I keep my left thumb on the focus ring (Fig. 5.30b) while eyeing the action and the distance displayed in the LCD.

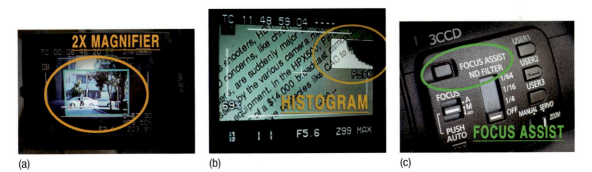

(a)   (b)   (c)

FIGURE 5.29
Most HD camcorders feature some kind of focus assist – notably a 2X magnifier or histogram.

---

[4] Liquid crystal on silicon finders offering high resolution can be especially susceptible to burn damage from the sun. They are also subject to a potentially annoying display lag when panning or tilting the camera. Most HD camcorder viewfinders remain a significant shortcoming regardless of the display technology.

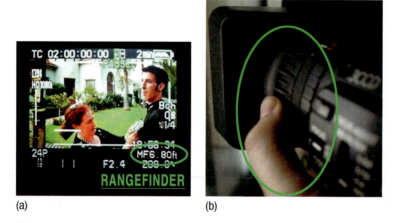

(a)   (b)

FIGURE 5.30
For shooting documentaries and reality TV, the best strategy for finding and keeping focus is by referencing the rangefinder in the camera viewfinder. Except for close-ups, you can focus effectively this way, supporting the camera and pressing the thumb against the lens ring.

Some JVC HD models utilize an effective three-color focus assist. When activated, the viewfinder image becomes monochrome and the *peaking*[5] around in-focus objects assumes an obvious easy-to-decipher colored fringe.

> ## DON'T GET BURNED!
>
> A typical sunny afternoon in Los Angeles. A director friend stepped up to my camera, looked through the viewfinder, and strolled away leaving the viewfinder pointing at the sun. I came back after less than sixty seconds at craft services, and there were massive orange-black blobs in my LCD viewfinder screen! That turned out to be the most expensive Snickers bar I've ever had!
>
> Depending on the intensity and angle of the sun, a camcorder's viewfinder may be irreparably damaged in as little as 3–5 seconds. The damage may not even appear until after the camera has shut down and cooled. I often wonder why camera makers don't just provide shutters on viewfinders instead of the silly warning stickers. It's only a matter of copying the pressure-eyecup system we've had on for years on film cameras.

STAND UP FOR YOUR WHITES

Our eyes can be remarkably adaptive when it comes to perceiving white. We go into a supermarket illuminated by banks of fluorescents and we don't see the noxious green hue. We blow the candles out on a birthday cake and don't notice

---

[5]To facilitate critical focus, many camera viewfinders feature a "peaking" function to boost sharpness. Camera viewfinders and LCD monitors feature a "peaking" function to boost sharpness in order to facilitate critical focus. The peaking level has no effect on the camera's recorded or output signal.

FIGURE 5.31
While the excessive warmth in this scene may not be apparent to your eye, your camera is a lot less forgiving. Color correcting in post is usually the most practical way to remedy such anomalies in documentary and most nonfiction projects.

the strong orange cast. These out-of-balance scenes appear "white" because our brain color compensates – the green curse of the fluorescents balanced by magenta, the warm orange candlelight offset by blue – all this done inside our brains without us ever being aware of it.

TO PRESET OR NOT PRESET

This is the question for many shooters. For documentary and most nonfiction work, I recommend utilizing your camera's *white-balance preset*; it is not the same as auto white balance, which is wrong, wrong, wrong in virtually all cases.

The trick here is to get as close as possible by selecting the *appropriate* preset. Use the 3,200°K preset for interior tungsten and near-tungsten conditions (as in Fig. 5.32) and the 5,600°K preset for daylight and near-daylight conditions. This matter of getting close in-camera is important because we want to avoid having to make dramatic color adjustments later.

Keep in mind as you go about your white balancing chores: shooting under fluorescent lights is *supposed* to look a bit green. Shooting at sunset is *supposed* to look a bit red. Don't white balance these nuances out of your visual story! (See Fig. 5.33)

FIGURE 5.32
Hollywood Boulevard at night. The mixed illumination is integral to the visual story and you'll most likely want to preserve that feeling. In most cases, the camera's white-balance preset can help you do this. Attempting to white balance every scene manually is unwise and will lead to crazy, inconsistent results.

FIGURE 5.33
When white balancing this warm scene in San Marco Square, we should compensate only enough to alleviate the excessive warmth, but not so much as to remove all sense of place and drama. It's worth repeating: don't balance your whites at the expense of your story!

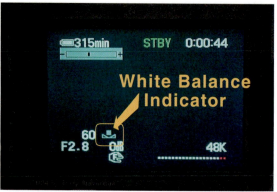

FIGURE 5.34
Typical white-balance icon found in prosumer cameras. When the icon stops blinking, the camera has applied the required compensation.

FIGURE 5.35
While most cameras offer the ability to white-balance manually, the manner of doing so varies from model to model. Often, the hodgepodge layout of buttons and dials leaves much to be desired.

SETTING WHITE BALANCE MANUALLY

Because the camera must know what you intend as looking white in a scene, manual white balancing is often necessary, especially for narrative productions. To perform a routine white balance, you direct the camera at any white surface – a white card is typically used – and zoom in as necessary to fill the frame. Press and hold the camera's white-balance button or dial. A wedge-like icon in the viewfinder (see Fig. 5.36) will blink and then go steady as the camera applies the compensation needed to render the white card reference as white on screen.

BLACK BALANCE

Auto black balancing (ABB) should be performed periodically to ensure that black in your picture is reproduced accurately. An incorrect black level may impart a noticeable hue in deep shadows and compromise the overall color palette. ABB effectively adjusts the zero level of the primary RGB (red-green-blue) colors. This operation is normally performed with the iris closed and/or lens capped; professional cameras close the iris automatically during the black balancing process.

It is not necessary to perform ABB with every setup. It should be done specifically, however, when the camera is used for the first time or after a long period of inactivity, when the ambient temperature shifts dramatically, when the shutter

FIGURE 5.36

Black balancing ensures that a pure "black" is recorded with a proper color gamut. It may also mask dead or damaged pixels by borrowing data from adjacent undamaged photosites. ABB (auto black balance) is typically initiated by a front-mounted toggle switch. In prosumer models, this operation is often performed during startup or in tandem with the auto white balance (AWB) function.

has been turned off, or if the camera is switched between progressive and inter-laced scanning modes.

Most importantly, ABB should also be performed after a long international flight since this may help to mask any dead or damaged pixels inflicted by errant cos-mic rays along the way. This only applies to CCD-type cameras; CMOS models are not susceptible to cosmic ray damage, or at least not in the same way.

AUTOWHITE ANYONE?

The illogic of autoeverything extends to autowhite balancing as well. Of course, our camera is superintelligent but how could it possibly know what is supposed to be white in a scene? Left in automode, our little servant will obligingly and continuously apply "correction" mid-scene to compensate for what it perceives to be a drifting incorrect white balance. Warm sections of scenes will be "rem-edied" by steadily adding blue. Cool portions of scenes will get the opposite treatment, receiving an unwarranted dose of red. We can imagine how the shifting color can wreak havoc in post as we struggle to build a visually coherent sequence. What a mess.

So here's the thing: our camera's autowhite feature is an anathema to good storytelling craft. After all, we are the masters of our domain. We control how our camera sees and feels the world, and the last time I looked, the world was not an endless series of neutral gray tones. So let's tell our camera what white is. Use the correct preset or set the white balance manually. Whatever you do, just remember the "white" your story requires may well have a dash of warmth or blueness in it.

ABOUT THE WHITE-BALANCE PRESETS

To facilitate white balance under "average" conditions, most cameras include one or more presets for interior and exterior conditions. The interior preset is intended to accurately capture scenes illuminated by standard tungsten lighting at 3,200° K.[6] This color temperature reflects that of a glowing tungsten filament suspended inside an airless glass bulb, the kind of lamp used commonly in professional lighting kits (Fig. 5.37). The metal tungsten is used because when heated to 3,200° K, it emits a very even spectrum of color – a near-perfect white light.

FIGURE 5.37
Tungsten lamps produce a near-perfect white light at 3,200° K. Your camera's sensor and processor are designed to respond ideally under this type of illumination.

FIGURE 5.38
A typical camcorder white-balance switch features storable A and B settings in addition to the 3,200° K preset.

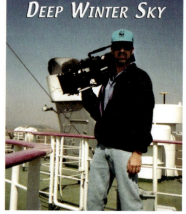

FIGURE 5.39
Scenes recorded under a clear sky may exhibit a strong blue cast, especially in the shadows. In winter, the color temperature may exceed 20,000° K in the shade!

---

[6]Color temperature is measured in degrees Kelvin, named after the British physicist Lord Kelvin, who first devised a system of temperature measurement based on absolute zero at zero degrees K. The Kelvin scale is identical to the Celsius system plus 273°.

(a)

(b)

FIGURE 5.40
Your camera's tungsten-balanced imager requires proper filtration for use in daylight. This is accomplished via a standard daylight (Type 85) conversion filter, which may be mounted physically inside the camera or applied digitally during image processing.

Color Temperature of Common Light Sources

Artificial Light:

Match flame	1700º K.
Candlelight	1850º K.
Sodium vapor streetlight	2100º K.
Household incandescent	2980º K.
Standard studio (halogen lamp)	3200º K.
Photoflood	3400º K.
Daylight blue photoflood	4800º K.
Fluorescent (Cool White)	4300º K.
Fluorescent (Warm White)	3050º K.
HMI	5600º K.
Xenon	6000º K.

Sunlight:

Sunrise or sunset	2000º K.
One hour after sunrise	3500º K.
Early morning/late afternoon	4300º K.
Average noon (Washington, D.C.)	5400º K.
Midsummer	5800º K.

Daylight (mix of skylight and sunlight):

Overcast sky	6000º K.
Average summer daylight	6500º K.
Light summer shade	7100º K.
Average summer shade	8000º K.
Partly cloudy sky	8000º–10000º K.
Summer/winter skylight	9500º–30000º K.

Source: *American Cinematographer Manual*, 6th Edition 1986.

FIGURE 5.41
Common lighting conditions and their approximate color temperatures. Standard "daylight" is the spectral equivalent of heating a tungsten filament to 5,600°K – a typical daylight preset found value in most cameras.

In nature, few sources match the 3,200°K standard. Common incandescent household lamps typically exhibit a color temperature between 2,600 and 3,000°K, which means scenes recorded under these lights will appear unnaturally warm if the camera's tungsten preset is used with no additional adjustment or filtration. Under such conditions, balancing the camera to a white reference adds the appropriate blue offset, thus compensating for the excessive warmth.

For exteriors, your camera applies standard daylight conversion and assumes a color temperature of 5,600° K, this temperature reflecting an "average" mixture of skylight and sunlight. The video storyteller understands that direct sun adds warmth to a scene, while the light reflected from a clear blue sky adds a noticeably cool cast.

SO WHAT IS WHITE?

The shooter storyteller understands that proper white balance is subjective. Shooters for shows like *Access Hollywood* have become quite adept at capturing celebrities coming up the red carpet, quickly re-whiting in advance of a particular star, by adding warmth or coolness to a star's "look" in accordance with the dictates of that evening's gossip mill.

Whiting the camera to a blue-tinted reference infuses subjects with a warm, flattering look. Conversely, white balancing to a reddish source has the opposite effect, instilling a cool cast on an actor perhaps playing a villain in his latest movie.

At first, the references carried by shooters were makeshift pieces of colored construction paper. Some shooters even collected scraps of paper to match particular stars. This is the Cameron Diaz. This is the Jennifer Lopez. You get the idea.

Now, if you're so inclined, you can purchase prefabricated cards in a range of warm and cool tints (Fig. 5.42a). It's an easy, inexpensive way to control white balance and mood, two areas that ought to be of primary interest to every shooter storyteller.

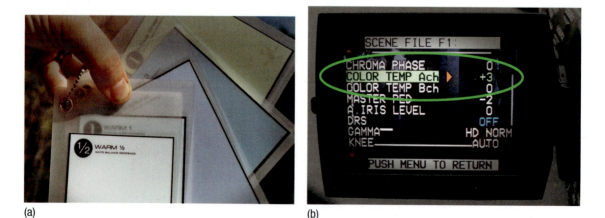

(a)   (b)

FIGURE 5.42
Commercially available "Warm Cards" (a) can help the shooter storyteller achieve a white-balance consistent with a desired mood. A similar warming or cooling effect can be achieved in the appropriate camera menu (b).

COLOR CORRECTION

In these days of powerful color correction tools, we need not be overly consumed with scrutinizing or tweaking our camera's white balance. In documentary and non-fiction environments, the important thing is to get reasonably close (Fig. 5.43a), as fine-tuning of color and density can usually best be achieved in post. The popular editing platforms from Apple, Adobe, and Avid all have superb color correction capabilities that can easily perform minor adjustments. Large shifts in color from

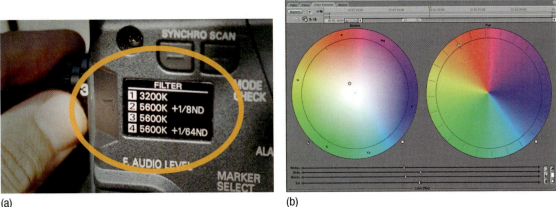

(a) (b)

FIGURE 5.43

(a) Use your camera's filter wheel to perform basic color correction for tungsten or daylight conditions; (b) More precise tweaking of color and white balance can best be performed in postproduction. For most nonfiction applications, the two-way color corrector in Final Cut Pro is adequate to address basic correction needs.

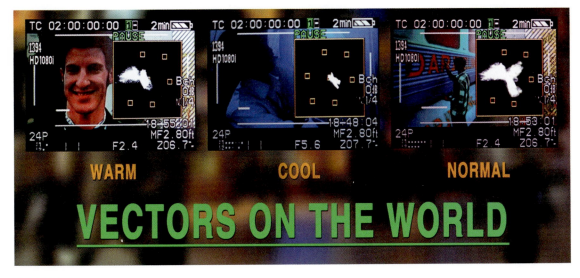

FIGURE 5.44

Several Panasonic camcorders feature a built-in vectorscope that can alert the shooter to an overly warm or cool scene. The image at right might or might not be correct — depending, of course, on one's particular storytelling demands.

day to night or night to day, for example, are another matter as the dramatic boosting of individual color channels can introduce noise and lots of it, thereby impairing downstream encoding to DVD, Blu-ray, and the Web.[7]

MANAGING VIEWFINDER CLUTTER

There seems to be no limit these days to the minutia displayable in a viewfinder or swing-out LCD: focal distance, zoom percentage, battery condition, optical image stabilization (OIS), audio levels – there is more than ample opportunity to totally obscure the image and edges of the frame (Fig. 5.45).

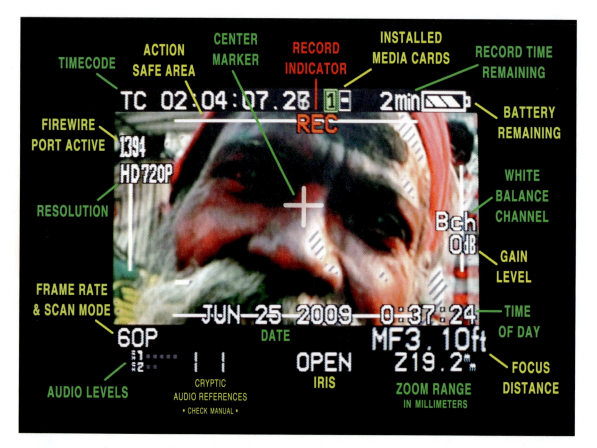

FIGURE 5.45

The point of any camera viewfinder is to facilitate framing, focus, and composition. This cluttered display appears to work against that imperative. For me, I prefer a more uncluttered view with only the essential functions displayed: timecode, memory card or tape status, remaining record time, battery condition, focus, zoom, iris settings, and frame rate. I also recommend displaying the *action safe area*, audio levels, and the center marker. When shooting talent, most viewers will accept a close-up composition as correct if the center marker is placed at or very near the subject's nose.

---

[7]For more on the rudiments of color correction techniques, check out *The Art and Technique of Digital Color Correction* by Steve Hullfish, Focal Press 2008, and *Color and Mastering for Digital Cinema* by Glenn Kennel, Focal Press 2007.

There is help now as many camcorders offer user-customization of display functions. We needn't enable the entire smorgasbord of gobblygook served up in the setup menus; rather, we need display only the essentials to monitor key parameters.

Some cameras provide framing guides for 16:9 and 4:3, as well as *title and action safe markings* to ensure sufficient headroom and proper placement of critical scene elements inside the frame. The action safe markers denote a 10% cut-in from each side, the title safe boundaries indicating a 20% cut-in. The theory behind title and action safe areas is the likelihood that some portion of the transmitted television image will be cut off in the home receiver or display. Modern TVs without overhanging physical cabinets seldom crop more than 7 or 8% of the picture, so a 20% title safe crop is overkill. In postproduction, I often push my title graphics into the title safe area. The shooter can keep this in mind as well.

The *rangefinder* is a very useful function to display in a camera's viewfinder. The numerical readout, in feet or meters, can greatly facilitate focusing by eye using the zone approach, a strategy I use almost exclusively when shooting with compact camcorders like the Sony EX3 in documentary or nonfiction environments.

The zoom range or percentage of zoom may be less critical to display, although some shooters of dramatic projects may need this data to ensure continuity. The zoom setting expressed as a percentage from 1 to 100 can be helpful to match frame size in a reaction shot, for example, or to ensure continuity in the event a scene or portion of a scene needs to be reshot.

It may seem obvious that the shooter should keep a watchful eye on the audio. Even with a sound recordist, it's still a good idea for shooters to verify proper levels and that audio is actually being recorded to the camera!

DON'T LAUGH – IT COULD HAPPEN TO YOU!

When rolling, always verify that the REC indicator is lit! verify the REC indicator is lit when recording! In the heat and of battle, it is not uncommon for a camera operator to forget to press RECORD! It has happened and will continue to – especially when operating solid-state cameras that are completely silent!

THE TIMECODE DILEMMA

Timecode is central to the workflow of the video storyteller as it provides a reliable means of referencing and synchronizing audio and video throughout a production. In the PAL television system,[8] timecode is a simple matter: video moves along at 25 fps and timecode invariably reflects that reality.

---

[8]PAL (phase alternating line) is an NTSC-based 50-Hz television system with a raster size of 720 × 576. Introduced in Europe in 1967, it is used widely throughout the world including most of Europe, Asia and Australia. Some folks claim that PAL with higher vertical resolution is superior to NTSC at 720 × 480. However, NTSC operates at a higher frame rate (30 fps rather than 25 fps) and thus delivers more samples or *fields* per second to the viewer.

In the NTSC system owing to the discrepancy between the nominal 30 fps and actual 29.97-fps frame rates, we must deal with *two* timecode systems – *drop frame* and *nondrop frame*. The existence of two timecode modes has been the source of misery and woe for decades.

TIMECODE TAKES OFF

It was the best of times. It was the worst of times. Timecode was born with the advent of the space program in the 1950s. Mission controllers watching for anomalies closely monitored the 30 fps television signals beamed back from space. In this context it made sense given the mission day to divide timecode into a 24-hour interval comprising hours, minutes, seconds, and frames.

This 1:1 system of counting frames proved practical when referring to mission events since one frame of video could be associated easily with a moment in time. The system of counting, however, did not account for the *actual* 29.97 frame rate of NTSC video, and so, this particular flavor of timecode posed a problem for broadcasters because it did not accurately reflect *elapsed* screen time, a matter of critical importance for timing programs of program on and off-air points. Thus, the demand was born for an alternative scheme based on the 29.97-fps rate, instead of nominal 30 fps used by NASA and others until then.

(a) (b)

FIGURE 5.46
(a) 1959 Mercury launch; (b) Ham the Chimp. The 1950s ushered in space exploration, monkey astronauts, and timecode. To track anomalies in flight mission, controllers embraced a 24-hour 30-fps video counting system.

FIGURE 5.47
Timecode consists of four fields: hours, minutes, seconds, and frames. A semicolon is commonly used in software applications to denote drop-frame (DF) timecode.

FIGURE 5.48
Just as the earth doesn't spin precisely at 24 hours per day, so does NTSC video not operate at exactly 30 fps. When timecode compensates for NTSC's actual frame rate of 29.97 fps, this is called *drop frame*. No actual video frames are dropped; the timecode is adjusted to compensate every minute (except every 10 minutes) by omitting frames 00 and 01 in the count. As for the calendar, we compensate with some exceptions every 4 years by adding an extra day – February 29.

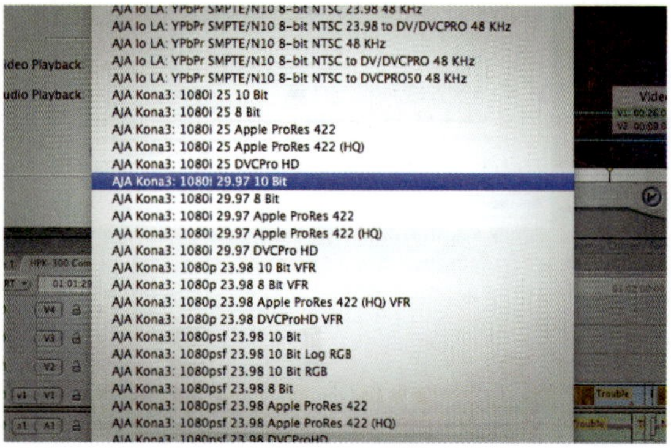

FIGURE 5.49
The evils of competing timecode schemes have sadly permeated the HD world. To enable easy downconversion to standard definition, it is common practice to shoot 60i/p HD with DF timecode. When shooting 23.98 fps (24p), nondrop frame timecode (NDF) always applies.

FIGURE 5.50
Which timecode mode is correct? If you're shooting for broadcast and need to precisely track running time, drop-frame TC is the better option. On the other hand, if you need to reference a continuous frame count, e.g. for closed captions or subtitles, NDF is the better choice. In most cases it really doesn't matter as long as your workflow consistently reflects one or the other. Remember: timecode mode does not apply when shooting 24p!

FIGURE 5.51
Some VCR displays use a single dot separator (rather than a colon) to indicate a DF recording.

FIGURE 5.52
The ability to assign timecode in-camera is essential for efficient organization and asset management.

WHEN YOU'RE OUT OF SYNC

When troubleshooting an out-of-sync condition, mismatched timecode modes should always be suspected. Capturing DF footage as NDF or vice versa will result in the program audio drifting out of sync at a rate of 3 seconds 17 frames per hour. This one insight will save you many hours of frustration over the course of your career and possibly earn you thousands of dollars. Please send your grateful payment to... ☺

RUNNING FREE

When synchronizing multiple cameras to a common timecode, the *free run* (F-Run) recording option is generally used. This setting advances the TC whether the camera is running or not. For routine single camera operation, the *record run* (R-Run) mode is more practical since timecode only advances when the camera is actually recording.

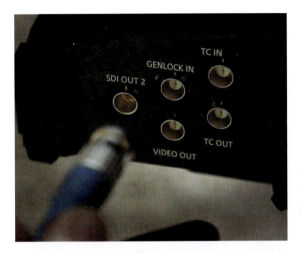

FIGURE 5.53
Multiple cameras with GENLOCK and TC IN/ OUT can easily lock together to share the same timecode.

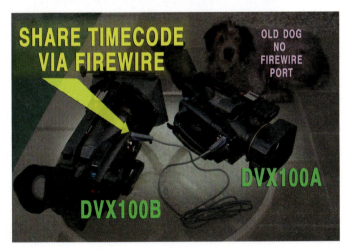

FIGURE 5.54
Synchronizing cameras without TC IN/OUT or GENLOCK may be possible via Firewire. However, the process of "jam syncing" may be convoluted and require many steps.

SPECIAL SHOOTING SITUATIONS

Given the features in today's camcorders, the shooter can look to these capabilities to expand his storytelling palette. Like the film cameras of yore, most modern cameras recording to solid-state memory are capable of shooting single-frame animation and stop-motion. The *intervalometer* has become a staple in everything from the most staid nature documentary to flashy

FIGURE 5.55
Among other things this iPhone application can calculate depth of field and help determine the correct interval for time-lapse recordings.

eye-candy bumpers for the evening news. Like frame rate and exotic focal length lenses, the intervalometer is best utilized in a subtle way to increase the *apparent* speed of slow-moving objects. These might include clouds streaming inland from the sea or the gentle movement of the sun's rays peeking around a building corner. The intervalometer typically provides a range of recording options from one frame every half-second to one frame every 10 minutes.

Selecting the appropriate interval requires experience and arithmetical prowess. A solid support or robust tripod is imperative, as well as having sufficient power available for the camera to cover a potential interval spanning days, weeks, or longer. Autoexposure, for once, may be an advantage depending on the length of the interval and the anticipated exposure fluctuations.

Many HD model cameras today including tape-based HDV types feature a prerecord (PRE_REC) function. This capability seemingly straight out of *The Twilight Zone* allows for the recording of picture and sound several seconds ahead of the shooter depressing the RECORD button (Fig. 5.57). The PRE_REC interval varies among camera models; most camcorders ranging from 3 seconds in HD to 7 seconds in SD.[9]

Solid-state cameras may also permit continuous recording to memory cards or hard disk. This LOOP capability is the only

FIGURE 5.56
Show me a world I haven't seen before! This time-lapse scene of a geyser was captured in Yellowstone National Park.

[9]Depending on camera model, PRE_REC may not be possible at all frame rates and capture modes, including 24p and 24p native formats. Be sure to check your camera's operating manual for specifics.

(a)

(b)

FIGURE 5.57
Some HD cameras feature a prerecord function that is ideal for shooting unforseen events like an elephant suddenly emerging from the forest or an attempted assassination in front of a California courthouse. With the camera set, uncapped, and properly focused, unanticipated action will be captured even if the shooter's attention was elsewhere for several seconds prior to pressing RECORD.

exception in these cameras that allows for recording over of previously recorded material. Otherwise given the many safeguards, it is impossible to inadvertently delete or overwrite existing files on a camera that utilizes a P2, SD, or SXS memory card.

OPTICAL IMAGE STABILIZATION

While OIS may be useful to reduce shake when shooting handheld, the feature must be used with care due to the increased risk of stutter or backlash when panning or tilting the camera. For routine operation, disabling OIS is usually a good idea.

MONITORING YOUR WORK

Shooting in HD, a high-resolution mounted atop the camera or located nearby is a virtual imperative for checking proper color balance, framing, and composition.

So what should a shooter look for in an on-board monitor? First, it must be compact and frugal on power, especially if patched directly into the camera. Most full-size camcorders feature a utility plug to power an on-camera light or monitor. Power consumption for a typical 8-inch LCD monitor should not exceed 20 W (at 12VDC). This is a reasonable power draw for a professional LCD display.

FIGURE 5.58
OIS is often useful for shooting out of moving vehicles or trains. On most compact camcorders, OIS can be enabled or disabled via an external button.

FIGURE 5.60
Some monitors feature focus-in-red peaking – an effective aide for seeing critical focus.

FIGURE 5.59
An on-board monitor is indispensable to circumvent the limitations of a camera's tiny viewfinder. In low light, the external display may be the only clue to what you're actually capturing.

FIGURE 5.61
Ahh. The beauty of seeing what we're doing. Panasonic monitors feature a built-in waveform and vectorscope for tweaking camera parameters in the field. A pixel for pixel function also assists critical focus by displaying the camera imager at native resolution, i.e., without scaling.

Be mindful of some monitors' substantial weight. While the increased mass may reflect a more robust construction, some displays are simply too heavy for the fragile handles of compact camcorders. Later model cameras from Panasonic and others have reinforced handles for this reason.

The newest LCD production monitors exhibit dramatically improved blacks, especially apparent in the deep shadow areas. Achieving solid black has been the bête-noire of LCD displays, as the fluorescent source backlight projected through a liquid panel produced a murkiness that made accurate color and contrast assessment difficult, if not impossible.

The latest-generation monitors reduce the murkiness and the once-common blue cast in the shadows by inserting a moment of black in the refresh cycle. This is one advantage of doubling the LCD's drive speed to 120 Hz, the improved blacks and reduction in motion blur being immediately obvious in sports and other high-motion environments.

FREQUENTING THE BARS

Whether you like to drink or not, you'll want to record 30 seconds of bars and tone at the head of every setup. If shooting to tape, this should be done for each new cassette and prior to beginning recording of actual program. The recording of bars and tone captures the state of the camera at the time of recording and will help ensure a proper audio and video reference through postproduction.

Not all cameras output standard SMPTE color bars, however, which you need to set up an analog monitor. The situation has improved in recent camera models, but there are a few laggards out there, so it's worth checking out the local bars scene as it pertains to your camera.

FIGURE 5.62
The SMPTE color bars at left are the industry standard. The nonstandard bars, right, are colorful but relatively useless. The zebras seen in the yellow swatch are set to 70%.

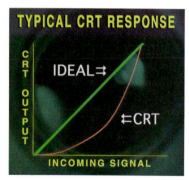

FIGURE 5.63
A straight green line reflects the ideal camera-display response. NTSC displays have a distorted response for which the standard definition camera or encoder compensates by skewing its response in the opposite direction. Not all cameras or DVD encoders apply this compensation (gamma correction) sufficiently or in the same way.

THE IMPERFECT CRT

In the ideal television system, there is a precise 1:1 relationship between what the camera sees and what the monitor ultimately displays. If equal amounts of red, blue, and green are fed into a camera, the same proportion of red, blue, and green should be evident in the display device.

The NTSC television system is rife with compromises, not the least of which is the (assumed) CRT display. Interestingly, your camera and LCD displays are capable of producing near-perfect images, but this perfection must be sacrificed to compensate for the anticipated distortion in the home CRT receiver. Although disappearing and banned in most countries out of environmental concern, the tube-based display and its legacy continues to wreak havoc in the guise of our standard definition NTSC and PAL programming, where many of us still find our bread and butter.

LIMITED GAMUT

While there is a single black level setup in digital space (Level 16), there are two in analog: 7.5 IRE in the United States and Zero IRE most notably in Japan. Some older DV cameras unfortunately output black via their analog jacks with Zero Setup. In these cases, the NTSC display set to 7.5 Setup yielded scenes with noticeably crushed blacks. The shooter must resist, then, the temptation to compensate in lighting or exposure, as the dark images displayed are not indicative of

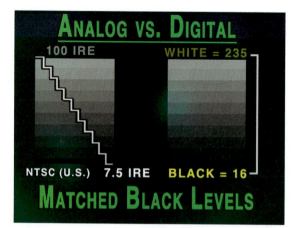

FIGURE 5.64
In 8-bit SD the digital range from pure black to pure white is 16–235. The more limited gamut should be considered if standard definition output to DVD, for example, is contemplated from an HD master.

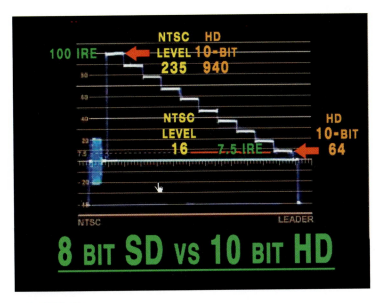

FIGURE 5.65
The equivalent 8- and 10-bit values for analog and digital video are noted on the waveform.

what is being recorded to tape. This means if you're still shooting with a Canon XL1, XL1-S, Sony DSR-PD150, Panasonic DVX100[10], or similar vintage camera, what you see on an external monitor is not necessarily what you're getting.

Shooting HD today we still suffer from the vestigial slings and arrows of the CRT.

Constrained by the NTSC and PAL standards, the CRT cannot display black values below digital 16 or white values above 235. The penalty for exceeding NTSC "safe" values is a dramatic increase in noise in the deepest highlights and brightest highlights as the CRT struggles and fails to display the wider gamut. Recording to a 10-bit format like AVC-Intra offers only a partial solution as it, too, must be hobbled in postproduction and limited to an output range of 64–940 (based on 1,024 assignable samples per channel) to accommodate a standard definition release.

---

[10]The output black setup error was subsequently corrected in the DVX100A model.

CHAPTER 6
Tweaking Your Story's Image

For many shooters, the creative mindset from decades ago still applies: do we want a film or video look? The rival looks connote a different feeling and sensibility. In general, the film look conveys a more dreamy transcendent feel and thus may be more appropriate for a narrative brand of storytelling, while the video look is more present tense or "immediate," and thus more suitable for news and nonfiction-type applications.

I entertain this mental wrangling before every shoot, as I settle on a look and adjust the camera menus accordingly. As in everything else, story and genre inform this decision most of all, so the proper look is part and parcel of the overall storytelling. Given the capabilities of many cameras today, we can create, in effect, a custom film emulsion for every project. It is a huge advantage not to have to depend on Kodak or anyone else for this, but it can also be a curse for the reasons stated earlier: too many choices can lead to paralysis like too many options at the In-N-Out Burger: it doesn't necessarily make for a happier burger buyer or more productive video shooter!

The film versus video paradigm has practical implications, as it impacts how a shooter implements various aspects of his craft. In the context of a video camera, the shooter invariably records at 60 frames or fields per second; all other frame rates including 24p being derived from that and appropriately played back later, ignoring the superfluous frames.

Traditional tape and disc-based cameras including DV, HDV, and XDCAM HD are video cameras and can only operate like one, limited by their mechanical transports that operate at a constant forward speed. These cameras support video connectivity and streaming via Firewire (IEEE 1394). Apple created Firewire in 1990 as a serial digital interface,[1] which enabled DV capture into an ordinary

---

[1]Firewire as a "serial digital interface" should not be confused with "SDI," the industry standard for uncompressed signals in standard and high definition. See Chapter 6 for more on SDI workflow.

FIGURE 6.1
Many HD cameras are capable of creating a highly custom look, akin to creating one's own film emulsion.

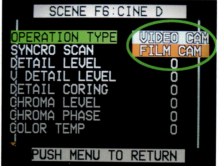

FIGURE 6.2
Shooting film or video? The two media convey a different look and mindset. Some cameras organize their menus this way as a means of strategizing image control.

FIGURE 6.3
The default settings of many cameras contribute heavily to video's presumed harsh brassy look. The shooter seeking to alleviate the curse can access an array of menu options to improve the look and feel of his images.

desktop computer. With the advent of solid-state cameras acting more like film cameras that record discrete frames, the relevance of Firewire has been significantly diminished.

Video cameras acting like film cameras have inherent advantages, notably the ability to record natively at various frame rates. This can improve the camera's low-light capability at lesser frame rates, while also reducing by more than 50% the storage requirements of (still) rather expensive memory cards. The flip side of this is that the camera isn't really shooting video – it's capturing data, which has implications with respect to workflow in an increasingly computer-centric IT world.

GETTING STARTED ON YOUR LOOK

When devising the appropriate "look" for a story, the first order of business is setting the camera *detail* (DTL). Detail level affects the perceived sharpness of a scene by placing a high-contrast edge around objects.

When detail is set too high, images rimmed with the hard edge acquire a crude unsubtle look that folks often associate with "video." When camera detail is set too low, images may appear soft and lacking in definition. Turning the detail off entirely is almost always a bad idea,[2] especially in lower-cost camcorders where maintaining adequate sharpness and contrast is a struggle even under the best of conditions.

When ascertaining an appropriate detail level, it's helpful to keep several factors in mind, including your story's intended display environment. For small-screen

---

[2]Turning off detail is not the same as a detail setting of 0, which means a *medium* amount of detail, half way between maximum and minimum.

venues – iPod, cell phone, and the Web – your visual story can support a higher detail setting than for large screen displays or digital cinema, where a hard edge is likely to be magnified many times and thus may appear more objectionable.

When shooting in film-like or cine-gamma modes, the master detail should typically be raised to compensate for the lower contrast and apparent loss of sharpness. Many cameras allow reducing the detail specifically in the flesh tones, which may be desirable to cover imperfections in an actor's complexion. Be careful not to dial the *skin detail* down too far, however, to avoid a ghoulish look. I knew a shooter who leaned on this gimmick a bit too much and transformed a leading actress's face into a soupy, undefined blob. That shooter is now selling shoes for a living on Staten Island.

Reducing the default detail in new cameras (especially Sony cameras) should be the first priority of every shooter as the elevated values favored by some manufacturers contribute to a hard plastic look. One reason manufacturers may prefer a high detail setting is to compensate for a camera's inexpensive optics that lack good resolution and contrast. Camera makers also apparently believe that unsophisticated shooters prefer the "sharper" hyper-real look. I'm told that's true in Japan. I don't think it's the case elsewhere.

In the natural world around us, objects transition gently from low- to high-contrast areas. This smooth transition is evident even in high-contrast scenes like the silhouette of a skateboarder (see Fig. 6.4) framed against the bright evening sky.

FIGURE 6.4
An excessively high detail setting rims the skateboarder with an unnatural hard edge.

GENTLE ORGANIC TRANSITION

FIGURE 6.5
Smooth transitional boundaries produce less harsh, more natural-looking images.

(a)   (b)

FIGURE 6.6
The hard edging around objects is an indication of excessive detail level. (a) This Venice scene at dusk was captured with minimal detail. (b) The blow-up reflects the same scene with high detail. Many cameras are shipped from the factory with elevated detail, a ruse intended to foster the impression of better optics and increased image "sharpness."

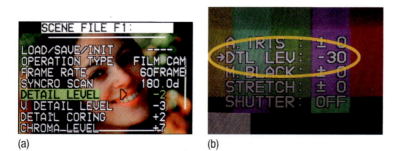

(a)   (b)

FIGURE 6.7
In mid-level Panasonic camcorders (a), the detail level may be increased or reduced in seven increments. Comparable Sony models (b) offer a range from −99 to +99, an initial setting of −25 to −30 being usually advisable. Note that a "zero" value means average or medium-level detail.

FIGURE 6.8
Dialing down skin detail helps conceal blemishes in the face and skin of your favorite Hollywood starlet.

FIGURE 6.9
Soft detail is analogous to the Unsharp Mask in Adobe Photoshop. When excessively applied, the thick lines can become objectionable. (Images courtesy of JVC.)

Be conservative when setting detail, especially in entry-level camcorders. For narrative projects, use a lower setting; for documentaries, feel free to increase the detail setting slightly, and as always, let good taste and the demands of your story be your guide!

GOING GOING GAMMA

After determining proper detail, next up is selecting an appropriate *gamma*. Camera gamma determines the range of tones reproducible in the straight-line portion of the characteristic response curve (Fig. 6.10). A lower gamma (i.e., less slope) enables more tonal gradation and may help retain shadow detail. A too low gamma, however, will produce lifeless washed-out images as the mid-tones and highlights are undesirably lifted along with the shadows. Conversely, excessive gamma may yield a high-contrast look with a surreal wax-like finish imparted to faces and flesh tones. Hey! If you're shooting *Invaders from Mars*, this may be exactly what you're looking for!

Today many cameras offer a range of gamma presets, including film-like or cine modes. The intent is to dramatically alter the camera's response curve to better reflect film's wider tonal response in the shadows and highlights.

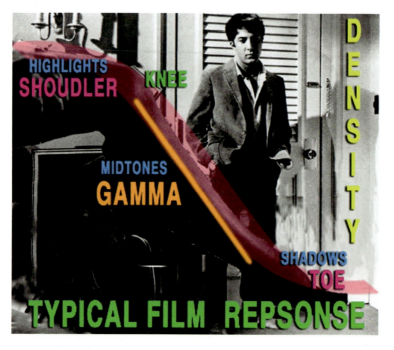

FIGURE 6.10
Don't get seduced by cine gamma! While cine gamma is designed to mimic the gentle toe and knee response of motion-picture film, it can introduce substantial noise in underlit areas of the frame.

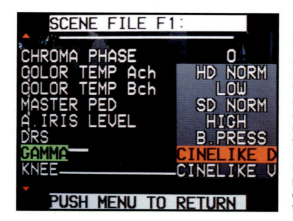

FIGURE 6.11
HD camcorders often feature several gamma presets. Panasonic's CINELIKE-D maximizes latitude at the cost of potentially increased shadow noise. CINELIKE-V produces a punchier look with higher contrast and less noise compared with the HD NORM setting. I prefer HD NORM (or STD) for most documentary work, as it delivers good performance in a range of lighting conditions with minimal noise in the shadows.

(a)   (b)

FIGURE 6.12
In cameras that support a user-defined gamma, most shooters prefer a "normal" value of 0.45. I prefer the increased punch of a slightly higher 0.50 gamma, especially when shooting in low-contrast film-like modes.

GOT DENSE SHADOWS?

Shadows communicate the essence of our visual story, delivering to the viewer a sense of genre, mood, and the protagonist's mindset. Overly dense shadows can work against our storytelling goals.

There are a number of ways to tackle the issue of excessively deep shadows. Adding appropriate fill light and camera diffusion[3] are common ways to help retain shadow detail. So can enabling a contrast, lowering gamma, or *black stretch* (see Fig. 6.13). Black stretch can improve shadow detail by producing

FIGURE 6.13
While many shooters use black stretch to enhance shadow detail, its counterpart, *black compress*, may be useful in some night scenes to suppress noise in underlit areas.

[3]See the discussion of camera contrast-control filters later in this chapter.

FIGURE 6.14
In newer camcorders, many functions including black stretch and black compress may be assigned to a User Button at the side or top of the camera.

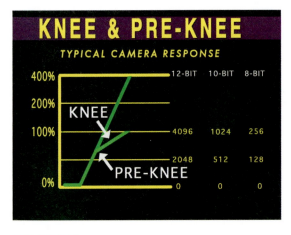

FIGURE 6.15
In some cameras, the shooter can set a pre-knee point where the slope lowers to accommodate greater detail and contrast range in the highlights. A typical pre-knee value might range from 85 to 95%. In cine modes, this value is much lower.

more shades of gray in the darkest areas of the image. The potential drawback is the increased noise in underlit areas, so black stretch should always be applied with care and with proper attention to adequate fill, which in most cases is the preferred strategy for managing too dense shadows.

WATCH YOUR HIGHLIGHTS

While shadow control is critical to your visual story, the retention of highlight detail is also pivotal. Unintentionally blown-out or *clipped* highlights are the sure sign of a novice shooter, so proper attention must be paid to an image's hotter areas.

Preservation of highlight detail is a function of your camera's *knee* setting. A gentler slope in the knee means more tonal gradations and, thus, better detail accommodation (Fig. 6.15). Analogous to black stretch in the toe, a gentle knee can improve the look of an interior scene that includes, for example, a bright exterior window.

A film or cine-like gamma reduces the knee dramatically to as low as 20% to accommodate as much highlight detail as possible. While this may be desirable and indicative of a traditional film stock, it may also produce images with dingy off-color whites, akin to not using enough bleach when doing the laundry; the whites never get really, truly white.

In comparison, an elevated knee above 90% may produce purer whites but at the increased risk of "clipping." The clipping of highlights is a significant hazard facing the video shooter, the loss of highlight detail being particularly difficult to ameliorate in post.

AUTOKNEE

A camera's *autoknee* sets the appropriate threshold dynamically, to retain as much highlight detail as possible on the one hand, and preserve the whiteness of the whites on the other. Today's 12- and 14-bit cameras sample far more picture information than can actually be recorded to tape or flash memory. Accordingly, the autoknee provides a mechanism (Fig. 6.17) by which some of the excess detail can be infused into the 8-bit recording as demanded by the various XDCAM HD/EX, DVCPRO HD, HDV, DV formats. How much highlight detail that can actually be retained, however, is a function of the knee and its slope, which in most cases is best controlled in automode (Fig. 6.18).

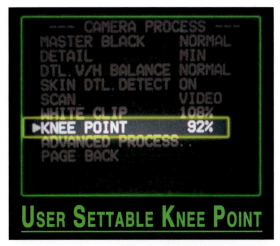

USER SETTABLE KNEE POINT

FIGURE 6.16
The pre-knee point is commonly expressed as a percentage. On some cameras, an external toggle allows shooters to disable the autoknee function. You will seldom want to.

FIGURE 6.17
The pre-knee point impacts the amount of detail retained after squeezing the oversampled image into the 8- or 10-bit space imposed by the recording format.[4]

FIGURE 6.18
The autoknee enables capture of increased highlight detail as evidenced in the car windows at right. (Images courtesy of JVC.)

---

[4]While most recording formats like DV, HDV, and XDCAM are 8 bits, Panasonic's AVC-Intra codec captures 10 bits to P2 flash memory.

FIGURE 6.19
Dynamic Range Stretch applies autoknee as needed to portions of the frame at risk of clipping. This can help in high-contrast environments typical of many sports venues.

Still, autoknee has a notable drawback as it affects the entire frame, pulling down the whites even in areas with little actual risk of clipping. For this reason, Panasonic developed Dynamic Range Stretch (DRS), which applies autoknee only to the portions of the frame that need it. For example in a sports stadium (Fig. 6.19), when panning from the dark stands to a sunlit field, DRS greatly reduces the risk of clipping in the course of the pan, pulling down the peaking values in the sunlit section to ensure a smooth gradient from dark to light and vice versa.

MATRIX

In keeping with the notion of creating one's own film emulsion, specific colors in a scene can be made more intense to create a specific look or support a storytelling goal. Professional cameras, including some prosumer models, offer various preset matrices for shooting under fluorescents or to simulate the color response and saturation of motion-picture film.

Consider the color matrix in our mind. Under ordinary fluorescents, we may not see the noxious green cast, but it certainly is there and the camera sees it, especially so. The matrix in the camera can be configured to de-emphasize the green spike just like our brains do; otherwise, the spike could overwhelm a scene if the default tungsten matrix were left in place.

The shooter may also want to use an alternative matrix to offset shifts in color due to elevated video gain. In low light, hue shifts are common, especially under mercury vapor and similar-type lighting, so a matrix more reflective of "seeing" under such conditions should ideally be applied. Changes in a camera's color matrix do not affect black or white levels.

(a)

(b)

(c)

FIGURE 6.20
As a storyteller, you can use the camera's matrix to punch up or tone down colors integral to your story. The muted color in Fig. 6.20a helps meld the cat with similar hues into the Roman canvas. The intense red rhino in Fig. 6.20b amplifies its dominant storytelling role. Same deal in Fig. 6.20c where the green umbrella IS the story.

CONTROLLING CHROMA

Color saturation (*chroma*) can strongly convey a sense of your story's genre. High chroma is generally associated with light comedies and satires; the climactic saturated scene of exploding consumer appliances in Michelangelo Antonioni's *Zabriskie Point* immediately springs to mind (Fig. 6.22).

The *news gamma* is often preferred by news directors who feel a hyper-sharp, saturated look conveys greater immediacy (Fig. 6.23). Conversely,

FIGURE 6.21
Typical color matrix menu in a prosumer camcorder. The matrix function in high-end models offers much greater precision and capability.

FIGURE 6.22
The high chroma deluge of exploding products in *Zabriskie Point* (1970) reinforces the film's storytelling and sexually charged theme.

FIGURE 6.23
High-contrast scenes with vivid color are indicative of news and reality shows. Some cameras feature a news gamma preset to facilitate this look.

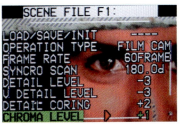

FIGURE 6.24
Typical chroma adjustment in a mid-level HD camcorder.

weak desaturated color or low chroma suggests a story told in past tense, which may be the correct tone, say, for a historical drama that takes place in the 1930s.

As in all things craft-driven, the camera's chroma is best applied subtly. Kick it up a click or two to add punch to a scene or knock it down several increments to fuel a period drama. Pushing chroma higher can be a way to increase apparent sharpness, but the compensation required later in post to correct the imbalance may introduce noise. Better to tweak the camera as required to achieve the desired look on location; it might be doable later during color correction but it won't be as simple or as free of noise.

YOUR STORY, YOUR MASTER PEDESTAL

The *Master Pedestal* lies at the beginning of the gamma portion of the camera response curve and affects black level and the density of shadows. A lower Master Pedestal creates deeper blacks and higher contrast, while a raised setting produces a washed-out look with weaker blacks and lower contrast.

Shooting with an elevated Master Pedestal may require raising the camera detail (DTL) to compensate for the apparent loss of sharpness. Lowering the Master Pedestal and applying negative gain (−3 dB) can reduce noise significantly along with the black level. Such tactics effectively reduce the sensitivity of the camera as well, so the smart shooter must also keep this in mind.

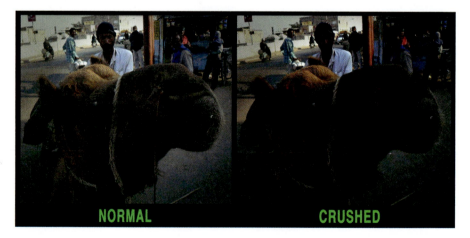

NORMAL   **CRUSHED**

FIGURE 6.25
Smug camel. Smug shooter. Crushed blacks drain life from images and suppress detail that may be crucial to your story.

NO GAIN, NO PAIN

In most cases there is little to gain from increased *gain*. Camera gain controls the sensitivity of the imager in analog terms by regulating the level of signal amplification. In most cameras, gain may be raised or lowered by selecting a low, medium, or high setting at the side of the camera body. When gain is raised, the camera's sensitivity and ability to capture detail is also raised but unfortunately along with the noise. Then, when compressing for the Web, DVD, or Blu-ray, the increased noise can contribute to a maelstrom of ugly picture defects, as the encoder is unable to separate unintended noise from intended image detail.

FIGURE 6.26
Undercranking can create amazing images in very low light. In Terrence Malick's *Days of Heaven* (1978), the actors slowed their performances to compensate for the 6-fps camera intended for 24 fps film playback.

When shooting in low light, increased camera gain should be the last resort, not the first, to achieve an acceptable range of gray tones. Many cameras offer increased gain up to +18 dB or even higher (Fig. 6.28), the copious noise at this level making such scenes suitable only for down-and-dirty news or surveillance applications.

Each +6 dB increase in gain, nets one-stop advantage in exposure. In broadcast cameras, *digital super gain* provides greatly improved functionality with less noise, the camera boosting the signal in the digital domain where the noise can be more effectively isolated from the picture information. Digital gain can produce markedly more usable images than the traditional analog method of amplifying the entire signal, desired or not, emanating from the imager.

FIGURE 6.27
In many models, gain values ranging from −3 dB to +18 dB can be assigned to the L/M/H toggle at the side of the camera. Not all cameras feature a negative gain option.

Some shooters prefer working with *negative* gain, which deepens the blacks and helps obscure the noise in weak shadows. Many recent camcorders including the Sony XDCAM EX feature a −3-dB setting, which decreases the camera's sensitivity a fraction of a stop along with the noise. The trade-off may not always be viable.

Rather than resort to increased gain, my approach to shooting in low light often entails *undercranking* the camera, that is, recording at a slower frame rate.[5] This

---

[5]Shooting at less than normal playback speed (24, 30, or 60 fps) produces accelerated motion on screen; capturing a scene at higher than normal playback speed, i.e., overcranking produces a slow motion effect.

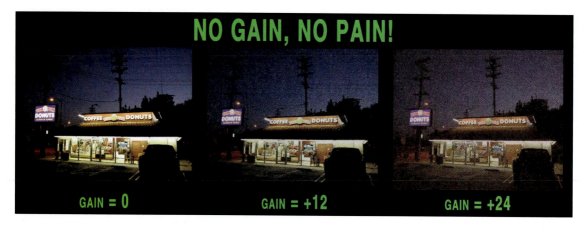

FIGURE 6.28
Be wary of shooting with elevated gain. The increase in noise can seriously detract from your visual story.

strategy obviously doesn't apply in dialog scenes or when shooting with a tape or disc-based camera that records in any case "over 60 fps," but it does work well with the new solid-state camcorders. Undercranking at 12 fps and recording in *native mode* proportionately slows the scan rate of the imager and effectively doubles the camera's low-light response when compared with operating at the normal 24 fps.

I'm often amazed by the degree of cheating we shooters can get away with! The great cinematographer Néstor Almendros shooting late after dusk would slow down his actors in combination with a slow cranking camera to gain the additional exposure. The technique used in the famous locust scene in *Days of Heaven* (Fig. 6.26) significantly extended the storytelling window, effectively and remarkably, well into the Magic Hour.

KEEP THE NOISE DOWN, WILL YA?

It may be the most serious problem facing documentary and reality TV style shooters: noise, and often lots of it, in dark shadows and underlit areas of the frame. With the advent of HD cameras' smaller, less responsive pixels, objectionable noise has emerged as many shooters' primary concern. While it's impossible to eliminate noise entirely, there are ways to mitigate it through proper camera setup, strategic use of physical and software filters, and controlled lighting.

It's important to address the noise issue in-camera because its potential negative impact will likely be multiplied many times downstream when encoding to the Web, cell phone, DVD, and Blu-ray. In general, noise may be defined as random single-pixel hits of data that are always present but not necessarily apparent. Potential sources of noise include the camera imager or processor, faulty Firewire or USB cable, even the recording media itself.

Standard definition cameras with relatively large pixels typically exhibit better shadow integrity with less noise than similar-class HD cameras. In compact camcorders, the tiny HD imager struggling in low light can often not distinguish the detail in the image from the surrounding noise, and with chaos in the ranks and error-correction running amok, the reconstructed frame played back later can get pretty ugly.

We discussed how compressing the blacks or lowering the Master Pedestal can take the noise down considerably. The effect can often be punishing, but if noise is the number one villain in your life and you don't mind throwing the silicon out with the bath water, the victory-at-all-costs approach may be a viable way to go.

Along these same lines it is usually best to avoid the cine-like modes that stretch the blacks to increase shadow detail but may also further exacerbate the noise in a scene's underbelly. This doesn't mean foregoing the cine-gamma modes altogether. It simply means you must pay closer attention to shadow integrity and make sure the shadows are well supported. Well-filled scenes are happy scenes, quiet and unobtrusive, where noise is not a serious visual storytelling impediment.

Another common strategy to reduce noise is dialing down your camera's Master Detail. This can help blur the edges of noisy pixels and render them less objectionable but at the price of some reduction in image sharpness and contrast.

A more effective approach, perhaps, is raising the camera's *detail coring*. Detail coring targets only the noisy pixels close to the baseline of the waveform, that is, in the deepest shadows where noise is most apparent and objectionable. In some camcorders, the detail coring and associated noise reduction is applied automatically as part of routine image processing. This approach has its advantages as images normally appear calmer and with less noise in low light.

When dialing up detail coring, be careful not to push it too far, since image detail is suppressed along with the noise residing in the same shadowy neighborhood.

Use just enough coring to be effective, but not so much to render the shadows sterile and devoid of life. Note that detail coring works by defocusing the edges around pixels and thus has little effect with the camera detail level set low. The coring option only really works at normal or elevated detail settings.

Of course, shadow noise can be especially objectionable in the faces of actors. In this case, the lowering of skin detail can be useful to tamp down texture along with any noisy pixels. As in all cases related to detail level, the reduction of skin detail must be done with care to avoid an unflattering mushy look. Remember it's not only your actor's image that is on the line!

FIGURE 6.29
No guts, no glory! Shooting in low light opens yourself up to capturing your best stuff! Don't be afraid of the dark!

FILTERING YOUR IMAGE

The savvy shooter storyteller knows the curse well – the impenetrable blacks, the blown-out highlights, the hard plastic edges around objects. For years, these were the hallmarks of DV that we had to put up with in exchange for the economy and opportunities that the format offered.

Today's low-cost HD, HDV, and AVCHD cameras contribute to the video curse in their own ways: inferior optics, hue shifts, and overzealous error correction all play their part. But whatever the reason for lackluster images, if you're going to derive the best performance from your trusty low-cost HD variant, you'll need to address the techno-esthetic issues head-on, and that includes, almost invariably, the strategic use of an appropriate physical or software-based camera filter.

GETTING PHYSICAL

With more sophisticated camera processors, the curse of low-cost digital video may seem like less of an issue. Indeed, the majority of cameras today require only minimal futzing to produce what most folks would consider a decent-looking picture.

Still, the savvy shooter storyteller understands the value of a properly *finished* image, and for most shooters, a physical camera filter is the best and most practical way to achieve it. This is because a physical filter placed in front of the lens treats the actual *captured* image, optimizing levels of detail, contrast, and diffusion that, in turn, enable the highest performance and efficiency in the camera processor.

Deliberately capturing a scene with an incorrect look and then hoping to fix it in post is a dubious strategy, since the unwanted attributes tend to be

FIGURE 6.30
The complex interplay of light passing through a physical filter cannot be completely recreated in software.

FIGURE 6.31
The newest generation cameras with CMOS imagers produce video of extraordinary sharpness, with a harsh look and propensity for copious noise. Proper image control and filtration can help mitigate these issues.

amplified after compression in-camera. Properly compensating in postproduction or inside the NLE may not even be possible as the countermeasures required to remedy serious shortcomings are likely in and of themselves to produce objectionable picture defects.

While many filters can indeed be approximated in software, the delicate interplay of light through a physical glass element is not a process that lends itself to a generalized postcamera solution. Considering a beam of light interacting with the thousands of tiny *lenslets* inside a Schneider HD Classic Soft, the character, color, and direction of the beam are impacted in a myriad of ways as it passes through and around the irregularly interspersed elements.

A physical filter's actual impact on an image depends on many factors, like the strength of a backlight, if it is striking the filter directly or obliquely, whether point sources in frame are sharply defined or more diffused, and even the degree of polarization in the sky. All these elements can profoundly affect the mood, look, and feel of one's visual storytelling.

CONSIDER FILTER LAST

The savvy shooter understands that a camera filter should be considered last, not first, with respect to controlling a story's look. It should be viewed as icing on the cake after the lighting has been tweaked, diffused, and appropriate camera setup options selected.

Here are a few pointers before reaching for your filter kit:

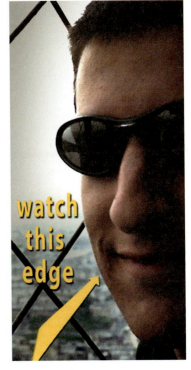

FIGURE 6.32
Try reducing the camera or skin detail setting to alleviate hard edges, especially in close-ups. The lowering of detail mimics the effect of a diffusion filter.

FIGURE 6.33
Consider adding fill light. Rembrandt probably never gave it much thought, but unfilled shadows can be the source of abundant digital noise.

FIGURE 6.34
Consider your story and the appropriateness of a deeply saturated color palette. For dramatic productions, a low-contrast cine gamma with muted color may be more desirable.

FIGURE 6.35
When geyser gazing, watch for erupting blown-out areas of the frame. You may need to adjust the camera's knee and gamma settings to accommodate the extreme dynamic range.

FIGURE 6.36
When downcoverting to standard definition, be wary of the usual NTSC troublemakers, like moiré patterns in wardrobe and combing effects in scenes containing many vertical elements.

FIGURE 6.37
High-detail scenes like this 1937 view of my grandfather's grocery may wreak havoc if captured in an interlaced format. Consider deinterlacing such scenes in postproduction, or better still, shoot progressively at 24p, 30p, or 60p.

FIGURE 6.38
The correct camera filter can dramatically enhance the visual storytelling, especially in landscape scenes.

FIGURE 6.39
The tiny droplets in a black mist filter may appear inadvertently on screen due to some cameras' enormous depth of field and confused autofocus system. While shooting wide-open and avoiding backlit scenes can help, shooters may also opt for an alternative filter type without a droplet pattern, such as the Tiffen Soft/FX or Schneider Digicon.

DESIGNED FOR THE TASK

While camera filters of various types have been around since photography's first days, the advent of chipsets only a few millimeters in diameter has necessitated a change in design to accommodate the more stringent demands. Not that a vintage diffusion filter or *net* can't serve today's video stories, of course it can. Storytelling with a camera is a craft, after all, and only you, the talented, gifted manipulator of light and shadow, can make the aesthetic determinations appropriate to your story.

Nevertheless, many older filters are not ideal for digital use because they utilize a soda lime glass that imparts a green tint, a trivial amount perhaps to film shooters, but a more serious matter to video folks owing to the potential for inaccurate color sampling and loss of saturation. The impact of the green glass is exacerbated in three-chip cameras whose green sensor is deliberately moved out of register to reduce artifacts in high-detail scenes.[6]

Modern filters designed for digital applications use a pure "water white" glass that does not contribute to sampling inaccuracies. From the shooter's perspective, a filter is a precision optic and must be produced in much the same way. While manufacturers today are very precise, this was not necessarily the case years ago; so older, less flat filters may produce waves of distortion in today's cameras, especially during slow panning. Older-style laminated filters should be especially avoided as they produce tiny focus shifts and banding patterns that lead to pixilation in the encoded video file.

FIGURE 6.40
Neutral density filters are available in a range from 0.3 to 1.2, the equivalent of one to four stops. By absorbing 50% or more of the incoming light, the ND filter enables a larger f-stop with reduced depth of field – usually a good thing!

The structure of traditional nets may also interfere with an imager's grid pattern, and thus exacerbate aliasing issues. Older-style black mist filters can be particularly problematic, as their highly reflective droplets can confuse a camera's autofocus system (Fig. 6.39). Some cameras simply freak out and interpret the scattered dots as a dirty lens, ratcheting up the error correction to compensate!

KNOW THE LOOK YOU WANT

For the shooter, of course, it's all about the "look". But what should that *look* like? Should it be soft and diffused as in a period romance or hard and

---

[6]See Chapter 3 for a discussion of spatial offset and related aliasing issues.

FIGURE 6.41
The tiny apertures required to shoot midday exteriors tend to exacerbate small-imager video's enormous depth of field. By enabling a larger f-stop, the neutral density filter (ND) assures optimal lens performance, image resolution and contrast.

unforgiving, as might be appropriate for a documentary about forensic science or news coverage of the latest City Hall scandal?

Shooting with as wide an aperture as possible is usually a good idea. Filter and net patterns are less likely to appear on screen, the reduced depth of field helps isolate key story elements, and the large f-stop eliminates the risk of diffraction and softening of the image.

In bright daylight, shooting wide open (or nearly so) requires a neutral density (ND) exposure control filter. Most cameras feature a built-in ND array (Fig. 6.42) that provides a two to four stop advantage. This obviates the need in all but the most extreme cases for a supplemental ND filter in front of the lens. Neutral density filters are gray in color and do not affect the color or character of a scene.

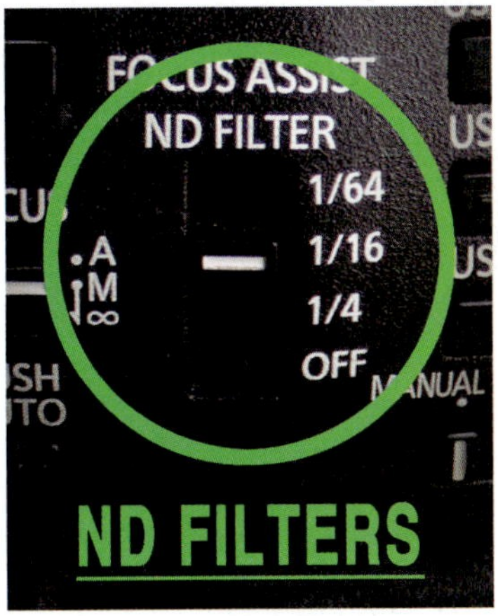

FIGURE 6.42
Many cameras now provide sufficient built-in neutral-density so a supplemental glass filter is no longer necessary. Be sure to engage your camera's ND when shooting in bright conditions!

AVOID SMALL F-STOPS

Shooting at narrow f-stops can have a significant negative impact on one's images, as all lenses are subject to diffraction and loss of contrast when stopped down. The bending and scattering of light through and around the tiny aperture (Fig. 6.43) can produce multiple internal reflections and a concomitant increase in flare. As a result, bright daylight scenes typically appear washed out or otherwise lacking in sharpness (Fig. 6.44).

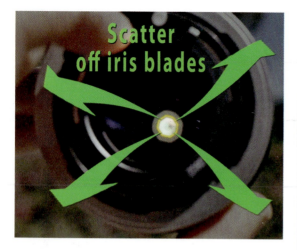

FIGURE 6.43
At small apertures, the edges of the iris appear to glow and act as many tiny light sources, scattering light and dramatically lowering contrast. For the shooter storyteller, inferior lens performance at small f-stops is another compelling reason to shoot early or late in the day.

FIGURE 6.44
This bright ski scene recorded at a minimum f-stop appears washed out due to severe diffraction.

A POLARIZED VIEW

The polarizer is among the most heavily used filters in the shooter's arsenal and for good reason: it is the only filter that can *increase* contrast and resolution. For this reason, the polarizer is indispensable for shooting land and seascapes, which tend to be low in contrast due to the many layers of atmosphere and the small f-stop typically used to record such scenes.

A polarizing filter increases contrast by reducing light scatter. This is accomplished by the filter's horizontal or vertical grid that blocks the off-axis waves not consistent with the polarizer's orientation. Because the northern sky (in the northern hemisphere) is partially polarized already, a suitably aligned polarizer can further darken the sky and increase the impact of clouds against it.

A polarizing filter is most effective at 90° to the sun. One way to determine the area of sky subject to maximum darkening is to point at the sun and note the direction of your thumb which points to the most polarized section of the sky. The *opposite* sky at 180° is also subject to maximum darkening.

When shooting exteriors under bright conditions, a polarizing filter can often improve an actor's skin tone by attenuating a portion of the sun's glare. The increased contrast may also, however, increase the visibility of blemishes, surface

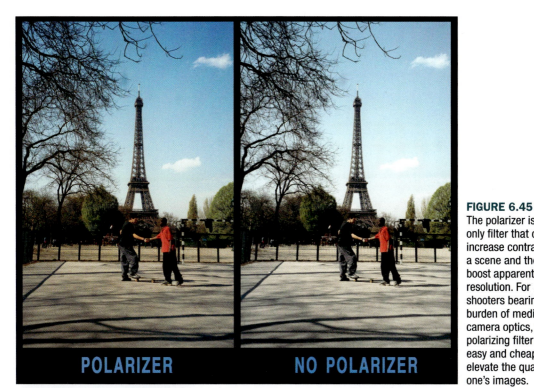

POLARIZER   **NO POLARIZER**

FIGURE 6.45
The polarizer is the only filter that can increase contrast in a scene and thereby boost apparent resolution. For shooters bearing the burden of mediocre camera optics, the polarizing filter is an easy and cheap way to elevate the quality of one's images.

Off-axis rays blocked

FIGURE 6.46
The polarizer's grid blocks off-axis rays, reducing contrast-robbing scatter. Polarizers come in both linear and circular varieties. Linear polarizers are more effective but may interfere with a camera's autofocus system and other functions. If autofocus is important to you, go with the circular type.

FIGURE 6.47
Polarizers reduce or eliminate window reflections that can add a three-dimensional sense to a scene. Don't automatically kill reflections and highlights that can be useful to your visual story!

veins, and other defects, so a polarizer should always be used with care when shooting talent close-ups.

SKY CONTROL

Our usual desire to record maximum texture is frequently challenged by bright areas of the sky that exceed the dynamic range capability of the camera. Blown-out areas of the frame including the sky and clouds convey an amateurish feeling that can distract or even alienate audiences from the storytelling experience.

A sky control filter with a soft, hard, or attenuated edge provides a means by which detail can be preserved across the frame from the deepest shadows through the brightest highlights. Graduated filters which taper to a clear section are available in range of colors, the most useful for me being the soft-edge blue, sunset, and 0.6 and 0.9 ND varieties. In general, we use a soft-edge grad for wide-angle landscapes; the hard-edge grad is a better choice for use with the telephoto to preserve a more discernible graduated effect.

FIGURE 6.48
Effective sky control is critical to avoid clipping and the loss of large areas of detail. At right, a soft ND 0.9 graduated filter darkens the sky and helps direct the viewer's eye to the compelling story inside the frame.

FIGURE 6.49
Sky control filters can reduce the risk of clipping in high-contrast exteriors. The attenuator used in the street scene at left is not intrusive; at right, the same scene without the attenuator. The filter's lack of a dividing line (and need to conceal it) is a major advantage.

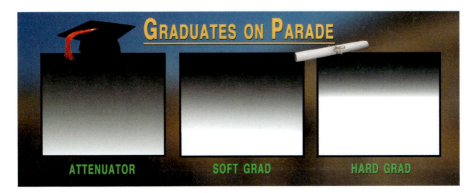

FIGURE 6.50

A graduated attenuator pattern is at left. The hard-edge grad (right) is used with telephoto lenses. The soft grad (middle) with a feathered transition is ideal for wide, establishing shots with large areas of sky.

FIGURE 6.51

You want blue sky? I'll give you blue sky! The soft edge of the graduated filter at right is concealed across the top third of the frame.

FIGURE 6.53

A sunset grad can add color and interest to scenes captured late in the Magic Hour.

FIGURE 6.52

Tiffen soft-edge blue graduated No. 2 filter.

HOW THEY STACK UP

Maintaining satisfactory contrast can be a challenge. While inferior lenses and the lack of a matte box or sunshade are contributing factors, the stacking of multiple filters can make matters worse by increasing the number of air-to-glass surfaces and potential internal reflections that lead to contrast loss.

If a warming effect is desired along with diffusion, I prefer a combination filter, like a Warm Pro-Mist or Warm Supermist that merges the two functions (Fig. 6.54). As a rule I try not to stack more than two filters. For example, I will commonly stack a star filter and weak Tiffen 1/8 Black Pro-Mist to soften the star's hard edges (Fig. 6.57).

FIGURE 6.55
The overused star filter is a favorite of sports and event shooters. A matte box with a rotating stage is essential for proper orientation of star and graduated filters.

FIGURE 6.54
The warming and diffusion functions are combined in this one filter, eliminating the need to stack the multiple filters that can reduce contrast.

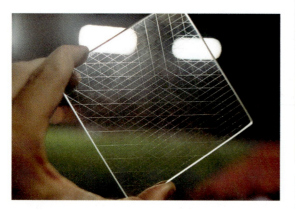

FIGURE 6.56
The Tiffen vector star.

FIGURE 6.57
Sometimes stacking of filters is unavoidable; here, a warm diffusion filter is used to soften the harshness of the star filter behind it. Note the position of the star close to camera reducing the likelihood of its pattern appearing on screen.

THE LOW-CONTRAST DILEMMA

In most cases, the shooter seeks to enhance contrast, and this is where proper lighting, superior optics, and a polarizing filter can help. Shooting in bright sun in the middle of the day without silks, fill cards, or supplemental lighting will almost certainly produce images with too much contrast, so you'll need a contrast reducing solution in your arsenal as well.

A low-contrast filter works by redistributing surplus values from an image's highlights into the shadows (Fig. 6.58). This lightening of the shadows allows the overall scene to be darkened proportionately, thus pulling down the hottest highlights to prevent clipping. This can be an advantage to shooters trying to capture high-contrast exteriors with little or no additional fill light.

However, the increase in dynamic range comes at a price. Blacks may become murky and contribute to a flat, lifeless image. This is because a low-contrast filter does not actually improve the inherent capture capabilities of the camera and lens system. A low-contrast filter can indeed expand the dynamic range by two stops or more, but the resultant washed-out look may not be acceptable.

The cine-like gamma option in many cameras works similarly, expanding the dynamic range and improving shadow detail while at the same time creating grayer, possibly less compelling and noisier images overall.

For the shooter preferring the low-contrast look, a weak low-con filter may work fine. Likewise for shooters looking ahead to a digital intermediate or

FIGURE 6.58
Low-contrast filters can help prevent clipping in the brightest highlights while coaxing greater detail from the deepest shadows. A noble idea, but be careful: too low contrast can produce washed-out images that lack sparkle.

FIGURE 6.59
A terrific choice for cityscapes at night, the ultracontrast filter can often eliminate the need for supplemental fill light. At right, the increased detail is apparent in the side of the hot dog stand. Scenes illuminated by practical sources, such as neon, stand to benefit most from the ultracontrast filter, which lifts underlit shadows without producing an obvious flare or pronounced diffused effect.

FIGURE 6.60
To conduct a proper "emulsion" test, find a cooperative subject and light her in a normal way. Then, referring to a proper monitor, gradually reduce the fill light and note the level of shadow detail discernible at each stage along with any hue shifts. Recognizing how your camera responds in deep shadow will improve your abilities as a visual storyteller and prepare you well for the lighting challenges ahead.

film out, the additional shadow detail could be an advantage, assuming any murkiness in the gray tones can be ameliorated in software.

Most diffusion filters incorporate a contrast-lowering component, so few shooters will need to invest in a set of low-con filters. Still, with the smooth, modulated images possible in today's cameras, a low-contrast filter may be all you need to achieve a satisfactory dynamic range when shooting "run-and-gun" in full sun.

THE EMULSION TEST

One doesn't normally think of performing an emulsion test when evaluating a video camera, but that's what I do when working with a new or unfamiliar model. In film, shooters will often test the responsiveness of a new stock to determine the level of shadow detail that can be retained at various levels of fill light. The same logic can apply here. By altering the gamma mode, black stretch and Master Pedestal in conjunction with the fill light, the shooter can gain insight into the limitations of the camera and its ability to capture critical shadow detail.

THE DIFFUSED LOOK

The preservation of shadow detail is a key responsibility of the shooter, and in this respect, the low-cost HD camera can be especially savage. To achieve the required reduction in file size, engineers target for disposal what they consider to be *redundant* or *irrelevant* picture details. Understanding that human beings can't see well into deep shadows, engineers tend to look there first for disposable information, the result being often a significant loss of shadow detail in scenes originating in HDV, XDCAM EX, or other highly leveraged format.

Low-contrast diffusion filters increase the relevancy of shadow details by lifting their pixel values out of the danger zone and making them less likely to

---

[7]Quantization is the process of organizing similar value pixels into groups where they can be rounded off, declared "redundant" and subsequently discarded. The main purpose of quantization is to identify and retain only those image details readily apparent to the human eye. How aggressively your camera pursues the discarding of "redundant" or "irrelevant" picture information is in part a function of its setup parameters, including black stretch, pre-knee, and other parameters. See Chapter 5 for further discussion of compression fundamentals.

be jettisoned during quantization.[7] As shooters, we strive to create a mood consistent with our storytelling, and so we need a filter strategy to service that need, beyond the pointless UV filter permanently affixed to the front of many cameras as a kind of see-through lens cap.

The one-size-fits-all diffusion filter of years ago is now largely impractical. Depending on a camera's chipset, processor, and menu settings, a filter that works well on one model camcorder may work poorly on another, as manufacturers make compromises and assumptions that run contrary to a shooter's best storytelling and creative instincts.

Today's cameras irrespective of price are capable of producing remarkable images indistinguishable in many instances from their top-end broadcast brethren. The trick is exercising the necessary high level of craft, which includes, among other things, selecting the right diffusion filter for your particular camera and setup.

DESIGNING THE IDEAL FILTER

Filter manufacturers look principally at three ingredients when designing their wares: refraction, diffraction, and scatter. Favoring one area over another, notable flaws in a camera's performance can be addressed and often ameliorated. This is what happened several years ago when veteran shooters discovered their time-tested Betacam filters did not translate well to the digital realm. The Tiffen Black Pro-Mist, for example, that served so reliably for over a decade produced a much cruder effect in DV cameras.

Manufacturers tackled the issue of poorly performing mist filters by effecting changes in the porosity and reflectivity of the embedded black droplets. By reducing the droplet size, the Schneider Digicon achieved the desired level of diffusion without the halation and loss of resolution that had been the case (Fig. 6.62).

Of course, no one filter can magically transform a mediocre-performing camera into a $2,50,000 acquisition tool, just as no one filter can magically transform a clueless shooter into Sven Nykvist. Still, most narrative shooters can benefit from diffusion of some sort, and that means facing a bewildering array of choices. In the Tiffen stable alone, there's the Pro-Mist, Black Pro-Mist, Soft/ FX, Black Diffusion FX, Gold Diffusion FX, Fogs, Double Fogs, and Softnets. Schneider has its own lineup of filter types, including the HD Classic Soft, Warm Classic Soft, Black Frost, White Frost, Soft Centric, and Digicon. Same deal with Formatt, the U.K. filter manufacturer offering a dozen or more diffusion options. Whoa, baby! There are just too many choices!

FIGURE 6.61
To reduce shadow noise, some on-camera diffusion is usually desirable, especially in dramatic productions. Most compact HD cameras can benefit from a weak Black Pro-Mist, Soft/FX, or Schneider Digicon filter. Remember the lowest strength filters will be likely the most useful to you. Less is more!

FIGURE 6.62
Akin to water droplets on glass, the micro lenslets (A) in the Schneider HD Classic Soft diffuse small wrinkles and blemishes while maintaining overall sharpness. Looking closer at the filter structure, the light (B) passing between the lenslets is unaffected while light passing through the lenslets (C) is diffused creating a mix of sharp and less sharp pixels in the same image.

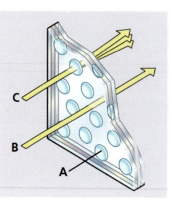

FIGURE 6.63
Use caution when using any type of net. At wide angle and at small apertures, its grid pattern may become hugely apparent on screen!

WHICH DIFFUSION FILTER?

TIffen Soft/FX

A practical all-purpose diffuser, the Soft/FX filter, is well suited for shooting high-contrast exteriors. The slight loss pf resolution is offset by the pleasing look. Tiffen Soft/FX filters are available in a range of sizes, including screw-in types for consumer cameras.

Tiffen Black Pro-Mist

A very light black mist filter can help reduce hue shifts in the shadows and suppress noise, especially in lower-end camcorders. Heavier mist-type filters should be avoided, however, owing to a pronounced "shower curtain" effect.

Tiffen Gold Diffusion/FX

The Tiffen Gold Diffusion/FX works well for stunning portraits and interviews. Its elegant finish and professional glean is seen frequently in broadcast and commercial applications.

Tiffen Softnet

It's old and no one talks about it anymore, but the Softnet 1B produces a great period look suggestive of a 1930s MGM epic. The Softnet 1S ("S" for skin) creates a comparable feeling but with enhanced flesh tones – a good choice when working with narcissistic celebrities.

Schneider HD Classic Soft

Imparting a tasteful, diffused look with no loss of resolution, the Schneider HD Classic Soft filter is ideal for shooting high-value talent – an excellent universal diffusion filter for dramatic applications.

Formatt HD Soft

The filter softens harsh outlines with minimal loss of detail and contrast. It's a good choice for mitigating the inherent harshness of CMOS-type cameras.

WARMING UP

A warming filter or *skin enhancer* can build credibility with an audience by making talent appear more human and alive. Because the shooter storyteller usually seeks to foster as much intimacy as possible with the viewer, a warming filter can play a key role in helping convey a person's humanity and caring nature. Just be sure to remove the filter when white balancing the camera to preserve the warm effect.

(a)   (b)

FIGURE 6.64
(a) By enhancing skin tones, a warming filter renders talent more appealing and helps draw the viewer closer to the story. The warming effect can also be added postcamera during the color correction process. The same scene (b) without the warming produces a more brooding downcast look.

OUT OF THE FOG

Cinematographers have long used fog filters to add atmosphere to otherwise sterile or lackluster landscapes. Historically, these filters have never been a real option for video shooters owing to these filters' often heavy and unnatural effect.

FIGURE 6.65
With the advent of HD and better performing cameras, traditional fog filters can again find practical use. In this Venice scene, the double fog introduces a natural-looking effect with minimal flare as evidenced in the foreground string lights. At right is the same scene sans filter.

Now, owing to the improved performance of today's cameras and higher density imagers, traditional fog and double-fog filters have again assumed a serious craft role, offering shooters a multitude of storytelling possibilities. Whether you're-looking to add a touch of atmosphere or a full-blown marine inversion, there's likely a strength and type of fog filter out there that can make it happen.

Fog filters come in two varieties: standard and double fog, the double fog type producing a greater sense of *actual* fog. Close-ups retain their sharpness despite the lower contrast and blooming of highlights. Of course, such effects should

TYPE	TIFFEN	SCHNEIDER	FORMATT	Remarks
Black Mist	Black Pro-Mist ⅛, ¼, ½, 1, 2, 3, 4, 5	Black Frost ⅛, ¼, ½, 1, 2	Black Supermist ⅛, ¼, ½, 1, 2, 3, 4, 5	Lowers resolution with moderate flare. Good for analog cameras. Black Frost creates more pastel, glamorous look and has less effect on blacks than Black Pro-Mist. Can be used for general tightening in weak grades. Higher grades not recommended for small-imager HD cameras.
White Mist	Pro-Mist ⅛, ¼, ½, 1, 2, 3, 4, 5	White Frost ⅛, ¼, ½, 1, 2	Supermist ⅛, ¼, ½, 1, 2, 3, 4, 5	Lowers contrast by lowering white exposure. Gently flares highlights without reducing resolution. Often used in tandem with soft effects-type filter for romantic look.
Ultra Contrast	Ultra Con ⅛, ¼, ½, 1, 2, 3, 4, 5	Digicon ¼, ½, 1, 2		Effectively raises black levels while lowering highlights. No loss of resolution or softening. Minimal halation and flare. Combined with in-camera gamma settings, a higher dynamic range can be recorded.
Lenslet	Soft/FX ¼, 1, 2, 3, 4, 5	Classic Soft ⅛, ¼, ½, 1, 2	HD Soft 1, 2, 3	Lowers contrast with no little loss of resolution. Keeps sparkle in eyes sharp. Causes highlights to glow softly in heavier grades. Good choice for general exteriors in weakest grades.
Circular Diffusion	Diffusion/FX ¼, ½, 1, 2, 3, 4, 5	Soft Centric ¼, ⅓, ½, 1, 2		Subtly reduces contrast without flare or loss of sharpness. Reduces visibility of blemishes and wrinkles in close-ups. Adds subtle edge-diffraction effects. Etched pattern may become visible in backlit scenes and/or when shooting at full wide-angle. Excellent for on-air talent.
Warming	Nude 1, 2, 3, 4, 5, 6 Type 812	81 Series	Warm Skintone Enhancer 1, 2, 3	Used primarily to augment skin tones. Warm effect is commonly merged with diffusion in single filter. Non-specific general warming can be added in post.

FIGURE 6.66
Cross-reference of diffusion and warming type filters by manufacturer.

always be tastefully applied in keeping with your overall storytelling goals.

CHRISTIAN DIOR TO THE RESCUE

Some shooters don't care for the look of a glass diffusion filter, preferring instead the increased flare from a real silk stocking. Applicable to cameras with interchangeable lenses, a small section of stocking can be stretched across the back element and secured with ¼-inch double-sided tape or a rubber O-ring. The rear-mounted stocking produces extreme blooming in the highlights, so you should consider the appropriateness of this in the context of your story.

Because the stocking color is infused into the highlight glow, I usually prefer a black net as it imparts an overall neutral cast. On the other hand, a flesh-color stocking offers the benefit of enhanced skin tones, a potential advantage when working with aged celebrity types.

For years, my stocking of choice has been the Christian Dior Diorissimo No. 4443, still generally available in Europe's high-end boutiques. (I acquired my stash several years ago in Paris at the Bon Marché on Rue de Sèvres.) If you go the stocking route, you should resist the temptation to use lower-quality hosiery, as the effect on screen will invariably appear crude and less than flattering.

THE POSTCAMERA FINISH

The shooter storyteller, as master of his craft, must be familiar with a range of imaging and compositing tools, and that includes increasingly various postcamera options. Your role as a shooter storyteller doesn't end until the DVD, Blu-ray or Web player sings.

For shooters, the temptation is obvious: why not achieve the desired look in post by simply applying a filter in the NLE or compositing tool? We've noted the complex interplay of light as it scatters, halates, and otherwise refracts through a physical glass filter and how these parameters are difficult to reproduce

FIGURE 6.67
A silk stocking behind the lens can produce dramatic blooming of highlights, which may or may not be appropriate to your story. Let good taste be your guide!

FIGURE 6.68
A swatch cut from a silk stocking is affixed to the back of the lens with a rubber O-ring. After replacing the lens, always check the lens backfocus! (See Chapter 8.)

accurately or convincingly in postproduction software. Yet, we must admit that image tweaking postcamera has become a fact of life, the shooter coming now under intense economic and practical pressures to delay many image-finishing decisions.

Years ago I recall a crusty engineer taking me aside to lambaste me: because prosumer video offers "less" resolution than "real" video, they'd say, I should refrain from using an on-camera filter since it can only further compromise resolution and complicate the processing and ultimate output of the project later.

The savvy shooter should reject this notion. Aside from the aesthetic considerations and the desire of shooters to control their own images and destiny, a modern diffusion filter does not necessarily reduce resolution. On the contrary, the shooter can take advantage of a new generation of filters (like the Schneider HD Classic Soft) that impart a pleasing diffused finish with no apparent or actual softening of the image.

Of course, there are times when appropriate diffusion must be applied postcamera. On some shows, like many live concerts, producers may opt to economize by not investing in diffusion filters for multiple cameras. Utilizing software to mimic the desired effect, the shooter can precisely tweak the level and nature of the diffusion after the fact. Final Cut Pro users even have the option of creating their own diffusion FX scripts for a custom look.

Postfilter application also makes sense for simple chores like adding a touch of warmth or coolness to a scene. The strategy works less well and not nearly as convincingly for fog and diffusion effects, as the complex interplay of light scattering and refracting through a physical filter cannot be precisely recreated.

FIGURE 6.69
My overstuffed filter case contains more than 125 individual filters; some, like the color effect types, no longer see much use.

FIGURE 6.70
One of my favorites, the tobacco filter, used to work well for historical re-enactments. The effect is now more easily applied in software.

FIGURE 6.71
Many software tools can approximate the look of a physical diffusion filter. Using a compositing tool like Adobe After Effects, the original unfiltered scene is duplicated and placed in a second track. A blur is added to the second layer and its opacity is adjusted to achieve the desired diffusion. You can experiment with the opacity and type of blur in the overlying track. The Unsharp Mask in Photoshop works in a similar fashion, mixing in and out of focus rays in the same layer.

ROLL YOUR OWN

For the shooter seeking a postcamera solution, there is a variety of software "plug-ins" available. Plug-ins are minisoftware applications that extend the capabilities of the host NLE or compositing tool. These days the various plug-ins can offer shooters an almost limitless range of image control.

Tiffen's *Dfx* plug-in features a long list of presets intended to mimic the look of popular camera filters, including the diffusion, color graduated, and infrared types (Fig. 6.72). The tool offers the traditional shooter a familiar, path from the intuitive world many of us knew and loved to the more abstract and largely opaque digital realm.

The Magic Bullet Looks Suite from Red Giant is a *tour de force* in software design. Beyond the ability to dial in any desired level of diffusion, saturation and color treatment, Magic Bullet integrates a host of distinct and *recognizable* looks. If you want a warm and fuzzy look like *Jerry Maguire*, there's a preset for it. If you want a heavy, diffused look like *Eyes Wide Shut*, you just dial it in (Fig. 6.75).

I occasionally use the software's browsing tool to parade a library of looks in front of a client. Not that shopping is ever in mine or anyone else's best interest, it can nevertheless be the ultimate fantasy trip for some directors, the ability to see and settle on a show's look by simply browsing through a catalog. It can be very reassuring to say the least for these fear-based creatures.

FIGURE 6.72
The Tiffen Dfx filter suite provides an array of familiar filter types. One advantage of the postcamera approach is the ability to apply an effect to only a portion of the frame.

(a)

(b)

FIGURE 6.73
(a) Bear Lake, Idaho through Dfx's day for night filter; (b) North Hollywood, California through a night scope.

FIGURE 6.74
Noise Industries'
FxFactory places
a great number of
diffusion and effects
filters at the shooter's
disposal, including
the ability to create
one's own.

(a)

(b)

FIGURE 6.75
The shooter storyteller
can select from a range
of presets in the Magic
Bullet Look Suite.
The warm and fuzzy
Jerry Maguire look
is seen in Fig. 6.75a.
The untreated frames
appear in Fig. 6.75b.

SHOOTERS, TAKE CHARGE!

The practice of finishing one's images in post is a process that fills many shooters with dread. On the one hand, the shooter storyteller is smart to embrace the latest software tools for the creative freedom and awesome possibilities they offer. On the other hand, the prospect of leaving unfinished images lying around a control room or media library is a threat to the shooter's reputation and livelihood. The shooter knows that despite the assurances of producers, clients, and stock library custodians, his or her untreated (or poorly treated) work will always, one way or the other, find its way in front of the public.

This crazy, digital world is evolving so quickly that it no longer makes much sense to be dogmatic about filters and when and where they should be applied. Times have changed, but the smart shooter still assumes responsibility for finishing the image, a process that only begins with capture into the camera but really isn't complete until some time later when the tweaked color-corrected show is ultimately presented to the world.

To control his destiny, the shooter storyteller needs a combination of in-camera and postcamera strategies. Remember, you are the artist, the painter of light, and the Vermeer of this digital age. It's up to you to decide by what standard you wish to be judged. Do you really want a bleary-eyed editor facing the deadline of his life applying finishing touches to your work? *Do you really think he'll bother?*

So take charge of your images! Coddle them, diffuse them, and tell stories with them. But most of all – *finish* them. However you do it – whether it's in-camera or postcamera – it is your image that is at stake.

CHAPTER 7
Going with the Flow

Spiritual teacher Eckhart Tolle, in his best seller treatise *A New Earth*[1], notably remarks we really only act out of two emotions: love and fear. If we aren't acting out of love, we're acting out of fear – and the new tapeless file-based workflow has instilled plenty of it. Our challenge as storytellers in this crazy digital-run-amok time is to confront our fear and replace it with, to the extent possible, love for the new technology. If we feel the pain of rapid change, of working with HDDs, SSDs, MXF, LANs, and P2 cards, it is because we are resisting that change. As Tolle points out: *what we resist, persists.*

Until recently, our stories originated invariably on videotape and we felt a comfort in the tangible nature of the medium. We knew tape well, even with all its foibles, and had a mature relationship with it, like a 30-year marriage. At the end of the day, we might gripe and snipe at our long-time partner, but then it's off to bed after supper and television – and all is well with the world. The familiarity was somehow reassuring.

ONCE UPON A TIME

In the current world of blue-laser recording and flash memory, the dragging of a strip of acetate and grains of cobalt across an electromagnet seems crude and fraught with peril. Dew or condensation can form and instantly shut a camera down. A roller or pincher arm can go out of alignment and cause the tape to tear or crease, or produce a spate of tracking and recording anomalies. And then there is the dust and debris that can migrate from the tape edges onto the surface and produce ruinous dropouts.

Today's tape shooters no longer face these perils to the same extent. Although clogged heads and the occasional mechanical snafu still occur, frequent dropouts

---

[1]*A New Earth: Awakening to Your Life's Purpose* (2005) by Eckhart Tolle. Read it. Learn from it. The business of life and video storytelling is all about overcoming our fears.

FIGURE 7.1
We could see it, feel it, and watch the innards turning. The mechanical world of videotape was comforting.

FIGURE 7.2
Who has the tapes?? Where are the tapes?? Each day after a shoot production folks everywhere nervously pose these questions. With the advent of tapeless cameras, the manner of handling and safeguarding "original" camera footage is new, unfamiliar, and fear-inducing.

FIGURE 7.3
Recording to top-quality media protects against dropouts and errors that can ruin crucial scenes. Remember DV and HDV tapes are fragile. Always handle these critters with love and understanding.

from edge debris are no longer a serious risk if we use high-quality media and not the dubious ilk available at your local Walgreen's or Rite-Aid. Of course, we shouldn't be using the cheap stuff for anything serious, but we swear we can't tell the difference, so why not scrimp?

Master-quality tape is now of such high quality that little if any debris remains from the slitting process during manufacturing. This debris, if not removed, tends to migrate onto the tape surface and lift the record head and cause dropouts and loss of data. Master-grade tape reduces this risk substantially, a fact that gains even greater relevance when recording to high-bit density HDV.

Of course, we should always exercise utmost care in tape handling and storage. Carelessly tossing loose tapes into the bottom of a filthy knapsack is asking for trouble – and we'll almost certainly get it. Shooting in less than pristine factories or on a beach amid blowing sand and grit, can also be conducive to dropouts as contaminants may penetrate the storage box, cassette shell, and the tape transport itself.

Dirt and other contaminants contribute to tape deterioration over time. The short shelf life of some MiniDV tapes (as little as 18 months!) should be of particular concern, as many producers routinely delete capture files from their hard drives and rely solely on the integrity of the camera tapes for backup and archiving upon completion of their projects. Videotape is not a viable archival format! (See a discussion of archiving options later in this chapter.)

BRAND LOYALTY

It is not advisable to mix brands of tape, as the chemical lubricants used by different manufacturers may adversely interact and cause head clogs or corrosion leading to dropouts. Be a loyal user of a single brand of tape if you can!

NO HITS, NO DROPOUTS, NO ERRORS

A dropout is a loss of data caused by the lifting of the record head from the tape surface, usually as a result of dirt or debris. Read errors have multiple causes, including aged or deteriorated tape, worn record or playback heads, or simply an elevated tape hiss that can obscure a signal. Shooters must recognize that while bit errors in the video stream may be correctible, similar errors in the *audio* stream are not, leading to a potential loss of critical dialog.

A LESS-SPECIALIZED WORLD

The tape-based world we knew and loved supported an industry of specialists in which creative directors directed, inspired writers wrote, resourceful editors edited, and god-like shooters shot. Our tools were specialized too, with every new camera and format demanding a new and usually expensive VCR. The

FIGURE 7.4
Director/writer/shooter/editor/sound recordist/on-air talent. The more hats you can wear, the more valuable you'll be in the new digital workplace.

FIGURE 7.5
Editing, compositing, color grading, sound design – you do all these things and more using the same box.

world we lived in was a mechanical place with belts and pulleys and cathode ray tubes, and million-dollar compositing tools like the 1990s Quantel Henry. Today, the Henry's once "advanced" features are accessible to virtually anyone with a PC or Mac and a modest knowledge of Adobe After Effects.

In this era of de-specialization, one person and one machine are increasingly doing it all. The tape-based world is rapidly giving way to a more file-based universe that requires fewer craftsmen specialists. This trend is being felt at every level of the industry, as national news organizations such as CBS, HDNet, and others look to their producers and correspondents to shoot and record their own stories. The demands of today's economy, fragmented audiences, and shifting distribution models are simply too great; the business of today's broadcasters, corporate producers, and feature filmmakers is requiring an ever-expanding *less* specialized skill set.

CAMERAS REFLECT CHANGE

Tape cameras faced many limitations imposed by the mechanical transport. Aside from their inherent fragility and need for periodic and costly maintenance, the spinning heads and tape mechanism necessarily operated at a constant 60 frames or fields per second. The Canon XL1 introduced in 1997 epitomized the tape

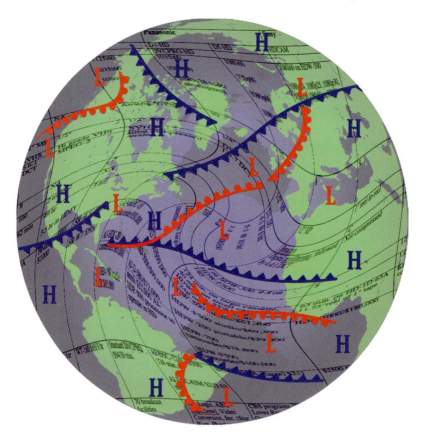

FIGURE 7.6
Like the weather, the world has seen more than a few video formats come and go.

FIGURE 7.7
Oops. A hungry VCR ate this tape!

FIGURE 7.8
No swallowed tapes in this puppy! And
this camcorder has a 5-year warranty!

FIGURE 7.9
Good-bye
mechanical
world! Tape-
less capture is
eliminating the
need for these
irksome beasts.

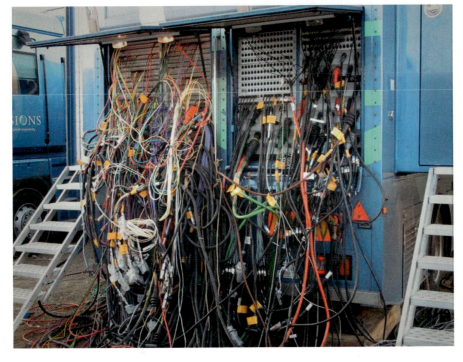

FIGURE 7.10
Hey! Who needs a
file-based workflow
anyway?

reality. Recording to a single format (DV) at a single frame rate (29.97 fps), the Canon XL1 offered ruggedness and excellent usability, but little versatility.

Zoom ahead 5 years to 2009, an eternity in digital speak. The Panasonic HPX300 recording to solid-state P2 cards is capable of capturing 24p in more than 30 different ways, at 1080, 720, and standard definition resolutions. The camera can also shoot Consumer DV, DVCPRO, DVCPRO HD, and 10-bit AVC-Intra, plus single-frame animation, and variable frame rates from 12 to 60 fps – a far cry from the hobbled tape-based cameras of only a few years ago (Fig. 7.11).

FIGURE 7.11
The Canon XL1 recorded only a single format (DV) to tape at 29.97 fps. Freed from the shackles of videotape and a mechanical transport, the Panasonic HPX300 can record a wide range of formats, frame rates and resolutions.

FILE-BASED RECORDING

The limitations imposed by tape transports motivated camera makers to devise clever ways to add functionality. Dual-use HDV cameras offered SD/HD capability without increasing bandwidth or exceeding the capabilities of the modest transport. The Panasonic DVX100 offered 24p capture in a tape camera by ingeniously repeating entire frames, not by blending fields, to create the 29.97 fps (60i) video stream required by the tape mechanism.

FIGURE 7.12

Flash memory recording has the advantage of no moving parts and a faster response time compared to tape- or disc-based cameras. Recording begins instantly without waiting for a physical mechanism to "get up to speed." On the other hand, optical disc recording provides an archival copy for backup – a consideration for Nervous Nellies fearful of inadvertently deleting original camera files from solid-state media.

FIGURE 7.13

Solid-state memory cards are extremely reliable. A 32-GB P2 card can store about 80 min of DVCPRO HD (or AVC-Intra 100) at 24 fps in native mode. XDCAM EX recording at 35 Mbps supports longer running times to SXS media, albeit at 8 bits in long-GOP 4:2:0 format. Future higher capacity cards will extend running times substantially.

FIGURE 7.14

For some shooters, SD memory may provide a low-cost alternative to proprietary SXS or P2 media. Most cameras recording to SD utilize the AVCHD[2] format. The JVC HM700 at right captures XDCAM EX and Final Cut Pro QuickTime files directly to SD media.

---

[2]AVCHD is a long-GOP H.264 variant format common to cameras from several manufacturers. Intended primarily for consumer applications, AVCHD requires exceptional processing and a fast computer for reliable decoding.

The advent of solid-state recording in the Panasonic HVX200 freed engineers and filmmakers from the tyranny of the fragile tape transport. A bevy of formats, frame rates, and resolutions could now be captured to flash memory, eliminating the constraints imposed by the impregnated strip of oxide, umpteen rollers, pressure pads, and spinning heads.

Video cameras could now capture *native* frames just like film; so 24p recording suddenly meant capturing 24 fps, and not the 60 fps or fields per second as had been required in tape- or disc-based cameras. The effect of recording only *keeper* frames was significant: as a practical matter, it meant a 2.5× increase in the storage capacity of expensive memory cards. But more importantly—and this is huge—it meant we were no longer recording video.

So began a quantum shift in our way of working. Many of us would continue to shoot video (of course) in whatever form as DV, HDV, HDCAM, and DVCPRO HD— only now file-based formats like Panasonic P2 and Sony XDCAM seemed to make a lot more sense. To bridge the emerging IT and former video worlds, Apple created ProRes 422 and Avid introduced DNxHD to provide a common editorial environment for video and data files, regardless of their source.

RECORDING TO OPTICAL DISC

In some ways, it's not much different than recording to tape: the physical mechanism imposes frame rate and resolution limitations; the disc requires a dedicated reader or expensive player; and start-up from stop and power utilization are akin to tape-based systems.

FIGURE 7.15
Like tape cameras before them, XDCAM HD camcorders require hauling of cases of recording media to distant locations. Solid-state cameras have no such requirement: you haul stacks of hard drives instead.

FIGURE 7.17
In a camera's thumbnail editor, clips may be deleted, marked for later use, or otherwise re-organized before offloading to a server or thumb drive. In P2 cameras, the displayed thumbnail can be exchanged for easier identification of a clip's contents.

FIGURE 7.16
Sony estimates the shelf life of blue-laser media at 50 years, compared to less than one-tenth that for some tape stocks. Although few shooters will do it, XDCAM discs can be reused 1,000 times.

Still, the disc recording camcorders offer many advantages associated with a tapeless workflow. Sony's XDCAM HD cameras and discs are extremely rugged and built to withstand the rigors of grueling assignments in distant and hostile lands. Clips can be accessed in a random manner with thumbnails referencing each clip, useful for preparing a *meltdown reel*. Good takes can be saved; the crap deleted.

Which brings up a salient point: each shooting day, many of us generate a large volume of footage, which is then off loaded to a hard drive. In editorial, the good takes are culled and the original material in its entirety is logged, labeled, offloaded *again*, and consigned to shelves or boxes in a closet or some Kansas cave. It's a colossal waste of time, money, and space to back up and archive terabyte upon terabyte of captured media, 98% of which we've *already* rejected. No wonder we face such immense media overload; we don't separate the wheat from the chaff soon enough.

RECORDING TO HARD DRIVE

Recording to a hard drive offers some workflow advantages because the drive can be mounted directly on a computer desktop without the need to transfer or further offload files. As HDV cameras begin to show their age, the ability to record to a compatible hard disc recorder (HDR) is an attractive option, extending the life of these cameras beyond the limitations of the HDV tape-based codec.

Hard-drive and solid-state drive (SSD) recorders offer a range of potentially useful options. For one thing, an HDD/SSD recorder enables *simultaneous* recording
to tape *and* hard drive, a distinct advantage for applications with fast turnaround
times, such as the preparation of rough cuts or DVD dailies on a commercial set.
Some HDRs can record continuously from tape-to-disk or disk-to-tape to further
extend recording times. For ENG, wedding, and event shooters, the *loop* mode
ensures that the camera will never run out of media, the same disk space being
recycled continuously, if desired.

The *AJA Ki Pro* (Fig. 7.18) records HD-SDI and HDMI[3] signals directly to a solid-
state hard drive in Apple's ProRes 422 10-bit codec. The onboard recorder has
inputs and outputs for every conceivable device; it can transform any 8-bit HDV,
XDCAM, or P2 camera into a state-of-the-art 10-bit 4:2:2 *uber-machine*.

FIGURE 7.18
The AJA Ki Pro records Apple ProRes 422 to an onboard
HDD/SSD or ExpressCard/34 installed memory card.

FIGURE 7.19
A solid-state (SSD) recorder affixes to the back of a JVC GY-HM700 camcorder. Although the
absence of hanging cables or fragile connectors is reassuring, the added size and bulk can be
inconvenient when operating in tight quarters.

---

[3]High Definition Multimedia Interface. See Figure 7.27.

WE SHOULD BE LESS FEARFUL NOW

With the reduced emphasis on videotape and quirky mechanical transports, we should, in theory, be *less* fearful of losing precious assets. Still, the new tapeless systems instill their own set of fears (mostly related to the practice of offloading flash memory media cards and wiping out the original camera files).

Nervous Nellies point to the inherent volatility of data files, and the need to store camera masters albeit temporarily on less than reliable bus-powered hard drives. The NNs point to the slow transfer process and the need for multiple redundant

FIGURE 7.20
With the advent of higher capacity flash memory cards, the need for panicked offloading of camera files has been mostly eliminated.

FIGURE 7.21
Shooters investing in a single HDD for off loading camera cards should invest in the best quality drive they can find. This is not a place to scrimp!

drives to ensure file integrity and peace of mind. For the neurotic among us, a tangible videotape or disc provides solace and reassurance, a security blanket in a digital age when critical data can neither be seen nor touched, and thus may be unknowingly mishandled, corrupted, or inadvertently deleted.

One can examine the source of the anxiety and blame our innately fearful dispositions. We shooters are like that, insecure and jittery. We worry about things and let fear dictate our thoughts: Do our imagers have enough pixels? Is long GOP going to diminish us as human beings? Are we subsampling our red and blue channels with sufficient abandon? These are the things that keep many of us awake at night.

The failure of a hard drive is not a prospect that sits well with shooters coming to grips with a solid-state workflow. Some fear is understandable of course. Even the best hard disk carries only a 5-year warranty, and most HDDs are guaranteed for only 1–3 years. Hard drive failure can be due to many causes including poor maintenance, subjecting the drive to excessive heat or shock, use of an incorrect or defective power supply, or failure of a *cheapo* connector or controller board. Whatever our trepidations, real or imagined, the shooter with aspirations of grandeur knows and feels one thing: the failure of an HDD is an occupational hazard that can strike any time and with devastating results.

THE ADVENT OF SSD

With no moving parts, the SSD confronts head-on the source of our anxiety. SSDs are reliable, feather-light, heat-resistant, and can tolerate extra-ordinary stress, including extreme G-forces.

Not constrained by a spinning platter or fitful mechanism, an SSD operates at the full bandwidth of a bus, or nearly so. That's 1,600 Mbps via eSATA at RAID 0.[4] If lingering fear still drives your desire for redundancy, a RAID 1 configuration with 100% mirroring can still sustain an impressive 960 Mbps. It's worth noting, however, that an SSD individually offers little if any speed advantage over a conventional hard drive.

The main bottleneck may be now the USB 2.0 interface, which at a nominal 480 Mbps is considerably slower than Firewire 800 or eSATA. For Mac users, Firewire 800 is the preferred interface for most data management operations; the eSATA option if available offering the fastest off-loading of camera files to an SSD.

In coming years, we can expect SSDs with greater capacities to drift lower in price while offering USB 3.0 at a blazing 4 Gbps. For tapeless shooters looking ahead, the greatest threat to one's material will not be failure of the drive, but physical loss or theft of the SSD itself.

---

[4]A Redundant Array of Independent Disks (RAID) consists of multiple hard drives that appear on the desktop as a single unit. Different RAID configurations, such as the popular RAID 5, balance the need for data protection versus speed and performance: RAID 0 striped data across multiple drives for maximum throughput; RAID 1 mirrors data across multiple drives for maximum (100%) protection.

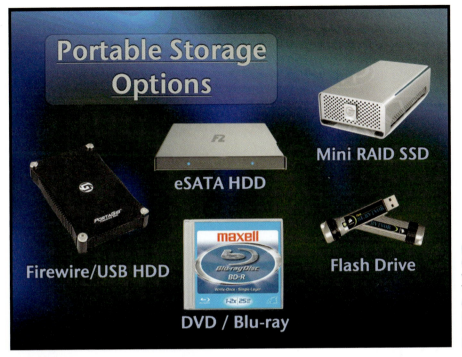

FIGURE 7.22
Coming soon to a
workflow near you!
The mini RAID can be
configured for speed
(RAID 0), safety (RAID
1), or JBOD (Just a
Bunch of Drives).

FIGURE 7.23
An idle SSD consumes
no power – except for
the illuminated LED!

INTERFACE, NOT IN YOUR FACE

It's not an exaggeration to say that Firewire changed the face of digital video. Built into nearly every Macintosh computer since 2000, Apple Firewire (aka *IEEE 1394* or *iLink*) delivered practical inexpensive desktop video to the masses.

Compared to USB or eSATA, which utilize file-based protocols, Firewire is a serial-digital interface (Fig. 7.25), interweaving audio, video, timecode, and machine control in a single *multiplexed* stream. As we rocket headlong into a file-based world, Firewire as a video streaming technology is beginning to lose its relevance. In its place, we see a rise in the fortunes of USB, the advanced v3.0 seemingly primed to dominate the new media landscape.

FIGURE 7.24
Solid-state storage options include high-speed thumb drives and SD memory; both are handy for off loading individual clips or a consolidated meltdown reel.

FIGURE 7.25
Firewire 4-pin versus 6-pin connection. The 6-pin Firewire connector is far more robust than the ridiculously fragile 4-pin type. Many manufacturers favored the 4-pin configuration because it precludes feeding power inadvertently into the camera.

FIGURE 7.26
HD-SDI/SDI has long been the preferred interface for professional video. The uncompressed 10-bit output frees the shooter from the shackles of compromised recording codecs like HDV.

HOST OR DEVICE

Whether recording to tape, flash memory, or optical disc, one thing is for sure: you're moving your files eventually to a hard drive or SSD. In DEVICE or file access mode (FAM), the camera acting like any other computer volume appears on the desktop. Files can then be transferred easily to a local RAID or server for subsequent ingestion into the NLE.

In HOST mode, the camera outputs directly to a hard drive or SSD without the need for a computer. Some cameras like the Panasonic HPX300 provide USB bus-power to an external drive (Fig. 7.28)

FIGURE 7.27
HDMI is an uncompressed serial-digital interface found in many handheld camcorders and consumer A/V devices such as Blu-ray players and big screen TVs. HDMI is rapidly gaining acceptance among professionals as well despite a notable drawback: HDMI signals do not carry timecode![5]

FIGURE 7.28
When operating in HOST mode, the storage device must be formatted in the camera's proprietary system, in this case, P2.

---

[5]It's starting to get messy out there in the HDMI ranks. As of mid 2009, there were five different versions of HDMI to choose from – HDMI Ethernet Channel, Audio Return Channel, 3D Over HDMI, 4K × 2K Resolution Support, and a new Automotive HDMI. Stay tuned. We're only up to version 1.4.

allowing crash offloading of files from camera to HDD in the field. In this case, the drive is P2 formatted (a variation of FAT-32) and can only contain the camera volume, not unrelated files like your favorite recipes, personal e-mail, or location notes.

NOT ONE WORKFLOW

Shooting tape, we blissfully followed a simple workflow: roll off a bunch of cassettes, hand them off to a production assistant, and submit an invoice. End of story. Nice.

Today, given the versatility of solid-state cameras and the vagaries of computers and the file-based environment, there is no longer one "industry-approved" workflow. In fact, there are many possible workflows (depending on your staffing, personal skill set and market niche), and you may well develop your own unique to your projects.

Shooting behind the scenes aboard a moving train for *The Darjeeling Limited*, I devised a workflow that made sense for the project. I had no reliable AC power, dirt and sand were everywhere, and my working space was extremely tight: wedged into the corner of a dank third-class sleeping car. Worse, I had only three 8 GB P2 cards for my HVX200 – a total of 1 h of running time – this making for some rather panicky off loading of cards in the course of my shooting day.

FIGURE 7.29
Given the rudiments of file-based workflow, every project may require a different approach. I set up this improvised off load station in the train workshop for "The Darjeeling Limited."

FIGURE 7.30
The encumbered conditions aboard a moving train dictated the choice of camera and a viable workflow.

THE PROMISE OF MXF

Conceived over a decade ago by the entertainment industry, the Material eXchange Format (MXF) was intended to facilitate the handling and management of media files, from image capture through postproduction and digital cinema. Unfortunately, given the 700-page "standard", there were bound to be implementation differences.

Panasonic's MXF format (called "P2") produces split audio and video files, with a randomly generated file-name to link them. Although this strategy creates elementary A/V streams that are useful in postproduction, it makes the handling and playback of these files difficult for computer users long used to moving, copying, renaming, and deleting files, more or less at will. The random file-names are particularly impractical, but changing those names disrupts the links inherent to the MXF structure.

ABOUT "STANDARDS"

A "standard" is what everyone ignores.

What everyone actually observes is called "industry practice."

Sony's XDCAM format also produces MXF files, which are incompatible with P2. The differences include significant variations in the folder hierarchy and how the A/V files are captured: XDCAM captures *multiplexed*[6] audio and video, a system of streaming particularly suited for the broadcast environment. In contrast, P2 maintains discrete audio and video streams, an arrangement ideal for production applications such as feature films, commercials, and long-form documentaries.

FIGURE 7.31
The Panasonic AG-HPX170:MXF file-based camcorder/encoder and capture device.

FIGURE 7.32
MXF's cryptic file names are required to maintain proper file association among the format's many components. In Final Cut Pro v7, the clip and subclip names assigned in-camera during a production are preserved, eliminating the cryptic references during Log & Transfer.

[6]Multiplexing is a process of interweaving multiple streams of data (in this case audio and video), into a single stream for easier handling and transmission.

THE BEAUTY OF METADATA

In 2005, a network news show aired a segment in which a plastic surgeon made what appeared to be irrational remarks during an interview. The doctor, not happy with his depiction, threatened to sue the network; but ultimately agreed not to do so on condition that the interview never run again. Four years later, an eager young producer at another show rediscovered the original broadcast and, unaware of the prohibition, reused portions of the doctor's unflattering comments. This time, in the face of almost certain litigation, the network fired the producer and settled quickly with the physician for a large cash sum. Just an unfortunate set of circumstances, you say?

Perhaps. But it could have been avoided. Such is the beauty and promise of *metadata* inside a file-based workflow. Metadata is data about data, and includes rudimentary clip information, such as frame rate and resolution to ensure proper playback. It can also include the serial numbers of the camera and memory cards, GPS tags, shooter and producer IDs, and custom file names and folders, instead of the usual cryptic stuff.

Shooters and producers can attach notes specific to a production, like location details, contact info, permit number, the nearest diesel fuel station for the

FIGURE 7.33
Metadata support is the major advantage of a file-based workflow. Custom fields permanently attached to a clip can accommodate a range of audio, video, and text notes related to a production.

generators, and the name of a nearby hospital for emergencies. The metadata can include voice and video memos from the script supervisor, editor, or production manager, and all of this can be treated like any other database: searchable, instantly accessible, and permanently attached to a clip – with use prohibitions if any immediately retrievable with a simple right-click of a mouse on the timeline of the NLE.

Robust metadata support is the critical cog in any effective digital asset management (DAM) scheme. For a recent Harry Potter trailer, producers conforming a shot for the digital intermediate[7] pawed through more than 120 different versions of the composited scene; no one could say with certainty which version was the one actually approved by the director! Adding a simple annotation to a clip in the metadata could have eliminated the anguish and expense of searching for hours through endless takes in the DI room.

PROXY VIDEO AND THE iPHONE

Whatever flavor of shooter storyteller we fancy ourselves, the ability to awe-inspire at the swipe of a finger can be mesmerizing, especially when trawling for new business. In this context, the iPhone supports playback of a demo reel or work-in-progress stored locally in the phone or streamed from a Web site via a high-speed network.

On-set, there's a growing impetus among shooters for the iPhone (and iTouch) to play a more active role, especially for playback of video dailies from P2 and XDCAM cameras. Some Panasonic P2 models, including the HPX300, can be fitted with a *proxy* encoder that prepares MPEG-4 audio and video for streaming to the Web or review of dailies on hand held devices like the iPhone. XDCAM cameras produce MPEG-4 proxies by default and so do not require a supplemental encoder card (Fig. 7.35b).

FIGURE 7.34
P2 file-folder structure. The proxy encoder in P2 cameras places the MPEG-4 A/V files in the appropriate folder.

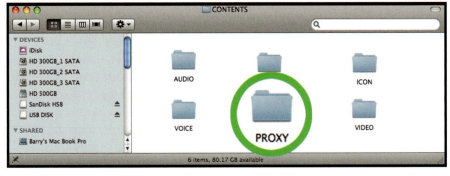

---

[7]Widely used for output of digital files to film for theatrical release, the Digital Intermediate represents a powerful convergence of technologies whereby scenes, or sections of scenes, are color-corrected, isolated, and composited with an extreme level of control and sophistication.

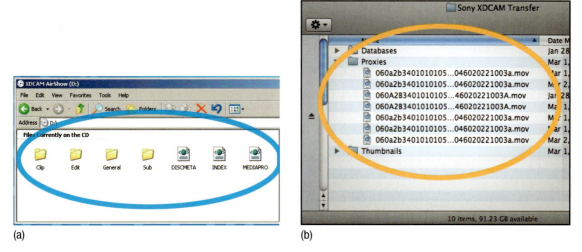

(a)   (b)

FIGURE 7.35
(a) XDCAM file-folder hierarchy; (b) XDCAM HD and EX cameras create low-resolution proxy files by default, and so do not require a supplemental encoder.

FIGURE 7.36
The process of creating video dailies is simple: Create a new playlist inside iTunes, drag in the proxy videos, sync to the iPhone. Voilà! Instant video dailies!

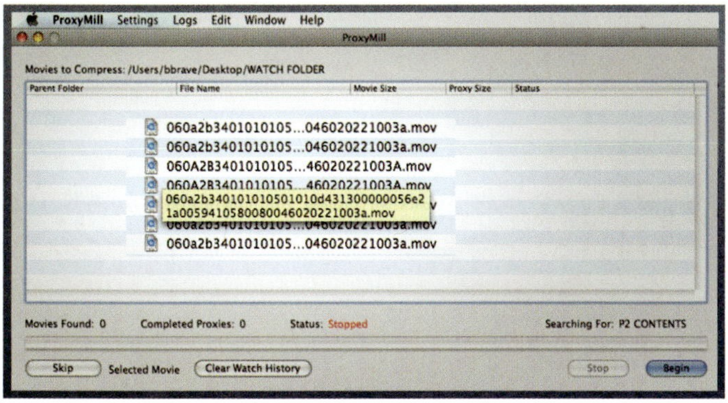

FIGURE 7.37
Even cameras without proxy encoding can take advantage of iPhone dailies. The Proxy Mill generates proper MPEG-4 files from P2 or QuickTime sources.

The preparation of iPhone dailies is similar for the Mac or PC. In the case of P2, the SD card containing the proxies is mounted on a computer using a common card reader. In Apple iTunes, a new playlist is created and named something logical, like "01_production_date." The proxy files from the SD card are then dragged into the playlist and synced to the iPhone in the normal way.

For XDCAM, the proxies are brought into iTunes from the disc or SXS card or retrieved after capture into Final Cut Pro. The "XDCAM Proxy Folder" may contain an amalgamation of clips from multiple reels, which can be input into iTunes as a single playlist.

THE ARCHIVING CHALLENGE

In the beginning, God created photographic emulsion, and all seemed right in the world. We'd shoot maybe 5 or 6 min of film for a 30 second commercial, and that was the norm. Producers saw little reason to shoot more.

Nowadays, of course, we are shooting more. A *lot* more. On some shoots the 27 cameras never stop, and so the question becomes what to do with all the footage after the smoke clears. In the past, the piles of tapes simply ended up on a shelf in a closet or carport somewhere, waiting, 8–10 years on average, for time to simply do its thing.

Today, we have no choice but to tackle in some way the archiving challenge. High-capacity hard drives may seem at first like a good option, being readily available and low in cost. But hard drives are fragile and prone to failure. They are, at best, a three to five year short-term solution.

FIGURE 7.38
Archiving once looked like this--!

FIGURE 7.39
-- and this!

FIGURE 7.40
Then this--!

FIGURE 7.41
-- and this!

Solid-state drives (SSDs) are certainly reliable and may hold promise in the future but their current high cost and relative low capacity make them impractical now. The long-term stability of flash media is also an open question: the jury is still out on that one.

Blu-ray disc may be an archival option for some folks, but write-speeds are slow and the media are currently limited to 50 GB is still rather pricey. Higher-capacity discs up to 330 GB have been promised, but these are yet to be delivered to market. In the same class of promised but not delivered, the *holographic video disc* (HVD) holds the potential of almost 4 TB of storage on a single 5-in. disc. Although some HVD units have shipped with a reduced capacity in the 300 GB range, their high initial cost and snail-like write-speeds have slowed the adoption of the new technology.

The most viable solution currently in this tapeless age is ironically – tape. Not videotape, but *data* tape – *LTO*[8] and *Super DLT*. These archival formats are proven entities and have in fact been used for years by banks, insurance companies, and the IRS. At least one major Hollywood studio rearchives its highest value properties every 7 years to LTO tape.

---

[8]Linear Tape Open (LTO) is a decades-old archival format favored by large producers including the major Hollywood studios. Digital Linear Tape (DLT) is similar to LTO, offering comparable functionality with greater economy for small and mid-level producers.

FIGURE 7.43
LTO Type 4 data tape with an estimated 100-year shelf life. Can archive 400–800 GB on a single cartridge.

FIGURE 7.42
The SDLT data tape drive is a relatively economical solution for archiving large volumes of digital assets. Suitable for schools and small production companies the drive can retrieve clips and subclips from the greater archive by referencing the MXF metadata.

The latest generation Super DLT drives (Fig. 7.42) have little in common with the cranky unreliable units of a decade ago. The new SDLT units mount on a desktop like any other drive and are network-aware, meaning they allow access to the archive via FTP from anywhere in the world. The new systems also feature a built-in directory for each tape, eliminating the former hassle of having to maintain and access a separate database that can, over time, get lost or corrupted.

CHAPTER 8

Your Window on the World

Your visual story depends on it. So does the quality and integrity of every image you capture. Your camera lens is your window on the world through which every element of your visual story must flow. Any way you grind, shape it, or filter it, your camera's optics are critical to your success and survival as an effective shooter storyteller.

It matters little from your audience's perspective which manufacturer logo is emblazoned on the side of your camera, which format or compression ratio you use, or whether you record to tape, disc, or hard drive. It is the quality of optics that matters most when creating compelling images. Your lens, dear shooter, is where your visual story meets the road.

In Chapter 2, we looked at how lens focal length can contribute to or detract from the shooter's intended story. The telephoto, by compressing space, increases the apparent size of crowds and the density of objects stacked strategically inside the frame. A short focal length or wide angle has the opposite effect, expanding a viewer's sense of scope by drawing nearby objects closer and pushing background objects further away. The wide-angle lens is therefore used for broad vistas and landscapes and in action sports to increase the sense of motion, especially in objects passing close to the camera.

For years, the *fisheye* has been the darling of the skateboard crowd. Its superwide perspective creates severe distortion, exaggerating the height and speed of skaters' jumps and gyrations – an effect obviously consistent with the intended storytelling. A very short focal length also minimizes the apparent shake of the handheld camera, a valuable benefit when shooting extreme sports from the nose of a surfboard or the handlebars of a rocketing motocross racer.

(a)

(b)

FIGURE 8.1
The extreme wide-angle fisheye increases the apparent speed and height of the skateboarder sweeping close to the camera. Support rods may be required for the oversize Century Xtreme, which features an astounding 180° horizontal field of view!

FIGURE 8.2
Lost in Venice. The wide angle in Fig. 8.2a effectively conveys the disorientation of my son in an unfamiliar city. By comparison, the long lens in Fig. 8.2b isolates him from the background, thus reinforcing his mental separation from the alien environs. Which story is correct? As a storytelling tool, the choice of focal length should ideally reflect your subject's mental state and point of view.

CONTROL OF CINEMATIC SPACE

The precise control of cinematic space is critical for effective storytelling, and nowhere is this more apparent than in action or chase scenes. To communicate clearly, your viewer must understand the geography of a scene, the location of the players, their direction of movement, and their relative proximity. Utilizing a telephoto lens can make a pursuer seem closer, the exploding boxcar behind him more perilous, the opening car door into the path of a biker more menacing. The wider lens in contrast expands space and thus minimizes these perils. It's your story. Use the power of lens perspective wisely.

FIGURE 8.4
Here the wide field of view reflects the exhausted state of this group of tourists in Venice.

FIGURE 8.3
The wide angle captures the emptiness of this Parisian park.

FIGURE 8.5
In San Marco Square, the young boy and pigeons appear to share the same cinematic space owing to the foreshortened perspective of the telephoto lens.

FIGURE 8.6
The long lens helps draw the billboard into this Los Angeles street scene.

HANDLE TALENT WITH CARE

Keep in mind: it's not merely a matter of framing a close-up any way we can, after all, a wide angle used close up can capture a subject with the same relative screen size as a telephoto from further away. No, the savvy shooter understands the implications of utilizing one focal length over another, especially for close-ups that do the bulk of our storytelling, a short telephoto *portrait* lens usually producing the most flattering representation of a subject's facial features.

FIGURE 8.7a
Oh, watch out! The peril of a car door opening into the path of a biker is amplified by the telephoto foreshortening.

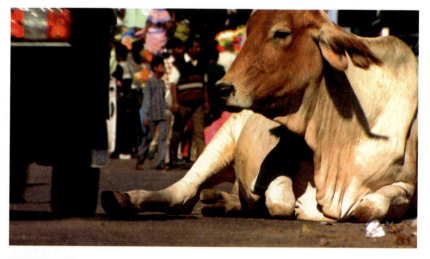

FIGURE 8.7b
Regardless of the lens perspective, this vehicle's wheel only missed the bull's hoof by a fraction of a millimeter!

FIGURE 8.8
Novice shooters may love the effect, but your narcissistic star will hate you forever. The wide angle in close-up grotesquely distorts facial features.

FIGURE 8.9
In contrast, the long lens unnaturally flattens the actor's ears and nose, producing a painted effect. This can undermine the intimacy we are (usually) trying to foster with our audiences.

FIGURE 8.10
A slight telephoto offers the most flattering perspective when shooting talent. The soft focus background contributes to the three-dimensional effect and helps direct viewer's attention inside the frame.

USE YOUR FULL BOW

Just as the accomplished violinist uses the full bow for maximum expression, so ought the shooter storyteller exploit the maximum capabilities of his camera and lens. In documentary work, I often utilize the full breadth of the zoom lens, first at full wide angle to establish a scene or capture essential action, then at full telephoto to frame the details and close-ups that advance the story.

Note I'm not talking about actually *zooming* in most cases but *reframing* – the variable focal length of the lens allowing me to recompose quickly without having to stop or otherwise interfere with the action to reposition the camera.

Shooters investing in a new camera should seek a model with a sufficiently wide field of view. Many camcorders with permanent lenses are inadequate in this regard, offering too narrow wide-angle coverage. Shooting with a 1/3-in.

FIGURE 8.11
Wide-angle adapters with large front elements may create a front-heavy condition and complicate the mounting of a matte box and filters.

format camera, like the JVC GY-HM700 or Sony HVR-Z7U, you'll need a minimum 4.5-mm wide angle.

If your camera has insufficient wide angle, you might consider a supplemental adapter that can increase coverage 30–40%. The practical use of such lenses varies. Some permit partial or total zooming, others don't. Some create barrel distortion akin to a fisheye, others don't. What works for you depends on the story you're trying to tell. Only you, the master of your storytelling domain, can make this determination.

FIGURE 8.12
When transitioning between wide and close shots, a hard cut is preferable to zooming, unless motivated for dramatic or stylistic effect.

Canon HF11	12x
Canon XH-A1s	20x
Canon XL-H1s	20x
JVC GY-HD250 (stock)	16x
JVC GY-HM100	10x
JVC GY-HM700 (stock)	17x
Panasonic AG-HMC40	12x
Panasonic AG-HMC150	13x
Panasonic AG-HVX200A	13x
Panasonic AG-HPX300 (stock)	17x
Sony HVR-A1	10x
Sony HVR-Z5	20x
Sony PMW-EX1	14x
Sony PMW-EX3 (stock)	14x

FIGURE 8.13
Optical zoom ranges for popular HD cameras. Some manufacturers' claims regarding optical zoom range should be taken with a grain of pulverized pumice.

GO LONG FOR THE TOUCHDOWN

While a proper wide angle is essential, the same might be said for a moderate-to-long telephoto, which offers the perfect complement. The instant narrowing of field of view can be highly effective, even thrilling, to audiences.

In documentaries, the zoom can be a valuable operational assist for shooters looking to adjust the frame between takes or questions in an interview. In reality TV, the subject's lack of predictability often makes it necessary to reframe while rolling to ensure adequate coverage, or exclude unwanted elements such as a boom pole protruding into frame.

Now, I know it's tough for many shooters to resist, but it's a discipline worth learning. If you zoom only when the story demands it, you'll be a far better shooter and storyteller for it. Zoom for visual emphasis, yes, or to sell a point or emotion, say, as in a contrite ax murderer's confession, but remember the zoom effect is highly unnatural and will certainly draw the viewer's attention. That may be OK and correct in the proper context and story. Story is our guiding light, the proverbial lens through which we must see and feel every creative decision.

BEWARE OF DUBIOUS CLAIMS

Just as most of us wouldn't buy a car on the basis of horsepower alone, we shouldn't automatically opt for a camera with the most pixels, best "minimum illumination", or the longest zoom range. What's the zoom range of a lens, anyway? 12x? 15x? 22x? Truth is, any lens can be a 50x or more if one disregards any notion of performance. Just omit a stop on the lens barrel zoom ring, and voilà! Suddenly, you got the bragging rights to a longer "improved" lens perfect for the next industry trade show!

FIGURE 8.14
The zoom range emblazoned on the side of a camera is often a fanciful exercise in creative marketing. Like "minimum illumination," a camera's stated zoom range can be any value – if performance is not a consideration. The 12x zoom on this Sony DSR-170, for example, feels more like 6x to me.

FIGURE 8.15
The loss of light and contrast with increased magnification is inherent to all zoom lenses. In low-cost optics, the severe "ramping" may produce soft unusable images.

The case of the overstated zoom range has craft implications for the shooter, as these lenses typically exhibit poor performance at maximum magnification. Telephoto scenes that lack brilliance and contrast can stick out like a sore thumb and disrupt your storytelling flow, so the shooter hoping to keep the viewer engaged would be wise to understand a lens' zoom-range limitations.

OPTICAL VERSUS DIGITAL ZOOM

It hardly matters that no one in the history of mankind has ever used a camera's digital zoom.[1] Manufacturers continue to tout the "feature" by pasting an impressive-sounding number on the side of their cameras: 400x Digital Zoom! 500x Digital Zoom! 700x Digital Zoom! Wow!

FIGURE 8.16
700x? Whoa! Some folks are impressed by such numbers. You don't have to be one of them.

While optical zoom actually magnifies the image prior to capture (Fig. 8.17b), digital zoom simply enlarges the pixels after capture to fill the SD or HD frame. The result is often a jumbled mosaic (Fig. 8.17c) akin to a scene from Antonioni's 1966 movie *Blow-Up*. The look of the impressionist may seem artsy to some people, but keep in mind that the pointillist effect (if intended) is far better implemented and with greater control in the NLE, Adobe After Effects, or some other compositing tool.

---

[1]Alright, I'm exaggerating a bit. Some cameras utilize the 2x digital zoom as a focus assist, and many shooters prefer the DZ to the optical extender in low light.

FIGURE 8.17a

FIGURE 8.17b
Optical zoom.

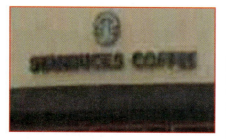

FIGURE 8.17c
Digital zoom. Cryptic, mysterious. What's the point?

FIGURE 8.18
An optical 2x extender incurs a light loss of two stops and markedly lowers contrast. In low light, the digital zoom at 2x may produce more usable images.

GOING WIDER AND LONGER

There are times when we should use the widest most distorted fisheye we can find – for a program, say, on haunted houses or mind-altering hallucinogenic drugs. There may also be times (in a Formula 1 racing tale or a sci-fi epic) when only the longest 5,000-mm telephoto will do. But these lenses are not common or subtle; and since we usually try to be unobtrusive in our work, we must exercise discipline when resorting to optics with such extreme points of view.

Many of us have had a long love affair with wide lenses. For news and reality shooters, they are our workhorses. They're versatile in uncontrolled spaces, like

Gene Simmons' kitchen for *Family Jewels* or in the rear seat of a racing squad car for *Animal Cops*. They add scope to expansive landscapes, like the endless desert stretching to the horizon and dramatically increase the grandeur and fluidity of Tiger Woods' swing. In short, these lenses provide the coverage and ooh-and-ahh shots that producers demand and keep us working. I love my wide-angle lenses!

But there's trouble also, especially in the super wides. Aside from aesthetic considerations and whether the extreme perspective is helpful or hurtful to one's story, the lenses tend to be heavy and bulky. As 2/3-in. zooms have expanded their wide coverage from 5.5 mm over a decade ago to 4.3 mm today, the corresponding increased weight and girth have introduced a bevy of headaches, including more severe vignetting, breathing and tracking issues, and uneven illumination across the frame.

Some light falloff to the corners may be apparent in even the best optics, like my Zeiss 10–100 zoom with which I blithely cruised the Amazon jungle and Arctic tundra for many years. At maximum aperture and full wide angle, this fabulous lens exhibited an obvious *vignette*,[2] an undesirable characteristic we shooters nevertheless accepted in exchange for this lens' otherwise extraordinary performance.

For today's shooter, a comparable perspective is needed with respect to the super wides. Because of the increased curvature of their front elements, the falloff of light from the center of the lens can be especially pronounced. This falloff is exacerbated in high-speed lenses and when shooting with a matte box, as the off-axis light reaching the corners of the lens and imager is further attenuated.

FIGURE 8.19
Terry Gilliam's warped wide-angle view of the world in *Brazil* (1985). The perspective helps sink the protagonist back into his environment.

FIGURE 8.20
In the climactic closing scene from George Lucas' *THX 1138* (1971), the extreme telephoto captures the cathartic escape from an oppressive subterranean world.

---

[2]*Vignetting* is a falloff of brightness or saturation at the periphery of an image. Some vignetting may be acceptable short of *portholing*, the more obvious impression of looking through a porthole.

FIGURE 8.21
How wide is wide enough?

FIGURE 8.22
The low-cost optics that accompany most prosumer camcorders can be the source of consternation for the video shooter.

Adding to this bagful of woe is the growing trend toward cameras CMOS-type imagers. Many CMOS designs utilize recessed photo sites that are like little "buckets" just deep enough to block strongly angled light from reaching the bottom of the site and the sensor surface. CCD imagers do not have this issue.

The move to wider lenses in recent years has unleashed a spate of conflicting demands on optics manufacturers. As shooters, we want the fastest, lightest, and sharpest lens we can find, with the widest angle and longest telephoto. We want stellar performance throughout the zoom range with a constant f-stop, flat field with no vignetting, and superb contrast to the corners. Toss in a 2x extender, internal focus, and the mechanical cams and followers to make it all work – and pretty soon, we're talking about some real complexity.

THE OPTICAL PERIL

The mediocre lenses that accompany most prosumer cameras pose a challenge to shooters vying to do first-class work. This "quality versus cost" trade-off should not be too surprising, given the manufacture of top-quality optics is a mature technology requiring costly and sophisticated processes. The few dollars that manufacturers allocate for the lens in a typical entry-level camera does not buy a whole lot.

So let's forget for the moment the virtues of CCD versus CMOS, HD versus 4, 5, or 6 K. You've thought way too much about your camera's fanciful minimum illumination rating, its 14-bit digital signal processor, and 4:2:2 or 4:2:0 color space. Truth is the quality of optics is most critical of all, in terms of what viewers can see and appreciate on screen.

FIGURE 8.23
Your lens is not an afterthought – it should be your first thought! Question is: what kind of images does your simian demand?

I recall reviewing the JVC GY-DV500 several years ago. The $5,000 1/3-in. camcorder was fairly impressive at the time, despite a look that tended toward the brassy and harsh. But fitted with a $10,000 lens, the camera no longer just looked decent, it looked great! Such is the power of good optics that can transform the look of virtually any camera.

This lesson should not be lost on the HD shooter. Today's cameras (irrespective of price) are so capable that lens performance must be considered first when evaluating a new camera. Such an evaluation cannot be achieved by merely perusing a manufacturer's spec sheet. Proper lens evaluation takes time and an understanding of the competing demands that go into a lens.

Logically, there's no way you'll find a $25,000 broadcast lens on a $2,500 camcorder. The world just doesn't work that way. We can hope, of course, and some camera makers have encouraged this notion by silk-screening the names of legendary lens companies on second-rate optics. But don't be fooled. When you spend only a few thousand dollars on a camera, there is something you're not getting; and that is, more likely than not, a lens that you can proudly hang your lens shade on.

Of course, we all want a lens that is lightweight and fast, with a long zoom range and close-focus capability. Problem is, these demands are often at odds with each other. Extending the zoom range, for example, tends to work against greater speed, and greater lens speed tends to work against maintaining low weight.[3]

Considering the compromises inherent to any complex lens, we shouldn't be surprised by the shortcomings in low-cost HD optics. Poor or nonexistent lens coatings, chromatic aberration, lack of sharpness, and weak contrast to the corners are real drawbacks that can negatively impact our images, especially when viewed at high magnification on a big-screen plasma TV or cinema screen.

WHY LENSES LOOK CHEAP

In my camera and lighting seminars, I sometimes use a resolution chart to demonstrate how a cheap lens can actually perform better with its front element covered with a layer of nose grease! The thin veneer, if applied carefully enough can serve as a crude lens coating that improves light transmission and reduces *flare*.

Normally when light strikes the hard glass surface of a lens, a portion of the beam (as much as 5 or 6%) is reflected. This loss of light is compounded in

---

[3]Increased lens speed – i.e., light transmission – is largely a function of lens diameter, which translates usually into increased lens weight and mass. Most shooters prefer lighter-weight lenses and equipment all around.

FIGURE 8.24
Don't try this at home. Rubbing a fine layer of nose grease over the surface of a cheap lens may improve its performance! High-quality lenses with advanced coatings obviate the need for such crude and demeaning tactics.

FIGURE 8.25
The Zeiss DigiPrime is a precision top-end lens constructed by hand with superior lens coatings. Any way you grind it, great lenses don't come cheap!

complex lenses with many elements, leading to an overall lowering of light transmission and speed especially in more complex lenses. More and better lens coatings reduce the light loss to as little as one-tenth of 1%, enabling intricate lenses to be made smaller and lighter while still maintaining high light transmission.

Superior lens coatings are expensive, however, so it's no surprise that many prosumer camcorders come up short. Increased internal reflections, and *flare*, significantly reduce the contrast and sharpness of the camera system, irrespective of the camera's native resolution, compression format, or imager type.

The quandary for HD shooters is this: a camera imager at 1,920 x 1,080, 2K, or 4K resolution, is capable of capturing an enormous amount of picture detail, which we presumably want. At the same time, the very high definition imager is capable capturing more lens defects, which we presumably do not want. This dichotomy with respect to resolution points to the need superior optics when shooting HD, if for no other reason that we see and resolve more lens performance issues at higher resolutions.

The most serious of HD lens defects is chromatic aberration (CA), an ugly fringing artifact found to some degree in all lenses regardless of price or sophistication. For HD shooters, CA is a major peril: it's the main reason that cheap lenses look cheap! (See Fig. 8.28)

Chromatic aberrations, referred to also as *shading* artifacts, appear commonly along the edges of overexposed light sources (such as streetlights or along the horizon line at dusk and other high-contrast transition areas). The fringing effect may be particularly noticeable at the long end of the zoom where lens aberrations are magnified. CA has always been an issue for shooters seeking sharp clean images, but the ragged edges of standard definition (SD) normally covered most if not all fringing artifacts. HD's smooth well-defined edges offer no such refuge.

WHY ONE-PIECE CAMCORDERS (MIGHT) MAKE BETTER PICTURES

Some shooters will have it no other way: they want a camcorder with an interchangeable lens. They want the flexibility to mount a long, short, wide, or better-grade optic as the need arises.

Yet, despite this insistence, only a small percentage of shooters actually take advantage of a camera's interchangeable lens capability; and when they do, they simply replace one mediocre lens for another. In such cases an interchangeable lens capability seems hardly worth it, given the compromises to image quality that tend to go with it.

Fact is that modest camcorders with fixed lenses usually perform better than similar-class cameras with interchangeable optics. The Panasonic AG-HMC150 (Fig. 8.26), fitted with a permanent 13x zoom, exhibits little of the breathing of focus one might expect in a very modest lens. Why? The soft spots and chromatic aberration known to the manufacturer are mapped out and digitally corrected, yielding a level of performance in a $3,500 camcorder that simply would not be possible in a camera utilizing low-cost interchangeable optics.

FIGURE 8.26
While offering less flexibility with respect to lens choice, camcorders with fixed lenses usually perform better than similar price cameras with interchangeable optics.

CHROMATIC ABERRATION COMPENSATION

For modest shooters taking advantage of cameras with interchangeable lenses, the challenge becomes how to extract the best performance from less than stellar optics. Panasonic wasn't the first camera maker to implement chromatic aberration compensation (CAC), but it is the first to do so in a relatively low-cost camcorder.

A CAC-compatible lens mounted on the HPX300 provides a unique digital signature: the camera identifying the lens model and type, applies the required chromatic aberration correction from a library of profiles (LUTs) stored in its memory. CAC does not correct for common lens defects like *tracking, breathing*

FIGURE 8.27
HD is fabulous! It can resolve enormous picture detail and fill our viewers' eyes with wonder. Unfortunately, HD also resolves more lens defects. Chromatic aberration compensation can help reduce the visibility of color fringing in high-contrast subjects like this wind vane in front of the moon.

FIGURE 8.28
Chromatic aberration is not art! Note the color fringing along the high contrast edges in this scene.

FIGURE 8.29
In Panasonic camcorders fitted with an interchangeable lens, CAC is applied automatically from a library of LookUp Tables (LUTs) stored in the camera's memory. Look for CAC to become commonplace in future HD cameras.

of focus, or flare,[4] but it does suppress the most serious fringing from chromatic aberrations. CAC is a feature worth looking for when considering an HD camcorder with interchangeable optics, especially if you often work at the long end of the zoom where CA is most objectionable.

MAKING PEACE WITH YOUR NOT-SO-HOT LENS

To compensate for mediocre optics, camera makers will often ratchet up a camera's default *detail level* to create the illusion of increased image sharpness. In Chapter 6, we discussed how the appropriate detail level is crucial for shooters seeking a more organic, less electronic look. Some caution should always be exercised, however, when setting a camera's *Master Detail*; if set too low, it can produce washed-out, poorly defined images, especially in conjunction with a weak lens.

---

[4]*Tracking* describes a lens' ability to remain centered on an object while zooming. *Breathing* refers to the loss of critical focus while zooming. The inability of a lens to maintain critical focus while zooming. *Flare* indicates the level of internal reflections that can reduce contrast and sharpness.

There's usually no point lamenting the low-cost lens permanently wedded to a camera. Better we should learn its shortcomings and (hopefully) find ways to work around them.

We've mentioned the *ramping* or darkening of the image that occurs at the long end of many zoom lenses. We've also cited the lack of quality coatings and CAC in cameras with interchangeable lenses. But beyond the requisite carping and shedding of a few drops of lens fluid, is there anything we can actually do to improve the quality of our images through mediocre optics?

HOW SWEET IT IS

Our camera's inexpensive lens may look okay on a small monitor, but large-screen projection is a different kettle of pixels. As more shooters display their work on a big screen TV or in a digital cinema, the high magnification will reveal hitherto unrecognized lens defects. The question becomes then for many shooters how to coax a decent level of performance out of what amounts to a very modest piece of glass.

Luckily, decent performance is possible even from the cheapest lens by identifying its *sweet spot*. Truth is, your camera's low-end optics may actually perform rather well at a given focal length and f-stop.

Of course, finding that sweet spot is not always so easy. The best way is to shoot a scene from your intended project, run it through the post-process (including color correction), and then display it in a large theatre. Large-screen projection will quickly reveal most serious problems such as breathing of focus, loss of contrast, poor tracking, and other common faults. On the big screen, you can run but you can't hide. Most lens shortcomings are painfully obvious under such scrutiny.

Still, such a test may not be always practical or economical. In the days before digital video, when cameramen were a revered and well-paid/overpaid lot, shooters would dutifully test every unfamiliar lens before a shoot. The lens was critical to our livelihood, after all, and our mortgages and car payments depended on capturing pristine images. Lens performance was too important to leave to chance or the whim of a manufacturer looking to cut costs – at all costs.

When evaluating a lens, it's essential to reference a high-resolution production monitor capable of displaying 1,000 lines or more. Such a monitor of at least 17 in. is one of the best investments you can make, the precision and peace of mind it offers being especially critical to shooters anticipating a big-screen presentation of their work.

High-resolution LCD monitors connected via HD-SDI[5] obviate the need for the laborious setup and calibration once required of analog tube displays. (See Chapter 5.)

---

[5]HD-SDI is the dominant digital video interface found on professional camcorders and other high-end equipment. A single cable carrying uncompressed red, green, and blue data streams are interweaved into a "multiplexed" signal, eliminating the handling of separate color channels.

LAYING DOWN WITH YOUR LENS

Assessing lens performance is critical to developing your prowess as a visual craftsman. Here is what works for my camera fitted with a manual interchangeable lens:

1. Start with the camera on a tripod focused on a distant object. I prefer a telephone pole, but any object with a hard vertical edge will do. Set the lens to "infinity" and check the setting. Can your camera find sharp focus? Cameras and lenses that focus past infinity should be rejected. I recently shot a car commercial with a lens that tracked okay but focused a bit past infinity. This bizarre behavior drove my assistant nuts and ruined several takes.

2. Now place your camera and tripod 6 ft. from a wall. Use a tape measure and be sure to measure from the imager's focal plane (Fig. 8.38a). Many cameras have this point indicated on the camera body; if not, you'll have to estimate.

3. You can use a professional *Chroma Du Monde* chart (Fig. 8.30) or you can retrieve yesterday's newspaper from the recycle bin and tape four pages to the wall (Fig. 8.30b). Be sure all four corners of the frame are covered. Depending on the camera's wide-angle this area will vary. At 6-mm focal length on 1/3-in. cameras, the image area will cover an approximate area 5-ft. wide by 3.5-ft. high.

4. Set up two lights at 45° and angle the lights to avoid hot spots. Zoom in and focus critically. Check the lens barrel for accuracy. Some lenses may not have a 6-ft. reference, so you might have to estimate or use an alternative distance. Any discrepancy should be noted to assure accurate focus and follow focus during production.

5. Now zoom out slowly while eyeing a high-resolution monitor. Note any breathing of focus in the newspaper text. Most lenses will soften slightly in the course of their travels. Watch for especially sharp sections and note any sweet spots. Also note while zooming any off-center shifting, as tracking can be a problem in some lenses.

6. *Now check backfocus!* I'll repeat this: **check backfocus!** Backfocus is a critical measurement from the lens rear element to the imager plane. The slightest imprecision in backfocus may prevent sharp focus at infinity and produce soft images especially at full wide angle at maximum aperture. Heat, cold, shock, and routine handling can all affect the measurement, and so it is imperative to check the backfocus distance regularly during production. Use a *star chart* (Fig. 8.33) available at low or no cost from lens manufacturers or DSC Labs (http://www.dsclabs.com/). The gradient patterns and fine lines in the star appear to snap in and out of focus on a high-resolution display.

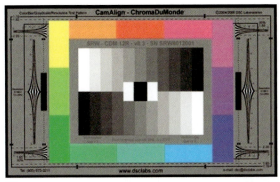

(a)

(b)

FIGURE 8.30
The Chroma Du Monde reference is an industry standard for color and resolution. You can improvise your own chart using sections of four newspapers taped to the wall (b). That pile of old newspapers you've been collecting may have a practical use after all!

FIGURE 8.31
Breathing problems? Many low-end HD lenses have mild to severe respiratory distress; have mild to severe breathing issues; rotating the focus ring should not produce a significant shift in field size nor should zooming exhibit obvious fluctuations in focus.

FIGURE 8.32
For 200 francs, can you recognize bad tracking when you see it? If your camera finder features a center crosshair, you can use it to check tracking. Place the marker over an object and zoom in fully. Does the object stay centered? If so, *tout va bien dans le monde!*

FOCUSING ON WHAT'S IMPORTANT

The ability to focus selectively lies at the heart of our visual storytelling, since the relative sharpness of objects communicates to audiences what is important – and, perhaps more fundamental, what is *not* important – in the frame.

Because precision machining of lens rings and components is expensive, camera manufacturers tend to look here to cut corners. Unsurprisingly, many prosumer cameras exhibit poor mechanical design and functionality. Focus rings in particular may be either nonexistent or shoddily constructed, thus denying the shooter the critical ability to precisely set and follow focus.

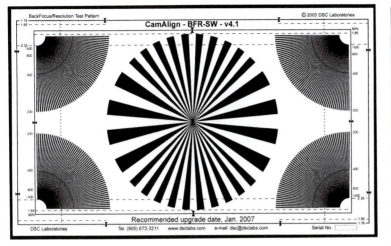

FIGURE 8.33
Checking backfocus, the star chart's fine grid appears to snap in and out of focus on a high-resolution display. For cameras fitted with an interchangeable lens, backfocus should be checked daily to ensure sharp images. This becomes especially necessary since many cameras' tiny viewfinders are incapable of providing this reassurance.

FIGURE 8.34
Focus ring on DSR-PD100a; focus ring EX1. Horror of horrors! The focus rings on many older cameras were completely useless. The knurled ring on this model spun continuously in both directions without any apparent effect on screen. More recent camcorders with a mechanical focus are greatly improved.

FOLLOWING FOCUS

For years, low- and no-budget shooters of narrative projects were hobbled by the inability to accurately follow focus. Today, there are rugged systems available from a variety of manufacturers, including Chrosziel whose follow-focus system is meticulously crafted. Its large knurled focus knob can be easily grasped by a harried, rain-soaked assistant, and its white marking disc can be removed and recalibrated for other cameras or lenses – a significant time-saver on projects where multiple cameras and lens combinations are used.

Of course, high-quality accessories do not come cheap. A good matte box and follow focus can run upwards of $1,500 or more; and with the appropriate support rods, mounting plate, and drive gear, one's total investment could easily exceed $2,000.

So, is it worth it?

Absolutely. Top-quality accessories like a matte box and tripod last for decades long after your shiny new *camera du jour* is relegated to a doorstop. If you're serious and intend to shoot and produce programs for a living (or serious avocation), it makes sense to invest in pro-level accessories. The superior craft that such gear enables will pay dividends for a lifetime.

FIGURE 8.35
An investment in top-quality accessories will pay you dividends for decades to come.

FIGURE 8.36
The follow focus engages a geared ring specific to a camera and lens combination.

FIGURE 8.37
Many one-piece camcorders now feature manual focus with repeatable markings for zoom and focus.

(a)

(b)

FIGURE 8.38
(a) Focal plane indicator on side of camera; (b) note the focal distance for cameras with integrated lenses (like this Canon) is usually measured from the front element – not the imager plane!

FIGURE 8.39
The typical camera on-board zoom control is notoriously balky, making smooth and tasteful zooms difficult or impossible.

THE MATTE BOX

The need for an effective matte box or lens shade cannot be understated. The low contrast inherent to many prosumer "package" lenses is made worse by stray light striking the front element at an oblique angle. These off-axis rays may be reflected internally, bouncing off and around multiple elements, substantially increasing flare and consequently lowering contrast and resolution.

Screw-in filters (Fig. 8.41) offer the advantage of low and easy availability, but the fumbling and risk of cross-threading when the chips are down (so to speak) can be disconcerting, especially in the face of a charging rhino or ego-maniacal director going berserk.

Slide-in square or rectangular filters in conjunction with a professional matte box (Fig. 8.42) allow more confident handling and enhanced creative possibilities. These capabilities include more accurate positioning of graduated and effects filters, and optimal rotation of the polarizer darkening the sky or controlling window reflections.

FIGURE 8.40
Enabling well-feathered zooms, a commercial-grade controller like this one features a pendulum rocker that does not exhibit the backlash or slop typical of consumer units. Of course, the smart shooter refrains from zooming without a compelling reason to do so!

Not all professional filters are available in screw-in sizes. This is particularly true of many Tiffen types, like the Black and Gold Diffusion/FX, as well as filters from Schneider Optics. (See Chapter 6 for more on the applicability of camera effects filters.)

FIGURE 8.41
Screw-in filters are awkward to handle, prone to cross-threading, and offer fewer creative possibilities than square or rectangular filters in a professional matte box.

FIGURE 8.42
Beyond serving as a filter holder, the 4 × 4 clip-on matte box provides protection from off-axis light striking the lens obliquely.

FIGURE 8.43
A chamfered filter tray prevents light leakage around the edges.

FIGURE 8.44
Don't take widescreen lying down! An appropriately proportioned matte box offers maximum protection for your visual story.

CLIP-ON VERSUS ROD SUPPORT

A matte box that clamps directly to the lens is more economical and convenient, but the extra weight may place excessive stress on the lens front element and lead to impaired optical performance or actual physical damage. If you're using a full-size matte box and follow focus, you'll need a proper rod-support system to ensure smooth operation and safely support the additional weight.

HANG OUT THE TRICOLOR

A French flag extends the functionality of the matte box by helping to prevent unwanted sun or backlight from directly striking the front of the lens. Some professional matte box systems provide for the simple mounting of a French flag using thumbscrews.

FIGURE 8.45
Allons enfants de la patrie...

USE OF CINE LENSES

There are times when a camera's mediocre optics will not suffice regardless of a shooter's expertise or insights. In such cases, one might consider the use of cine or 35-mm SLR lenses instead.

Costing many thousands of dollars, cine lenses (Fig. 8.46) invariably employ superior coatings, finely machined cams, and the finest optical glass. Overall performance with respect to light transmission, resolution, and contrast is often dramatically better than the low-cost prosumer fare one might be used to, with cine lenses' stated specs regarding speed and zoom range in general more accurate and honest.

The use of cine and cine-style lenses may also improve a video shooter's work-flow. Commercial-grade optics from Fujinon and Canon (Fig. 8.47) feature large brightly inscribed witness marks that can be easily seen and logged by an assistant or script supervisor across a set. Top-end lenses also feature integrated gear rings for precise follow focus and zoom. Of course, film shooters are long used to such functionality, but this capability until recently had been tough to come by in the modest low-cost video realm.

From a technical perspective, digital lenses differ significantly from their cine brethren. While film lenses focus on microscopic grains of silver, digital lenses must focus on a CCD or CMOS sensor, where pixel size is several orders of magnitude larger. Indeed, for years SD shooters saw little reason to improve

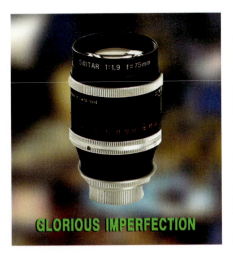

FIGURE 8.46
Cine lenses – oh how we love thee! Replete with flare, chromatic aberration, and distortion galore! For many shooters, the less hardened look is preferable to the harsh images typical of low-cost HD cameras.

FIGURE 8.47
In contrast to film, digital lenses must consider a camera's stationary image sensor and intervening prism in three-chip designs. Cine lenses typically feature large bright markings and integrated gear rings for zoom and focus.

FIGURE 8.48
C'mon guys! Most video lenses still sport miniscule markings, as if to keep f-stop and distance settings a tightly guarded secret!

the performance of their lenses, since the low resolution of NTSC and PAL television systems was thought to be the limiting factor.

Today with the advent of inexpensive high-definition camcorders, it's only logical that video storytellers would turn to cine lenses as a viable alternative to mediocre HD optics. Keep in mind that most cine, and 35 mm SLR lenses, were never designed for digital applications. Covering a mere 1/3-in. sensor area (actually 6 mm) in camcorders like the JVC HM700 and Panasonic HPX300, these lenses engineered to cover a much larger frame must work proportionately harder since only the tiny center of the lens is used. As a consequence, the resulting images may appear washed out or lacking in contrast, unless a specialized lens adapter is used.

Contrary to popular thinking, most cine-designed lenses are inferior to optics engineered specifically for digital applications. Due to the random nature of film grain, mechanical registration errors in the gate, and uneven flatness of the film plane, many lens defects including chromatic aberration, color fringing, and darkening to the corners of the frame are effectively concealed, particularly when compared to a static high-resolution electronic imager that reveals unabashedly all defects large and small.

The story is our guiding light, our reason for being, and final arbiter of all creative and technical decisions. We have only tools, not rules, and so it's important to recognize the advantages of working with film lenses in the digital sphere. Cine lenses deliver a softer more organic look, infusing a notion of past tense into the visual story. Shooting with film lenses is simply another tool in our storytelling arsenal. We may have to stop down a bit more to achieve good contrast, but we can live with that. The important thing is to understand the ramifications of utilizing film lenses, especially older lenses that tend to exhibit increased flare and a softer color palette. Who knows? This might be exactly what our story demands!

EXCESSIVE DEPTH OF FIELD

Selective focus can be a powerful storytelling tool, and so it is unfortunate that small-imager camcorders are unable to capture clearly defined focal planes. An understanding of depth of field (i.e., how much of a scene is in focus from near to far), is imperative; the rigorous control of focus having been a key discipline for traditional photographers imaging on film formats ranging from 8 x 10 to thumb-size type 110 Instamatic. Compared to video cameras with imagers as tiny as 3 mm, the film formats with their larger imaging areas required longer focal length lenses to produce a comparable *field of view*. The reduced depth of field, stemming from use of these longer lenses, narrows the visual story's focus and helps guide the viewer's eye to what's important inside the frame (Fig. 8.51).

FIGURE 8.49
What's the story here? What's this frame about? The extreme depth of field inhibits the shooter's ability to isolate key story elements. With the entire frame in focus, the visual story you intend may be less clear.

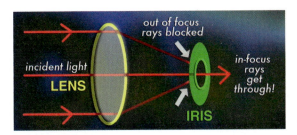

FIGURE 8.50
A narrow aperture allows more in-focus rays to reach the camera sensor, resulting in greater (usually) undesirable depth of field. In most cases, the shooter should use as wide an iris as feasible in order to realize best camera and lens performance, and ameliorate the depth of field issue. In bright conditions, the camera's neutral density filter is critical to achieving these goals.

FIGURE 8.51
The longer lenses used for larger-imager cameras produce less depth of field, which can enhance the three-dimensional effect that most shooters seek.

TAMING THE DEPTH-OF-FIELD BEAST

We've noted how excessive depth of field (DOF) is an ongoing problem for the video storyteller. The camera's tiny imager and short focal length lenses produce too much focus and so work against the establishing of well-defined focal planes. This means close-ups critical to our story are less effective as back-grounds stay sharp. Compositions also suffer as the viewer is unsure what to exclude from the visual story.

One solution to the excessive-DOF dilemma is a lens adapter that allows a high-quality 35-mm cine lens to be mounted on a small-imager camcorder; the goal being to preserve the cine lens' original narrow depth-of-field attributes.[6]

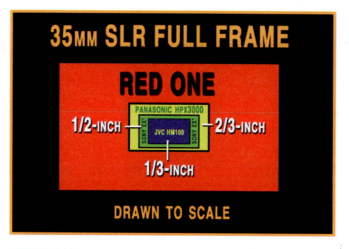

FIGURE 8.52
For many shooters the larger camera imager produces a more favorable depth of field. Here we see the relative size imaging areas for various film and video formats. The actual diameter of a 1/3-in. sensor is 6 mm; a 2/3-in. sensor is 11 mm.

FIGURE 8.53
A shallow depth of field can help attain the look and feel of a top feature film or commercial. This scene captured through a supplemental lens adapter preserves the narrow depth of field of a 35-mm cine lens.

FIGURE 8.54
A special adapter like the P & S Technik Mini35 allows the mounting of robust high-performance cine lenses on a compact HD camcorder.

[6]Depth of field is defined as the range of objects in a scene from near to far said to be in reasonable focus. Small f-stops (i.e., f8, f11) will reflect increased depth of field and large f-stops (i.e., a smaller number, f1.6, f1.8, etc.) will produce a narrower range of objects in focus.

Most lens adapters operate in a similar fashion, employing either a spinning or oscillating ground glass. With the cine or SLR lens set at full aperture, the image forms on the ground glass inside the adapter with the shallow DOF intact. This image is then relayed to the camera sensor through a series of optics fitted with a supplemental iris to control exposure, the setting of this iris having no bearing on the recorded image's previously established narrow depth of field.

When shooting with a lens adapter, the camera iris should not be stopped down beyond f4 due to the likelihood of seeing the grain in the adapter's ground glass as well as any dust that might have settled there. Bear in mind that 1/3-in. HD cameras can only record maximum resolution at full or nearly full aperture; when stopped down past f4, their performance is impaired, capturing images indistinguishable in many cases from standard definition! The lowering of sharpness can be attributed partly to the increased diffraction[7] at smaller f-stops and physical imager considerations that can play into the equation as well.

Maintaining critical focus can be a challenge with these adapters, especially in HD cameras with tiny 1/3-in. imagers. The diligence and precision required to focus and hold focus on an oscillating/rotating ground glass, is a potential major

FIGURE 8.55
Like most lens adapters, the Letus requires scrupulous attention to critical focus throughout a shooting day. A 17 in. or larger HD monitor is highly recommended! the Letus requires scrupulous attention to focus. A 17 in. or larger HD monitor is required for peace of mind!

FIGURE 8.56
A low-cost solution for sure, SLR lenses often perform poorly in video applications due to insufficient contrast.

FIGURE 8.57
Oops! What's going on? Many 35-mm adapters produce an inverted image, which can be disconcerting!

---

[7]See Chapter 6 for further discussion of diffraction and the perils of shooting with small f-stops.

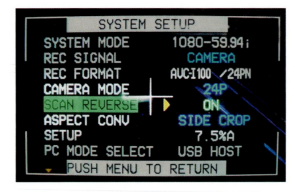

FIGURE 8.58
Some cameras like the Panasonic HPX300 feature a scan reverse option to correct a lens adapter's inverted image.

chore and incovenience (given the usual stresses of a shoot and the inevitable jostling of the apparatus).

I've remarked how the shooter storyteller must always seek the right tool for a job. In most cases, I find little advantage to utilizing a lens adapter: they tend to be unwieldy, use lots of power, and may result in substantial loss of resolution stemming from focusing on the internal ground glass. In the end, it may simply be too high a price to pay for a more favorable depth of field. Of course, only your story can determine that for sure.

CHAPTER 9
Making Light of Your Story

When we put a frame around the world, we are making a conscious decision to exclude what is not helpful to our story. Proper lighting craft mestoryans applying the same principle.

Our lighting should accomplish two things: to enhance the three-dimensional (3D) illusion by maximizing texture, and to direct the viewer's eye to what is important and relevant inside the frame.

The mantra to "Exclude! Exclude! Exclude!" is integral to our lighting craft because so much time and effort is expended modifying, controlling, and otherwise *removing* light from a scene. We accomplish this with the control devices such as barndoors, cutters, cookies, and *Blackwrap* and by altering the character and direction of the light using diffusion and color-correction strategies, Chinese lanterns, foam cores, blue and orange gels, and the rest.

Lighting is an exercise in logic, derived from the story and the opportunities and limitations that story imposes. In many cases, we merely reinforce the direction and quality of light already present. If there is a lamp on a CEO's desk, we place our light and direct it appropriately to mimic the lamp's effect. Of course, we may model and diffuse the light to present the CEO in a flattering way – if that is our story. But it is the lamp on the desk that provides the motivation for lighting the scene; the shooter simply builds on what is already there (or logically could be there).

On location, we are often required to exclude a dominant light source; by blocking out intrusive large windows, for example, that may be working against good modeling in our subject. This technique of adding *negative fill* may seem at first like an oxymoron, but it is common industry practice in order to establish firm control of the visual story (Fig. 9.1).

FIGURE 9.1
Exclude! Exclude! Exclude! Understand the wisdom! When lighting a scene, always consider removing light before adding more.

FIGURE 9.2
Today's digital cameras perform best on minimally illuminated sets, which are in any case faster and simpler to set up and more comfortable for talent. The more favorable depth-of-field in HD helps de-emphasize distracting background elements.

THINK SMALL

You don't need much to light well. The great cinematographer Néstor Almendros, who photographed many notable films including *Kramer vs. Kramer* (1979) and *Sophie's Choice* (1982) used only a mirror and a small Fresnel[1] to light most scenes. Employing fewer lights mean greater control and more manageable shadows. It means fewer cutters, C-stands, and gobo arms to control unwanted spill, which in turn speeds setup time and saves money on crew. These efficiencies can greatly enhance your value as a shooter and likely lead to bigger and better work assignments in the future.

Aesthetically, there are many advantages to thinking small. Shooting at low light levels enables a narrower depth of field due to the larger f-stop, thus serving the shooter grappling with the challenge of establishing clearly defined focal planes. Lower light levels also translate into a more comfortable working environment for talent and crew (Fig. 9.2). And there is the reduced chance of tripping circuit breakers for productions that must draw power from standard wall outlets on location.

---

[1] The Fresnel is a tightly focusable instrument that employs a ridged lightweight lens invented by French physicist Augustin-Jean Fresnel. Originally developed for lighthouses, the Fresnel lens is much thinner than conventional convex lenses and thus transmits more light, which accounts for its greater efficiency.

Minimum Illumination for Popular HD Camcorders

(manufacturer provided data)

Canon HF11	0.2 lux (Night Mode)
Canon XL-H1s	3 lux (24F)
*Canon XL1-S	2 lux
JVC GY-HD250	Not Specified
JVC GY-HM100	3 lux
JVC GY-HM700	Not specified
*JVC GY-DV300U	2.65 lux (LoLux mode)
Panasonic AG-HMC150	3 lux
Panasonic AG-HVX200A	3 lux
Panasonic AG-HPX300	0.8 lux
*Panasonic DVX100A	3 lux (+18dB)
Sony HVR-A1	0 lux (Night Mode)
Sony HVR-Z5	1.5 lux
Sony PMW-EX1/EX3	0.14 lux
*Sony DSR-PD170	1 lux (+18dB)

* These are standard definition camcorders.

FIGURE 9.3
Shooters should look warily at manufacturers' stated "minimum" illumination ratings because acceptable performance is seldom a consideration.

FIGURE 9.4
Do you see the problem here? This camera boasts a fabulous "minimum" illumination rating!

FIGURE 9.5
Unless you're shooting *Godfather IV*, you probably don't need truckloads of lighting and grip gear. Think and light small. More gear = less work accomplished during a shooting day.

SHOOTERS WHO LIGHT, EDIT, PRODUCE, AND WASH WINDOWS

In an era of one- or two-person crews, when the shooter storyteller is asked to wear many hats, the ability to work with simple lighting is crucial. In my own work, I prefer small focusable Fresnels to higher-power open-face instruments that produce more light but less control. For The History Channel several years

FIGURE 9.6
Less is more! Fresnel instruments offer precise focus and control which, in conjunction with a four-way barndoor, can eliminate the need for a multitude of flags, cutters, and cumbersome grip gear.

FIGURE 9.7
Open-faced instruments produce a lot of light over a broad area, and can be used with a soft box or for illuminating a green screen or cyclorama.

FIGURE 9.8
The shooter's basic kit comprised of four low-wattage 150 W/300 W Fresnels.

FIGURE 9.9
A good investment? My "Inky" serial number 22 manufactured by Mole-Richardson in 1927 has been handed down to me through multiple generations of cameramen.

ago, I recall shooting entire episodes of *Sworn to Secrecy* with a four-head 150 W Fresnel kit!

Things were different in the prehistoric days of my youth when I earned my living by shooting industrial films on ASA 25 16-mm film. The "standard" travel kit for lighting consisted of four open-faced Lowel lights fitted with 1,000-W lamps. Such relatively high-wattage gear was necessary to achieve a basic exposure – indeed, in many situations, any image at all.

With the advent of low-light sensitive cameras, the Big Bang approach to lighting is no longer the only or preferred way to go. For some shooters, old habits are hard to break, however. I recently witnessed a macabre shoot in which the veteran DP dragged two 1,200 W HMIs, three 4 × 4 bounce cards, three large cutters, two 5-ft. *meat axes*, seven C-stands, a 6-ft. piece of track, and a Western dolly into a 10 ×12 ft. windowless room. Aside from the personnel and hours needed to accomplish this Herculean task, what did the DP then do? Flag the lights. Squeeze the barndoors. Drape the heads with black foil and drop in three double-wire scrims. He spent over 2 h cutting the lights down to a reasonable and manageable level. Do you see the logic? I sure don't.

The preamble to the Shooter's Constitution is clear on this point: *When in the course of lighting events, it becomes necessary (as it usually does) to exclude, exclude, exclude; it sure saves a lot of time and effort if you're not using ridiculously too much light in the first place.*

HMI LIGHTING: EXPENSIVE BUT WORTH IT

For years, I traveled the world with a small tungsten Fresnel kit and two 400 W HMI[2] PARs. An HMI *parabolic arc reflector* is the shooter's dream light – strong enough to punch through a 4 × 4 diffusion silk, yet efficient enough to plug

FIGURE 9.10
My 400 W PARs have served me for almost two decades on projects throughout the world. The instruments' high initial cost has been recouped many times in rental fees – and peace of mind.

FIGURE 9.11
I demand rugged gear that can withstand the rigors of a torrential downpour.

[2]HMI (Hydrargyrum Medium-Arc Iodide) lighting uses an arc lamp with a ballast to provide ignition and control of the arc. Five times more efficient than tungsten lighting, HMIs provide a very high-quality daylight source.

FIGURE 9.12
Low-wattage HMI and tungsten units may be plugged into a standard wall outlet, a major convenience when shooting in diverse locations.

FIGURE 9.13
HMIs provide the option of bounce or direct lighting. At night, several instruments can be used to create pools of light or lift overall illumination.

FIGURE 9.14
The proficient use of fewer but higher quality instruments is the key to developing an efficient work style. The HMI PAR uses drop-in lenses to define its beam and character.

FIGURE 9.15
Today's LEDs mimic the look and feel of an HMI at a fraction of the cost. This "bi-focus" unit can be configured singularly or in a multiple array, outputting a variable blast of hard and soft light.

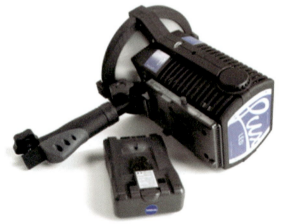

FIGURE 9.16
This self-contained LED light packs a lot of punch for news and reality shooters.

multiple units into an ordinary household outlet. For interiors, the PAR can be bounced off a white card to simulate a natural window source, or, for exteriors, used directly through a silk or grid cloth to provide a flattering facial fill. The 200 W or 400 W HMI PAR is one of the most useful (albeit pricey) instruments you can own.

HMI lighting can instantly elevate the look and feel of one's images; and unlike other gear requiring a sizeable investment, the impact of HMI lighting is immediately obvious on screen and thus readily billable to clients. A small HMI costing a few thousand dollars may seem extravagant, but for the working professional, it is not. Packing up ten times the punch of conventional tungsten lighting, the HMI PAR's power and versatility can often eliminate a trunk full of less useful gear. For the itinerant shooter, this efficiency alone justifies the considerable investment.

FLUORESCENTS AND THE GREEN PLAGUE

Fluorescent lighting for film and video used to be a perilous proposition. The fixtures ran cool, used little power and threw off tons of light, but who cared? The color balance was horrible, exhibiting a sickly green hue. Facial shadows and dark skin were particularly susceptible to the insidious green spike, requiring shooters to apply a wash of healthy light, often from a pricey HMI.

In 1993, I recall shooting at a popular health club in New York City. Of course, there were the usual banks of fluorescents in the ceiling, emitting the horrid green pall. Employing the wisdom of the time, I dutifully balanced every one of the *220 tubes* in the club, fitting each lamp with a *full minus green* gel. This compensated for the green all right, by bathing the entire club in a deep magenta, not unlike a bordello.

Naturally, this drew more than a few scathing looks from the ad agency rep; and the spot's young director, who regretting hiring me, demanded that I rectify the "mess" pronto. He simply couldn't believe that his smiling workout babes would appear normal on film. I tried to reassure him, pointing to my Minolta Colormeter, but his eyes kept telling him otherwise.

The fluorescent green plague is often exacerbated by the tubes' unfavorable overhead placement. To satisfactorily capture such scenes, the shooter usually employs an eye-level fill by borrowing a few diseased lamps from the ceiling to provide a frontal or side illumination. This strategy has the advantage of maintaining consistency in the fill light, albeit with the miserable green curse intact.

In theory, *Cool White* fluorescent lamps are supposed to mimic daylight, but this is only to the unsophisticated eye, which is a lot more forgiving of spectral deficiencies than the CCD or CMOS sensor in your camera. The reviled green spike is integral to all fluorescent tubes that employ mercury vapor. In many ways, it's a pact with the devil, as the lamp's high efficiency comes at a steep aesthetic price.

In the last several years, fluorescent tube manufacturers have made significant progress developing new phosphors to compensate for the green curse. But as manufacturers drive the lamps harder to achieve greater output, the off-color spike has increased proportionately, necessitating the formulation of yet another generation of compensating phosphors.

Kino-Flo and other manufacturers have developed their own line of fluorescent tubes, mixing a potpourri of phosphors to produce a color-correct lamp that

THE GREEN PLAGUE

UNCORRECTED   CORRECTED

FIGURE 9.17
The green plague is evident in this fluorescent-lit market. At right is the scene after white-balancing the camera, a process that adds the required magenta. If shooting talent close-ups, the overhead fluorescents should be supplemented with a side or frontal fill to avoid dark eye sockets.

FIGURE 9.18
Found ubiquitously in commercial establishments throughout the world, the Cool White fluorescent produces a lot of light at low cost. Problem is, all that light comes with a potent green curse.

FIGURE 9.19
Color-correct fluorescents make powerful and efficient soft lights. Balanced lamps without an apparent green spike are available in tungsten and daylight types.

FIGURE 9.20
Some fluorescents feature a highly directional beam more characteristic of a Fresnel than a broad array.

appears balanced to the eye. This should give solace to shooters prone to angry outbursts at the sight of the slightest green emanating from a fluorescent instrument.

Beyond the noxious green hue, there is also the potential for *flicker,* a hazard associated with discharge-type lighting in general, including LEDs. The ugly pulsating effect is seen most commonly in out-of-sync streetlights and neon signs when shooting at nonstandard shutter speeds, or when shooting NTSC (for example, in 50 Hz countries).

Today, high-frequency ballasts have largely eliminated the flicker risk in professional lighting instruments; but proper caution should still be exercised when shooting under ordinary fluorescent, neon, or mercury-vapor in areas known to experience power irregularities.

FIGURE 9.21
Blasting hard, undiffused light at your subject is lazy, unprofessional, and suggestive of adult entertainment. Don't even think about lighting like this – even if you are shooting adult entertainment!

THINK BIG

When working with talent, a large diffused source is usually advisable to soften facial shadows and suppress undesirable texture in the skin. As shooters, we usually seek to maximize texture when composing and lighting our scenes, but this is generally not the case when shooting close-ups of talent, especially narcissistic talent.

It matters that low-cost HD can wreak particular havoc with your favorite star's flesh tones. Compression anomalies, hue shifts, and shadow noise can contribute to a pattern of ugly contours not unlike an open pit mine – hardly a great way to treat your leading lady!

A broad source directed through a silk or *grid cloth* produces a flattering near-shadowless wash of light that can help attenuate HD's sometimes objectionable harshness. For narrative projects, the advantages of a broad soft source cannot be overstated, as much of the excessive error correction in prosumer camcorders is mitigated.

SOFT IS KEY

We've discussed our usual goal to maximize texture in our compositions and lighting. In practical terms, this means paying close attention to the smoothness, depth, and direction of shadows. Shadows, after all, communicate our visual themes; the quality, presence, or absence of shadow detail contributing to the viewer's perception of genre and mood. Shadows lie at the heart of our storytelling craft, the vehicle by which we as shooters are ultimately judged.

FIGURE 9.22
Because soft light dominates the natural, spiritual, and man-made worlds, the shooter usually mimics this quality in gently modulated shadows. Remember: more than anything else, shadows tell your story. Always treat them with dignity and respect!

CHOOSING A SOFT LIGHT

A soft source may be achieved through a silk or diffusion gel, by bouncing off a white card or foam core, or by employing a dedicated "soft box" or fluorescent bank. However you accomplish it, an effective soft light must be a part of every shooter's basic kit.

Color-correct fluorescent banks are a common sight on feature and commercial sets, as they can provide a broad soft key or fill light when shooting aboard moving trains, for example, or in institutions and offices, and large public areas like airports.

A fluorescent tube's rapid falloff may also be helpful as a backlight. While a Fresnel may project a hard shadow back onto the set or talent, a broad fluorescent produces a smooth shadowless beam without the bulk or hassle of a light box

or bounce card. Such economy in tight locations, such as office cubicles and supermarket aisles, is a major advantage of utilizing broad fluorescent sources like a *two or four-banger* Kino-Flo or *Gyoury* wand system.

The Gyoury system is built around the concept of a wand (Fig. 9.27) – a tube assembly that may be detached and mounted in difficult or hard-to-reach locations like along a bathroom mirror, beneath a computer screen, or even inside a refrigerator. The wand inside a China ball provides a flattering soft fill for walking shots in episodic TV and event-type shows like political conventions and award ceremonies, the mobile source producing a frontal wash with a very distinct professional gleam.

FIGURE 9.23
A large white bounce card serves as an excellent inexpensive soft key.

(a)

(b)

FIGURE 9.24
(a) A light box mounted on a 400 W HMI PAR. This is one of my favorite setups – an instant broad window source producing a beautiful soft light. The Old Masters in their northern-facing ateliers would've killed for a portable northern-facing window! (b) Vermeer's seventeenth century *Girl with a Pearl Earring*.

FIGURE 9.25
Two- and four-bank fluorescent broads are common fixtures on feature film sets. Here, almost two dozen instruments were built into the walls of the dining car of *The Darjeeling Limited*.

FIGURE 9.26
Multiple balloons and Chinese lanterns are often used to illuminate large areas like a city street or crowded meeting hall. This scene is from *Crossing Over* (2009). [Photo courtesy of Airstar Space Lighting]

FIGURE 9.27
The Gyoury wand produces a flattering soft source.

FIGURE 9.28
One or more tubes may be all you need to light a car interior at night.

SPILLING THE BEANS

One downside of utilizing large sources like a soft box or bounce card is the need to control the copious spill. In most cases, this requires the placing of one or more *flags* to protect a nearby wall or set element. Although a Fresnel with a focusable lens offers better control (and therefore less spill), its beam is harsher

FIGURE 9.29
Large soft lights often require multiple flags or "cutters" to prevent unwanted spill. Given the effort to erect and adjust such flags, a shooter with many setups per day may prefer a small Fresnel that is more easily trimmed and controlled.

FIGURE 9.30
Bear in mind when scouting that confined locations are tougher to light and manage. In some cases, lights can be directed through exterior windows – a strategy that works well for many interior sets.

and more likely to produce an objectionable shadow, especially on small sets and in confined locations (Fig. 9.30).

Shooting in tight spaces usually requires longer setup times and a larger grip complement to rein in the unwanted spill. For this reason, many filmmakers prefer shooting on a soundstage; the errant spill from multiple instruments simply falls off into space and produces no ill effects. In most corporate, documentary, and reality-style programming, the shooter is afforded no such luxury. The location is what it is – and we have to deal with it.

TYPES OF DIFFUSION GEL

For the shooter storyteller, the adept use of diffusion gel is critical for controlling a light's character and depth of shadows. Many varieties of diffusion gel are available, but most shooters only need three types of diffusion gel in their kits: a strong diffuser for on-camera fill and keying talent, a moderate diffuser to provide a bit more edge when needed, and a light diffuser to take the curse off strong directional sources. Diffusion gel may be purchased in long rolls or in a single 20-in. by 24-in. sheet at any film and TV supply house.

Alternatively, if you're like me and want to save a few bucks, you can rummage through the trash of a feature film or TV show that happens to be shooting in your city or town. The gel discarded each day from a typical commercial set is enough to supply most video shooters for multiple lifetimes.

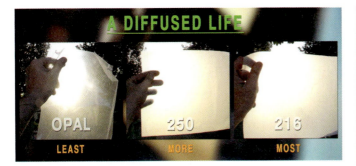

FIGURE 9.31
The three gel types essential to every shooter are opal, #250, and #216. Be sure to carry at least several sheets of each on every shoot. Lee Filter references are understood and are often used generically. Rosco produces a comparable line of diffusion gel.

FIGURE 9.32
In this typical setup, a 750 W "Baby Baby" fresnel is directed through a #216 heavy diffuser.

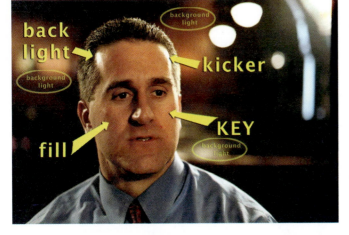

FIGURE 9.33
Keying through a heavy diffuser produces soft gentle shadows.

FIGURE 9.34
A lighter diffuser retains the direction and character of the setting sun.

THE JELLY ROLL

While scavenging through the trash of *Rocky XXII*, you might also avail yourself of other forlorn gel lying amid the detritus. These scraps can help outfit your *jelly roll* – an elastic pouch that is one of the most valuable pieces of gear you can own (Fig. 9.35). My 12-in. jelly roll contains an assortment of diffusion, color-correction, and "party" gel gleaned from various trash cans over the years.

For color correction, I keep on hand a range of CTB[3] (blue) gel, from one-quarter to full blue, the latter ostensibly but not quite converting a tungsten 3,200° K source to daylight.

CTB is the most used gel in my kit, as tungsten sources must frequently be "blued" to add texture when backlighting talent or to represent the effect of daylight or moonlight spilling into a scene. Typically, I add only a hint of blue, e.g., "half blue," to reflect a cool source in or out of frame. In most cases, I don't transform a tungsten source completely to daylight because I want to preserve the *feeling* of mixed light sources as we perceive and experience them in life. Conversely, when working with HMI or LED sources in tungsten conditions, I add a half CTO (orange) gel to alleviate the blue cast while still preserving the daylight feeling streaming from an exterior source. In fact, I often mix warm and cool lighting in my scenes, painting with CTO and CTB gel to add texture while maintaining the faithful interplay of light emanating from warm and cool sources.

Although full CTB is intended to convert 3,200° K tungsten sources to daylight, the effect in practice is quite a bit less than that when compared with actual daylight or the output, say, from an HMI. If true daylight balance is your goal (and it may well be), an actual HMI, LED, or color-correct fluorescent is required. Also, due to high heat absorption, the full blue CTB is subject to rapid fading,

FIGURE 9.35
I never leave home without my jelly roll! At least one replete with 10–20 sheets of diffusion, color-correction, and party gel should be a part of every shooter's basic repertoire.

---

[3]CTB = Color Temperature Blue; CTO = Color Temperature Orange.

so the wise shooter is sure to include extra sheets in his kit.

In addition to diffusion and color correction, the third variety of gel in a shooter's jelly roll is the "party" type often used to add a splash of color to otherwise sterile scenes. These gels, like the swatches of paint in an artist's palette, reflect a shooter's own creative impulses. In my roll, I keep an assortment of violet and rose gel to add color and/or texture to backgrounds, especially in corporate environments that tend to lack visual panache. The deep crimson is one of my favorites, instantly injecting intrigue, if not full-scale alarm, into any scene. A little goes a long way, however, so shooters should use such heavy effects sparingly, and as always, with utmost good taste and attention to one's overall storytelling goals.

CTO CORRECTION GEL		
Full CTO	converts 5500° K.	to 2930° K.
1/2 CTO	converts 5500° K.	to 3440° K.
1/4 CTO	converts 5500° K.	to 4060° K.
1/8 CTO	converts 5500° K.	to 4800° K.

CTB CORRECTION GEL		
Full CTB	converts 3200° K.	to 5700° K.
1/2 CTB	converts 3200° K.	to 4270° K.
1/4 CTB	converts 3200° K.	to 3550° K.
1/8 CTB	converts 3200° K.	to 3400° K.

FIGURE 9.36
Blue CTB increases the color temperature and makes a light appear cooler; orange CTO decreases the color temperature and makes it appear warmer.

THE STANDARD SETUP

In our work and in our lighting, we shooters normally strive to promote the *illusion* of a third dimension. Accordingly, when shooting a talking head, we direct our subject's look between the camera and the key light (Fig. 9.37). Thus, the viewer is peering into the subject's facial shadows, which, revealing an appropriate amount of texture and detail, evokes the story (Fig. 9.38). One or more

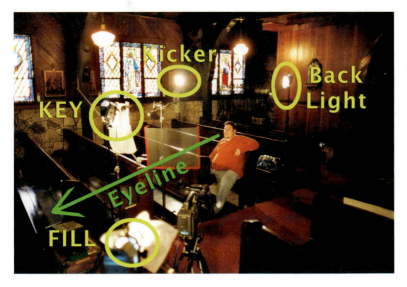

FIGURE 9.37
In a typical setup, the subject directs his look between the camera and the key light. The key and fill lights are fitted with a heavy diffuser, while the backlight and "kicker" are gelled with lighter diffusion to preserve their directional character. Most interior and exterior scenes are set up in this way, the shadow produced by the key light across the face maximizing the 3D illusion.

FIGURE 9.38
The kicker from screen left is stronger and more focused, simulating the effect of the window source visible in frame.

small Fresnels can then be placed three-quarters behind on either side of the subject to add highlights to the hair and wardrobe and to achieve separation as needed from the background. The background, in turn, is painted with a tightly focused Fresnel fitted with a party gel or *cookie* to add visual interest. [More on cookies and snoots later in this chapter]

LIGHTING FRONT AND CENTER

To reduce the texture apparent in actors' faces, the shooter will typically place a diffused light source close to the lens axis or atop the camera. As a frontal light produces no visible shadow, many defects in the face and neck of actors (such as acne scars, wrinkles, and dark lines) are de-emphasized.

A proper fill light may also play a vital storytelling role by placing a strategic point of light in an actor's eyes. Illuminating (or not) the eyes of an actor, reporter, or other talent is critical as the eyes are the point of entry to a character's warmth, credibility, and humanity. Likable characters with whom your audience identifies should have well-illuminated eye sockets and a distinct glint in the pupil of the eye (Fig. 9.39a). Conversely, characters who are despicable or villainous might exhibit dark, unfilled eyes; thus cutting off the viewer's potential identification with them (Fig. 9.39b). Your job as a shooter is to rigorously control these cues, which go directly to the genre, mood, and fundamentals of your storytelling.

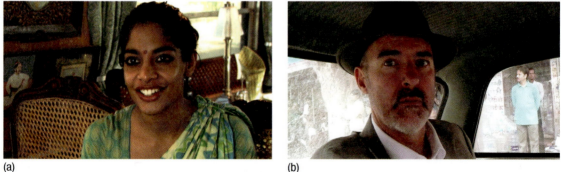

(a) (b)

FIGURE 9.39
(a) Proper front fill illuminates the eyes, making talent appear warmer and helping to establish intimacy with the viewer.
(b) Lack of frontal fill can make your favorite actor appear sinister. Maybe this is what you want!

HAVING YOUR FILL

The proper application of fill light can be tricky. Too little fill may lead to excessively dark shadows and a potential increase in noise in underlit areas of the frame. Too much fill can produce a washed out, deer-in-the-headlights look with a strong artificial feel (Fig. 9.40).

For shooters accustomed to working with film, the extra fill typically required when capturing HD is something of an Achilles' heel, as *some* front light is almost always necessary when shooting in a compressed HD format. Sometimes a little fill applied passively with a bounce card may be all you need to return a portion of the key light and lighten the facial shadows. An ultracontrast-type filter[4] may also help by transferring surplus values from the highlights into the darker image areas, thus potentially eliminating the need for an active or passive fill light.

ON-CAMERA OPTIONS

We have various on- and off-camera devices for adding appropriate frontal fill. Depending on the desired intensity, portability, and relative softness, a small Fresnel with diffusion or a China ball (Fig. 9.41) suspended at the end of a painter's pole can work fine.

FIGURE 9.40
We want our young starlets to look great, but too much fill can appear unmotivated and produce an unnatural look. Exclude! Exclude! Exclude! It applies to lighting most of all!

FIGURE 9.41
A China ball at the end of a boom pole is used to provide a soft frontal illumination in this walking shot captured at dusk.

---

[4]See Chapter 6 for a discussion of ultracontrast and other camera and software filters.

FIGURE 9.42
This on-camera LED is frugal on power yet packs a surprising punch.

FIGURE 9.43
This micro-LED is inexpensive and convenient, operating on four standard AA batteries.

If on-camera solution is preferred, the shooter can opt for a ring light or handle-mounted LED (Fig. 9.42) or miniature 10 W HMI. In any case, you'll want a camera light that packs enough punch to produce a natural wash even through a layer of moderate to heavy diffusion.

LIGHTING IN PLANES

When lighting a scene, every light has a purpose, just like every element in a composition must support the story. In general, we illuminate each plane independently. We place the key to tastefully model our subject in the mid-ground. We light our background (usually) to achieve separation and help lift our subject from the canvas. In addition, we light our foreground to help frame and direct viewer attention to what's important in the scene, i.e., the correct visual story.

Analogous to a layered Photoshop composition, the planes are treated independently so the shooter can precisely tweak a scene's look. A hard raking light may be used across the background to add texture and separation. A soft front light may be used at mid-ground to preserve detail in a subject's facial shadows or suppress unwanted texture in an actress's face.

FIGURE 9.44
Lighting in planes: it's an idea worth pursuing.

Lighting in planes can be a challenge to the documentary shooter who must often shoot in narrow or confined locations. As one light can

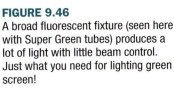

FIGURE 9.46
A broad fluorescent fixture (seen here with Super Green tubes) produces a lot of light with little beam control. Just what you need for lighting green screen!

FIGURE 9.45
This scene's multiple planes should be lit and controlled independently for maximum control of the visual story.

seldom optimally light multiple planes at once, the video shooter is constantly looking for ways to control the unwanted spill and the cross-contamination of one plane's light into another.

LIGHTING FOR GREEN SCREEN

One area where even illumination is a must is in green screen applications. When lighting for green screen, I typically use multiple soft boxes or fluorescent broads to ensure a uniform wash. The evenness of this wash can be verified using a *waveform monitor* (Fig. 9.48a), a key tool with which every serious shooter should be familiar.

FIGURE 9.47
On many jobs, I carry a 6 × 7-ft. collapsible panel, which is useful for shooting an actor or reporter from the waist up on location.

The green screen doesn't have to be bright 55–60% is ideal, just more saturated than anything else in the frame, including the actors' wardrobe. I use a *vectorscope* to check the saturation, which should be at least 40 units greater than the foreground. Utilizing too much or too little light on the green screen makes it more difficult to achieve the required 40-point separation in the vectorscope.

Note that conventional light meters may not always be accurate when utilizing fluorescent lighting. This is due to the green spike that produces an incorrect (too low) meter reading. In this case, the fluorescent green curse is an advantage as Kino-Flos fitted with Super Green lamps emit a pure green light, which means less contamination from other colors falling on the screen.

Even if you don't have access to a waveform, you can use your camera's *zebras* to achieve a relatively smooth illumination devoid of hot spots. Shooting green screen

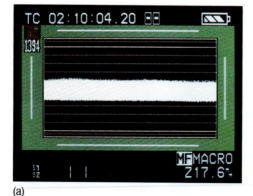

(a)

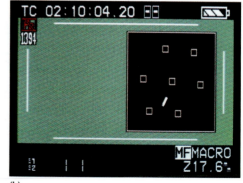

(b)

(c)

FIGURE 9.48

(a) The waveform built into some cameras and monitors can be used to achieve a smooth green screen illumination of 55–60%. The vectorscope (b) verifies optimal saturation at least 40 units greater than the foreground action. In a pinch, your camera zebras (c) set to 60% can facilitate a reasonably even wash.

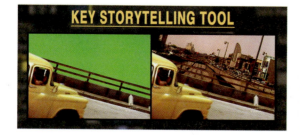

FIGURE 9.49

While dedicated tools such as BorisFx and Autodesk Combustion are widely available, many rudimentary keying operations may be accomplished nearly as well utilizing the popular desktop editors. [Images courtesy of Autodesk]

in tight spots can be particularly challenging because the spill from a broad lighting can easily contaminate wardrobe and flesh tones. It's always best to use the largest green screen surface feasible and keep your subject as far from it as possible.

Some cameras and monitors notably from Panasonic feature a built-in waveform and vectorscope and are therefore especially well-suited for green screen work. Software solutions like Adobe OnLocation can also provide the reference "scopes" via the Firewire interface to input data from the camera into a laptop or desktop computer.

WHY GREEN?

Green screen is favored over blue screen for several reasons. First, primary green occurs rarely in our everyday world, so we needn't usually worry about inadvertently keying out our starlet's beautiful blue eyes. Of course, if you're shooting sun-dappled leprechauns in a rain forest, you might consider an alternative keying color – red, blue, yellow, amber, white, and black. All will work.

Still, there is another compelling reason for using green: the green channel in digital video is not compressed. Compression invariably introduces noise, which can complicate the execution of a clean key. Given that the human eye is particularly sensitive to green sitting squarely in the middle of the visible spectrum, engineers do not normally toy with the green ("Y") channel because discarded detail "corrected" later may be readily apparent to viewers. In NTSC, DV's red and blue channels are sampled at only one-fourth resolution in the 4:1:1 color space. The uncompressed green channel represented by the "4" is thus the best choice for keying in standard definition.

The same mindset applies when shooting HD in 4:2:0 or 4:2:2. Either sampling scheme can produce an acceptable key; the 4:2:0 used in HDV and most XDCAM variants still samples the green channel at full resolution. On the other hand, the 4:2:2 color space in XDCAM HD 422, DVCPRO HD, and 10-bit AVC-Intra cameras have the advantage of increased blue and red sampling at 50% of the green, so these cameras should produce keys with much smoother edges. Images captured in the 4:2:0 space are hobbled in this regard, providing the same precision as 4:2:2 images, but only every *other* vertical line.

My preference for shooting 4:2:2 is simple: it's the preference of our Creator and our physiology. It's how our eyes are designed with *rods* embedded in our retinas that measure the brightness of objects and *cones* that assess the color. Because our retinas have twice as many rods as cones, the 4:2:2 approach that samples *luminance* at twice the rate of *chrominance* closely approximates how we see the world, all other differences and points of view aside.

Consider the wisdom: when we enter a very dark room, we can discern much more easily the shape of an object than its color. This makes sense from an evolutionary perspective: we first recognize in the dark the form of a predator before noticing the color of dress she is wearing.

While blue is also a viable option when green is not available, the color red is not usually a good keying choice owing to the amount of red in flesh tones. Black or white keying is also possible, and may be the only option when a *chroma-key* screen must be improvised on a location in front of a black or white wall.

An alternative to the traditional blue or green screen, the *Reflecmedia* system utilizes a lens-mounted LED ring light (Fig. 9.50) to illuminate a special fabric, which appears gray to the eye (Fig. 9.51) but registers as a solid blue or green to the camera. The fabric comprised of millions of tiny beads efficiently reflects the ring light source but rejects any stray off-axis light. The system thus requires virtually no setup time and eliminates the need for the usual broad green screen lighting.

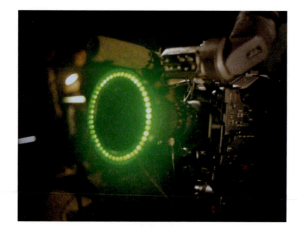

FIGURE 9.50
When used with a special screen, Reflecmedia's LED ring light eliminates the need for additional lighting when shooting blue and green screen.

FIGURE 9.51
The Chromatte screen appears gray to the eye, but blue or green to the camera, depending on the ring light color. The screen's beaded surface consists of thousands of tiny lenslets that reject off-axis light so stray shadows are not a problem. In this scene, we see splashes of green spilling onto foreground objects – a potential drawback of the camera-mounted ring light system.

The ring light approach also allows placement of talent very close to the screen. This is an obvious advantage to the shooter who must shoot in tight locations, such as a network production trailer or press box.

GET A GRIP

One can think of grip gear and the various lighting control paraphernalia as the ultimate expression of our storytelling imperative to *exclude, exclude, exclude*. We use our Fresnels, HMIs, LEDs, and fluorescents to place light into a scene, and we use our cutters, cookies, snoots, and *BlackWrap* to take light *out* of a scene by trimming, feathering, and crafting it to our visual story.

Like composition, selective focus, and field of view, proper lighting communicates to the viewer what is essential in the frame. Excluding light from a set element, prop, or actor's face informs the viewer: don't look at this. It's not important. Nothing to look at here.

We've already discussed how the viewer's eye is naturally drawn to the brightest object in the frame. This is a holdover apparently from our prehuman days as drosophila[5] when we were drawn inexorably to incandescing lightning bugs. Today, this notion of attention-grabbing lightning bugs is helpful to keep in mind when applying the tricks of the grip trade.

---

[5]From Wikipedia: "Drosophila is a genus of small flies, belonging to the family Drosophilidae, whose members are often called 'fruit flies" or more appropriately (though less frequently) pomace flies, vinegar flies, or wine flies." Shooters talk about irrelevant stuff like this all the time. Get used to it.

FIGURE 9.52
Watch your step! This is C-stand clutter! If you're serious about lighting, you'll stumble on this scene often.

FIGURE 9.53
The C-stand provides solid support for bounce cards, nets, cutters, and other lighting control gadgets. Here, it supports a microphone boom.

Every shooter can benefit from a basic grip and lighting control package, which at a minimum should consist of several C-stands and a medium flag kit. Such a complement is critical to controlling spill by cutting off errant light, especially at the top, bottom, and edges of the frame.

Transporting weighty C-stands is not always practical, however. If a shoot requires grip gear in a distant city, I try to rent a package locally and save the hassle of transporting hundreds of pounds of chromed steel in checked baggage. The same applies to unwieldy expendables like large sheets of foam core and show cards. Packing these items onto airplanes no longer makes much sense, given today's exorbitant excess baggage charges and the relative easy availability of these items in most large cities.

FLAGGING IT

A medium-size 18-in. by 24-in. flag kit (Fig. 9.54) consists of several cutters, a triple, double, two single nets, and a silk. Such kits are inexpensive and will last a lifetime.

KOOKS, COOKIES, AND CUKES

They're all names for a *cookaloris* that can add texture to flat or otherwise uninspired scenes. Every shooter with a few notches under his battery belt has reached for a kook now and then to break up a shadowless wall or other large

FIGURE 9.54
Medium 18 in. × 24 in. flag kit.

FIGURE 9.55
In most cases we place the most light on the subject's face. Here, a double (red) net feathers the light off the priest's bright collar, which might otherwise divert attention from the clergyman's heartfelt story.

flat surface. Kooks constructed of plywood are available as commercial products, or they can be improvised using strips of gaffer's tape, or more simply by poking a few holes in a piece of BlackWrap.

Known popularly by its trade name, *BlackWrap* is a malleable black foil (Fig. 9.57) with unlimited uses. Affixed to the back or sides of a light or clipped to its barndoors, the aluminized foil can help eliminate or reduce spill. It can also be used to fabricate a makeshift *cookie* for projecting a pattern on a bare wall, or improvising a snoot for narrowly illuminating a set element like a painting or photograph hanging in the background. I knew a shooter at NBC who kept the same well-worn pieces of BlackWrap in his package for his entire 25-year career! Job after job, year after year, he kept pulling out the same tattered old kooks. Not bad for a few pennies (or not even that!) investment.

Along with the gel for your jelly roll, you'll also find in the trash of a major production an abundance of slightly used BlackWrap. Go ahead and avail yourself. You'll feel on top of the world.

FIGURE 9.56
A single net at the end of a gobo arm feathers the light off the edge of a set.

FIGURE 9.57
The black foil referred to as BlackWrap is a practical and inexpensive way to control spill in tight locations. Adept use of the foil reduces the need for C-stands, cutters and other unwieldy grip gear.

(a)

(b)

(c)

FIGURE 9.58
(a) The shadowy pattern of a cookaloris is the signature effect in many *film noir* movies.
(b) A commercial cookie is usually made of plywood, but a "kook" can also be fashioned out of malleable black foil. BlackWrap can easily be cut and twisted (c) to produce an improvised window kook.

BEING SNOOTY

A small Fresnel fitted with a *snoot* (Fig. 9.59) may be used to illuminate individual set elements, like a wall painting or a Ming vase on a dresser. The highlighting of objects in this way is critical to creating visual interest and texture in the background of scenes.

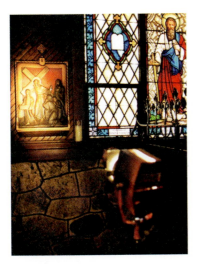

FIGURE 9.59
Snoots are often used to narrow a beam on a painting or other set element.

FIGURE 9.60
To adjust this low tech 1920s era snoot, you squeeze and warp the malleable copper opening.

CLAMPING DOWN

It was something of a status symbol among National Geographic shooters to carry the most beat-up grip gear imaginable. This mantle of status applied particularly to the various clamps we carried that proudly bore the imprimatur of *experience*. Their ratty condition (it was thought) reflected the pain endured in far-flung battle-borne adventures. To this day, I still carry an assortment of mangled clamps just to maintain this impression: pipe clamps, Mafer clamps, gator clamps, C-clamps – all beat to heck. My scissor clamps are especially full of personality,

FIGURE 9.61
The resourceful shooter carries an array of clamps to tackle any mounting challenge. I also keep a small suction cup (far left) in my package for mounting a small light on a car hood or other smooth surface.

FIGURE 9.62
Industry pros cutely refer to a clothespin as a "C-47" – a one-time catalog designation. The extension cord is a "stinger." An overhanging tree branch placed into a scene, we call a "Hollywood." Using proper lingo will increase your perceived prowess as a shooter and contribute to the omniscient halo above your head.

(a)

(b)

FIGURE 9.63
Apple boxes (a) are extremely useful on a set, from supporting a light or monitor to elevating an actor slightly to gain eyeline. The "pigeon" plate (b) screwed to an apple box or set wall can support a variety of grip gear.

these clamps being the darling of every shooter who has ever interviewed a CEO in an office with a suspended ceiling. Of course, I also carry a few dozen clothespins, the common spring kind. They count as clamps, too.

TAPE LIVES!

We've discussed recording to flash memory, optical disc, and hard drive, and we've sung the praises of the new and glorious tapeless workflow. But in at least one area, we continue to use tape – and lots of it.

Every shooter must be familiar with a range of industry utility tapes. *Camera tape* is especially useful, as it may be safely applied to camera bodies and lens barrels without fear of damaging the finish or leaving a gummy residue. The shooter should be sure to have at least one roll of 1-in. white camera tape on every job. Just stay away from the cheap stuff. Pro-grade camera tape is widely available from any film or video supply house.

Gaffer's tape is a heavy-duty cloth adhesive *not* for use on cameras, lenses, or electronic gear of any shape or form. Its powerful grip will easily remove the paint from light fixtures, apartment walls, and priceless works of art. Gaffer's

(a)

(b)

FIGURE 9.65
White camera tape is a must on every job. Use it for marking zoom and focus on a lens barrel or as ground markers for blocking talent. Hang a well-used roll from a cara-biner on your belt and the world will regard you as a seasoned pro.

FIGURE 9.64
(a) One sure sign of a pro shooter is the range of tapes he or she carries on the job. Paper tape is not as strong as gaffer's tape but is much gentler on surfaces and leaves no sticky residue. Gaffer's tape should not be confused with gooey household duct tape (b) which mustn't be used nor seen near professional equipment of any kind!

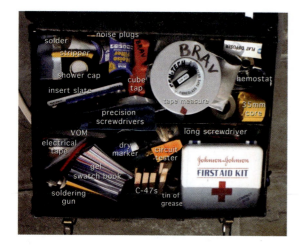

tape in gray or black is intended for heavy-fisted tasks like sealing shipping cases or covering a rough seam on a dolly board. It should not be used to secure cabling to floors or walls, as the sticky adhesive can make a nasty mess in short order. Look for a brand with a high cloth content to reduce the potential mess factor.

THE DITTY BAG

Every shooter worth his lens cap has a small case or *ditty bag* that he carries religiously to every job. I take great pride in mine, having rescued many panicked producers and productions over

FIGURE 9.66

My Ditty Bag

I've carried the same ditty bag (more or less) on jobs for the last 30 years. Below is a list of its contents, modified for the digital video age:

- Small diagonal pliers
- #1 and #2 Phillips screwdrivers
- 1/2 in. and 1/4 in. flat screwdrivers
- Needle-nose pliers
- Slip-joint pliers
- Wire stripper
- Jeweler screwdriver set (Swiss)
- Torx screwdriver set T1–T6
- 6-in. vice-grip
- 6-in. crescent wrench
- 8-in. crescent wrench
- VOM multimeter
- Awl
- Precision tweezers
- Assorted Sharpie markers
- Dry-erase marker
- Superglue
- 2 or 3 grease pencils
- 1/4 × 20 and 3/8 × 16 hardware
- Metric/SAE nut driver set
- Assorted BNC/RCA adapters
- 8-in. steel ruler
- Lens tissue and fluid
- Spare tripod touch-go plate
- Tube of lithium grease
- Jeweler's loupe
- Sewing kit (steal from hotel room)
- Safety pins
- Carabiner
- Velcro strips
- Space blanket
- Soldering gun with lead-free solder
- Star chart and gray-scale
- Can opener
- Corkscrew
- Jeweler Phillips screwdriver set (Swiss)
- Eyeglass repair kit
- 3 two-prong adapters
- 2 multitap outlet adapters
- Screw-in bulb socket adapter
- 12 C-47s
- LED flashlight
- Earplugs
- Protective eye gear
- Insect repellent
- Sunscreen, 45 SPF
- First Aid Kit
- Metric/SAE Allen wrench set
- Rosco and/or Lee gel swatch
- Cable ties (various sizes)
- Cloth 50-foot tape measure
- Lens chamois
- WD-40 lubricant
- Emery cloth
- Pepto-Bismol/Kaopectate
- Shower cap (for lens)
- 35-mm film core (nostalgic)
- Spare 9V, AA, and AAA batteries

the years. Everything from resoldering a power cable and replacing a hard drive in a laptop to treatment of diarrhea, it's all part of being a competent shooter and team member. On many shows, your resourcefulness in time of need can earn you hero – almost godlike – status.

GETTING YOUR FILL

Capturing well-balanced scenes under bright sun has always been a challenge to shooters owing to the extreme contrast range. Working with low-cost camcorders, the shooter faces a particular challenge; these models' narrow dynamic range exacerbates the loss of detail in dense shadows and bright highlights, both can similarly appear devoid of life. For the shooter toiling in the glare of the midday sun, it's a lose-lose situation at both ends of the camera's characteristic response curve (Fig. 9.67).

FIGURE 9.67
Dense impenetrable shadows. Clipped blown out highlights. Shooting in full sun can be an exercise fraught with peril.

FIGURE 9.68
When shooting late in the day, the soft raking sun adds warmth and texture. Your small-imager HD camera eats this stuff up!

FIGURE 9.69
Properly filled shadows facilitate compression in-camera by easing the transitions in challenging scenes. The result is much improved performance from even modest HD cameras.

FIGURE 9.70
A collapsible silver or gold reflector should be a part of every shooter's basic kit. Some versions have a white surface on the flip side – a very useful feature.

FIGURE 9.71
Shooting in far off lands requires considerable ingenuity when facing tough lighting challenges.

THE CRAFT OF INGENUITY

I said it before: you don't need much to light well. But you do need a sense of craft and a little ingenuity. On a recent dramatic production in East Africa, without a single actual working light, I was obligated to shoot several scenes inside the homes of Ugandan families, who lived in dark apartments inconveniently located on the upper floors of large buildings.

Under the intense equatorial sun, the exteriors were tough enough, requiring large diffusion silks and careful placement of reflectors to illuminate some *very* dark eye sockets. The interiors posed a different kind of challenge, however. The

FIGURE 9.72
The sun late in the day can be a gorgeous source of light – and it's free.

kitchen and bedroom sets were located high above a parking lot in the deepest recesses of a building away from large windows and potential sources of natural light. The reality of the situation was apparent: I had far too much light outside and far too little light inside.

With no grip truck or conventional lighting, I considered what I *did* have and that was people: lots of young Ugandans, Kenyans, and Tanzanians, eager to participate and add their imprimatur to the production. In addition, I had mirrors. Lots of mirrors. In Kampala. There was a factory there.

So that became the solution: banks of mirrors with two-man teams (Fig. 9.74a) delivering the sun from the outside parking lot into the upper windows of the building, then bouncing that beam down a dark corridor to the base of the stairs, where the last mirror team (Fig. 9.74b) filled the space with a magical

FIGURE 9.73
… reflect it down a long hall onto a landing by some stairs. Who needs pricey light kits and grip trucks?

(a)

(b)

FIGURE 9.74
Mirrors can be powerful tools to illuminate deep shadows or deliver an intense blast of sun to interior locations. At right, an interior bounce crew takes a break.

FIGURE 9.75
Intense sunlight bounced off multiple mirrors delivered a high-quality light to this interior hallway. This scene is from the Uganda production *Sins of the Parents* (2008), directed by Judith Lucy Adong.

golden glow (Fig. 9.75). The scene could not have been lit better with a 20-ton grip truck, seasoned Hollywood crew, and spate of HMIs!

The Sun is a beautiful thing. There's lots of it to be had in most places in the world, and it's free – if you can control it, harness it, and deliver it to where you need it.

I'm a shooter. It's what I do. Like breathing. So, after almost three decades of crashing a viewfinder to my face, I've developed an intimate relationship with my craft – one built understandably on the power of my images to tell compelling stories.

So, it is perhaps ironic that I've acquired the awareness that no matter how fabulous my leading lady may appear or how sinister the Mafioso capo from Staten Island might look on screen, the lack of clean audio will instantly torpedo the storytelling and drive the audience from their seats. Every shooter must know and be keenly aware: audiences will tolerate bad picture but NEVER bad sound!

SOUND ADVICE FOR THE VIDEO SHOOTER

In writing a script, we weed out unnecessary scenes and dialog. In composing a scene, we frame out elements that are potentially distracting or not relevant; and in recording sound, we also stay true to our mantra to exclude, exclude, and exclude. By moving a mic closer to the subject or otherwise excluding extraneous sounds, the soundman is saying to his audience, "Listen to this! This sound is important! This dialog matters to the audio story!"

For most shooters, a substantial investment in audio gear would appear to be illogical. After all, we are concerned primarily with our images, and good-quality audio seems like something that ought to just happen, like the changing of the seasons or day turning to night. Of course, recording proper audio is no fluke, and most of us realize that superior sound and superior images go hand in hand. As visual storytellers, we understand that a good mixer, cables, and microphone are in every way as essential to the shooter's craft as a camera, lens, and tripod.

It is understandable that camera manufacturers would focus almost exclusively on video because we shooters tend to pay scant attention to a camera's audio section. Beyond the issues of distortion and poor frequency response, noise can be a significant problem when recording audio directly into the camera. The

FIGURE 10.1
Capturing good sound is one of the best things you can do to improve the look of your pictures! So treat your soundman well! If you haven't got a soundman, may the force of a good on-camera or wireless microphone be with you!

FIGURE 10.2
The external audio controls are the frequent source of noise in many camcorders. Although recent models feature much quieter pots and preamps, it's still a good idea not to exceed 50% when recording directly to camera.

gain controls in low-cost camcorders are often the source of static or buzzing, so shooters should make it a habit not to set these pots above 50%. Poor quality cables, jacks, and adapter plugs are also major noise contributors. Don't scrimp in this area of cables and connectors if you can avoid it. For the news and documentary shooter tending to operate alone, the recording of crisp, clean audio can be a particular challenge that requires utmost focus and attention; and, of course, the appropriate professional gear.

BAD CONNECTIONS = BAD SOUND

For shooters working with consumer cameras, poor-quality connectors can be an ongoing source of frustration. Indeed, many of us know from hard-won experience that cables and connectors are a primary cause of failure in the field. This is due, in part, to the normal wear and tear and the physical stress to which these connectors are regularly subjected.

For the pro shooter and ersatz audio recordist, the ubiquitous 1/8 in. miniplug (Fig. 10.3) is Public Enemy Number One, providing a less than robust connection at a critical juncture with the camera. Common miniplug-to-XLR adapters (Fig. 10.9) offer only a partial solution, facilitating a professional interface on one side while retaining the fragile (unbalanced) miniplug on the other. The heavy XLR adapter weighing on the minijack may also contribute to an intermittent condition.

WANTED

FOR CRIMES AGAINST
HUMANITY

1/8-inch MINI-PLUG

FIGURE 10.3
Keep an eye and ear out for this villain and always approach with care! Avoid unnecessary plugging and unplugging to reduce wear and intermittent connections.

1/8" mini jack

1/8" mini jack

FIGURE 10.4
The 1/8-in. miniplug has accomplices. Two known female cohorts are shown here.

FIGURE 10.5
The proper handling of cables is critical to ensure noise-free recordings. For storing, cables should be loosely coiled with an alternating back twist to ensure they lie flat and free of damaging kinks.

MIND YOUR CONNECTIONS

Consumer RCA-type plugs and jacks (Fig. 10.6) offer easy interoperability with home-based gear, but separate easily when subjected to the stress and strains of a busy shooter's day. For this reason, the BNC twist-bayonet and industry standard XLR connectors are preferred.

FIGURE 10.6
BNC and XLR connectors provide more secure connections than the RCA consumer type.

A TIGHT SQUEEZE

FIGURE 10.7
As camcorders have shrunk in size, the real estate available for robust connectors has diminished. The placement of the audio connectors on some models seems like an afterthought.

FIGURE 10.8
For the itinerant shooter, an assortment of audio and video adapters is a wise investment. The right one can save a shoot or career!

FIGURE 10.9
On cameras fitted with the dreaded 1/8-in. mic input, a low-cost XLR adapter may be used to attach a professional microphone. The adapter does not convert an unbalanced camera to a balanced system, nor does it eliminate the fragile 1/8-in. plug that can often lead to trouble.

KEEP BALANCE IN YOUR LIFE

Shooting can be fun, but you have to keep some balance in your life. That means paying attention occasionally to your spouse, boyfriend, girlfriend, or kids. It also means opting for camera gear if you can with professional *balanced* audio.

The difference between balanced and unbalanced audio is a function of a third conductor. An unbalanced connection has only two wires: the signal (+) and the ground. A balanced line has three conductors: the signal (+), the antisignal (−), and the ground. An audio cable over long runs can act as an antenna and serve as a potent noise collector, thus the need for a noise cancellation strategy.

Balanced audio cables are shielded to resist noise and loss of signal. The third conductor carries a parallel signal 180° out of phase, which is flipped back into phase at the camera connection, effectively restoring a clean signal by canceling out noise that might have been introduced along the way. The use of an unbalanced component at any point in the system defeats the noise-cancelling strategy of the entire system.

Thankfully, an increasing number of camcorder models are offering balanced audio with rugged integrated XLR connectors.

MIXING IT UP

If you've been reading this book, you know I don't stand 1/24th of a second for flimsy gear masquerading and marketed as "professional" equipment. As a veteran shooter with a large mortgage and two hungry, mostly unappreciative kids, I demand a lot from my tools that I use and depend on everyday. These tools have become part of my family, and I rely on them in much the same way, for better and for worse, through thick and thin, for richer and for poorer. You get the idea.

When it comes to audio, your mixer is control central where you set levels, monitor audio quality, and apply limiting, padding, and filtration. Its layout of controls must be logical and easy to decipher. I'm a stickler for usability, and when a piece of gear is frustratingly designed, it is quickly relegated to a closet, back shelf, or eBay. A mixer's gain and fader knobs must have a solid feeling and be large enough to grasp even with gloved hands – a particular need for documentary shooters in wintry, icy cold conditions away from the coziness of a comfy studio or corporate boardroom.

Also, while we're discussing shooting on location, the mixer's output meters should be clearly visible in bright sun (Fig. 10.10a) whether at the beach or atop an alpine peak in glaring snow.

Of course, we want to work with the best equipment we can, but that may not always be possible given the economic realities. In a budget mixer, we can still look for a unit with a good signal-to-noise ratio, ample headroom in the recording section, and a decent limiter.

Mixers with insufficient headroom are problematic because they require recording at lower levels to avoid clipping, which can increase *hiss*. Mixers with poorly designed limiters can also produce unsatisfactory recordings; if pushed too far, loud passages may overwhelm the inputs and slam the limiters, producing severe distortion. This is why it's often safer to set a more conservative recording level.

In general, shooters should take advantage of a mixer's *safety limiter*. Because the limiter's threshold is not normally reached, it normally has no effect on a recording. However, in noisy unpredictable environments like barroom brawls or crazed screaming matches in *Operation Repo*, the limiter kicks in gently to prevent clipping.

As in all areas of the technical craft, the audio workflow should be thoroughly tested before a shoot, with the uncompressed sound files from the camera imported into the NLE and reproduced over a high-quality monitor in a quiet environment.

One good measure of a mixer's performance is its low-frequency response. The best field mixers use balanced transformers to provide isolation from the incoming source. Input signals are transformed magnetically; there is no electromechanical connection, as in the case of low-end mixers. For the shooter working primarily in reality TV, superior low-frequency response is integral to capturing clean professional audio.

Ideally, a mixer should interface easily with any microphone you might own (Fig. 10.10b). In my case, I continue to use my 25-year-old Sennheiser MKH-416, a trusted and devoted friend that has accompanied me literally to every continent on earth. From arctic cold to Amazon heat and humidity, this mic has earned its place in my family of Most Trusted Stuff; its ruggedness, reliability, and performance is unimpeachable. Your field mixer should be in this league.

All told, your mixer should ameliorate, not exacerbate, the noisy pots and preamps that plague many low- and mid-range cameras. It should feature

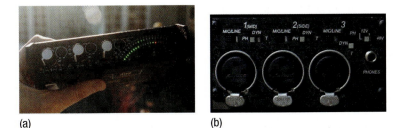

(a) (b)

FIGURE 10.10
A rugged two- or three-channel mixer is the centerpiece of a shooter's audio package. The display in this model (a) is clearly visible even in bright sun, a major advantage for shooters and sound recordists operating under diverse conditions. The mixer should accommodate a range of microphone types (b) without external adapters, cables, or bulky boxes.

FIGURE 10.11
This low-cost two-channel mixer may be an option for shooters who typically use a boom and wireless lavalier and seldom have need for a more elaborate configuration.

FIGURE 10.12
To reduce background noise from traffic and wind, the shooter should enable the mixer's high-pass 80-Hz filter. There is usually little audio worth recording below this point, especially in dialog scenes.

multiple microphone inputs (Fig. 10.10b) with a wide gain range to accommodate various line levels. A range of 75 dB from mic input to line output is ideal. For most shooters, a mixer with a built-in 80-Hz (high-pass) filter is desirable because we usually want to suppress low-frequency noise such as wind and traffic.

SHOOTING DOUBLE SYSTEM: IS IT STILL NECESSARY?

This question comes up often: Because the audio capability of recent camcorders has improved so dramatically, is there any reason *not* to record directly into the camera?

It all depends. For most projects, given the expense and inconvenience, there is probably little advantage to using a dedicated audio recorder. For corporate, documentary, and reality fare, the camera provides sufficient functionality and performance to enable capture of pro-caliber audio through a good-quality mixer or directly from a wired or wireless microphone. However, for many narrative projects and commercials, *double-system* recording continues to be the most attractive option for garnering the highest quality sound possible.

The lack of timecode in low-cost compact flash and hard drive recorders (HDRs) (Fig. 10.14) isn't normally a significant problem because the crystal reference in these machines is sufficient to maintain synchronization. As a practical matter when shooting double system, be sure to record proper head and tail slates, and feed a *guide track* into the camera for reference later in the NLE and for possible backup.

Shooters should also take care when shooting double system at 24 fps. Different cameras may record audio at different speeds. Most specify 23.976 fps, but some may capture at 29.97 fps, especially tape-based models. When shooting

FIGURE 10.13
Many feature film productions prefer shooting double system owing to the greater flexibility and superior audio quality. Recording double system requires a dedicated sound recordist and boom operator.

double-system, it is imperative to conduct proper synchronization tests before the first day of shooting. In this particular minefield, no one likes surprises, and there tend to be plenty when synchronizing double-system recordings from inexpensive prosumer devices.

AUTOMATIC LEVEL CONTROL

In every way, I've asserted the importance of exercising manual control of your craft. Whether setting appropriate exposure, white balance, or focus, only you the talented painter of light can legitimately make these determinations. With respect to audio, the same logic applies: disabling your camera's *automatic level control* (Fig. 10.15) is almost always advisable, as this will prevent unwanted background noise from ramping up during quiet passages. I say "almost always" advisable because with the advent of the one-man-band shooter storyteller, there is a practical limit to what one individual can reasonably expect to do with skill and aplomb. In some cases, Automatic Level Control (ALC) may be the only option for capturing satisfactory audio, for recording the ambience of passing traffic (for example), or the roaring crowd at a sporting event.

When setting levels manually, you should set the highest level feasible without clipping. The −12 dB reference in most cameras doesn't leave much headroom for loud passages, so the onus is on the shooter or soundman to capture proper audio in the first place. Remember just as in digital video, the detail not captured in clipped or distorted audio is lost forever. It cannot be recovered later in post.

FIGURE 10.14
Recording double system to a flash or hard drive recorder is a good way to circumvent the mediocre audio sections in some low-cost camcorders. Be sure to input a guide track into the camera to facilitate synchronization in the NLE.

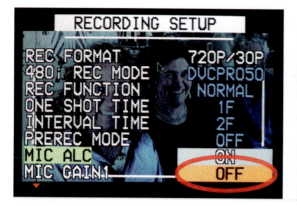

FIGURE 10.15
In most cases, *Automatic Level Control* (ALC) should be disabled in your camera's setup menu. Many professional cameras have an external switch to enable/disable ALC.

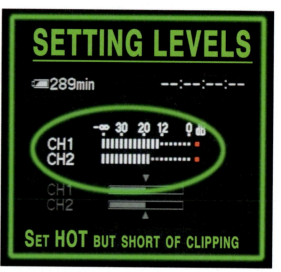

FIGURE 10.16
Differential audio setup CH1 and CH2. Referencing channel that is 26 dB below channel 1 offers the shooter protection against sudden loud passages.

FIGURE 10.17
In many camcorders, the headphone output may be adjusted to reflect either the live (slightly delayed) audio or the synchronized-to-picture recorded audio.

Cameras may combine the left and right microphone inputs in a single 1/8-in. jack or maintain the channel separation in individual XLR connectors. Although dialog is usually recorded in mono, it is common practice to split the incoming audio into two channels, the second channel set 6 dB lower (Fig. 10.16) to accommodate unexpected loud outbursts. Many shooters use a common configuration of placing the lavalier (or wireless) on channel 1 and a boom on channel 2.

FOR THE LOVE OF MIC

The shooter's goal of achieving clean, noise-free recordings begins with optimal microphone placement. Locating the mic too far from a subject or positioning it significantly off-axis will elevate the background noise and yield unusable sound. Shooters should know that mic placement is too critical to leave to an untrained person or reluctant friend pressed into service to "hold the boom." Not recognizing the value of proper microphone placement will quickly sink the viability of any production, or at the least, lead to some very expensive and time-consuming dialog replacement sessions down the road.

CHOOSE YOUR WEAPON

Of course, no shooter can be expected to assume all the responsibilities of a dedicated boom man and sound recordist. We have enough responsibility as it is! Still, I suggest that camera folks carry a basic sound package – a wireless

(a)

(b)

FIGURE 10.18
The short, shotgun microphone (a) is the workhorse of film and video production. A large zeppelin-type windscreen (b) provides protection against the wind and physical impact.

FIGURE 10.19
The directional short shotgun mic provides satisfactory audio for subjects relatively close to the camera. I used a camera-mounted mic to shoot the behind-the-scenes show for *The Darjeeling Limited* (2007).

FIGURE 10.20
Most cameras' built-in mic is omni-directional and is only really useful to record ambient sound.

FIGURE 10.21
Good sound is too important to leave to the camera's internal mic! For palm-sized camcorders or a DSLR set up to capture video, this microsize short shotgun can work well.

lavalier, short shotgun mic, boom pole, cables, and a small mixer. Having this capability is crucial to grabbing an unanticipated interview, say, when stepping off an airplane in a distant city, or in the middle of the night when your real soundman is recovering from a drunken stupor. My philosophy is simple: arrive on location ready to shoot. This means carrying the essentials with me on the airplane – camera, lens, battery, recording media, and audio – to get the shot.

FIGURE 10.22
Practice makes perfect. The placing of a lavalier on talent requires tact and expertise. Always ask permission first before approaching living talent and affixing a mic over or under wardrobe!

GOING WIRELESS

Every shooter regardless of specialty can benefit from a wireless mic in his or her basic package. The practical advantages are obvious – especially for the *bande à part* operator, who, lacking a dedicated sound or boom man, will often find the wireless to be the only practical way to capture clean professional sound.

In general, I'm not a fan of low-cost wireless systems, as they tend to sacrifice robustness through the use of plastic parts prone to breakage. More

FIGURE 10.23
Being unobtrusive and lightweight, the slot receiver adds little weight and bulk to the shooter's load. The Panasonic HPX300 features a wireless slot – the first in a modestly priced professional camcorder.

FIGURE 10.24
An external microphone select switch controls input source.

importantly, the economy units tend to exhibit a higher noise floor and a proclivity for interference. This loss in audio crispness and fidelity communicates an amateurish feel to an audience. Remember, as shooters we are concerned foremost about our images, but the quality of audio can never be compromised!

Every wireless microphone system faces the same challenges with respect to potential RF interference. This is particularly true in urban centers where the airwaves are full of radio transmissions of every type, from cell phones and TV remotes to emergency services and baby monitors.

To confront this menace, a wireless system must have superior filtering and preferably dual inputs. The two channels can provide for discrete mics as would be required for a reporter and his subject, or be linked to a single frequency for increased range and robustness of signal. *A diversity-type* receiver offers the additional benefit of automatically selecting the cleaner of the two inputs. I like this notion. As a shooter, I understand the importance of clean audio, but I do have other things on my mind. Usually.

FIGURE 10.25
External wireless systems must be Velcroed or otherwise inconveniently attached to the camcorder body. Be careful while shooting with such protruding accoutrements, which may interfere with your creative mojo or become entangled with an actor or grip.

YOU ARE SURROUNDED!

Inputting multiple-channel audio is now commonplace, with up to four channels possible in many camcorder models. With the advent of DVD and Blu-ray and the exponential growth in home theaters, the demand has increased for

FIGURE 10.26
This microphone with six elements
encodes multichannel 5.1 Dolby to
stereo, which can be captured into any
camcorder or stand-alone recorder.

FIGURE 10.27
Such beauty in simplicity! Philip
Cacayorin's elegant 360-degree
Stereophile 3D microphone uses
paired glass panes and two ordinary
lavalier mics inside a passive
enclosure.

capturing six-channel surround sound in-camera. Entry-level camcorders such
as the Sony HDR-SR11 and Panasonic AG-HSC1U already have the capability
to capture Dolby Digital 5.1, with sophisticated surround-type microphones
from several manufacturers becoming increasingly available for higher-end
camera models.

CHAPTER 11
Supporting Your Story

Like the Great Masters of centuries ago, the video shooter today provides a unique window on the world, a proscenium arch through which we expose, compose, and exclude what is not essential to the story. It is through this portal and upon this stage that we as shooters apply our sweat and the many rudiments of good storytelling craft.

Visually compelling stories demand rigorous control of the frame. You shake the frame and weaken its walls if you better have a good storytelling reason.

Despite this, as MTV has well demonstrated, the unsteady camera can occasionally work quite well. Because *shakycam* obscures what the shooter storyteller is up to, the viewer must work harder to figure out what the heck is going on. This can have the ironic effect of more fully *engaging* the viewer, as noted in Chapter 2; the obfuscation of intent is a powerful and seductive storytelling technique. Unfortunately, long after shakycam stopped serving any legitimate storytelling purpose, many shooters keep at it, and at it, and at it. The pointless gyrations then become more about the *shooter* than supporting a good story. Truth is, most times the unsettled camera is just plain distracting and an impediment to good storytelling – a once clever gimmick run amok.

Appropriate support of the camera and frame reflects the impetus of your story. Is the frame anchored solidly in reality, as in most establishing shots or landscapes, or does the handheld camera more accurately reflect the point of view of a deranged serial killer?

Compelling visual stories almost invariably require solid support. We want to draw the viewer's eye into the canvas and help him identify the relevant elements. Attracting unwarranted attention to the *edges* of the frame runs counter to the tenets of good storytelling craft. The smart shooter knows that robust camera support is imperative to maintaining the integrity of the frame and the story housed in it.

FIGURE 11.1
Sometimes the use of a tripod is not possible – or warranted. In the streets of 1980s Poland my shaky handheld camera served a legitimate storytelling goal. My shaky handheld camera served a legitimate and necessary storytelling goal.

FIGURE 11.2
Establishing shots like this London night scene demand a well-supported camera.

FIGURE 11.3
Epic scenes like the launch of a Saturn V rocket were never meant to be captured handheld!

FIGURE 11.4
My close-up of this hawk has been used many times in music videos and commercials. Close-ups pay the bills, and solid camera support gets me those close-ups!

FIGURE 11.5
The level (or unlevel) camera can be a potent storytelling tool. The skewed angle (b) suggests the mindset of an unbalanced person.

In my own career, I developed my love of tripod decades ago as I faced the perils of Communist Poland's dying regime. The 1980s were a tumultuous time in the streets of Eastern Europe; and being able to scurry and set up a tripod quickly meant I could use a longer lens to capture soldiers perched atop their armored vehicles or the dispirited faces of the populace grinning and bearing it, and waiting in endless food line. It wasn't always possible to stay married to a tripod amidst a riot when things got a little hairy; but from a craft perspective, the solid platform enabled more intense close-ups than would have been possible shooting handheld. It's really a simple matter: solid camera support gets me the close-ups I need to tell compelling stories.

GETTING A HEAD IN SUPPORT

If you're serious as a shooter and video storyteller, you'll want to invest in the most rugged professional *fluid head* you can afford (Fig. 11.6). Fluid heads use a silicon dampening system to enable smooth pans and tilts. The viscous liquid is forced through a series of drillings, like the oil inside an automatic transmission; the intent is to provide a predictable amount of resistance regardless of ambient temperature. On some models, incremental drag dials (Fig. 11.7) enable fine-tuning the resistance and torque, the amount of drag being selectable and repeatable. In this way, the shooter can gain confidence in his or her ability to execute consistently smooth moves. Like the clutch action on a car, the feel from vehicle to vehicle may vary; but once you are accustomed to the clutch on *your* car, the driving experience becomes seamless and second nature.

Although a low-cost *friction head* may seem like a viable option, a well-designed fluid head is the serious shooter's best choice; its precision engineering, low weight, and robust construction are critical to withstand the rigors of real-life conditions. The action should be glitch-free, impervious to the elements, with no perceivable backlash – the tendency of some heads to bounce back slightly when handle pressure is relieved. Pan-and-tilt locks should be of the lever type with large surfaces to facilitate operation, even in extreme cold through thick gloves.

Although some shooters may require a head that is small and mobile, the head should not be so lightweight as to preclude the use of long lenses for sports and wildlife applications. Smoothness of operation is especially important for sports and wildlife; so a fluid head should be checked for "stickiness" throughout its range, including when set to "zero" drag. Needless to say, any stickiness can render the head ineffective.

Depending on one's needs and particular niche, some shooters may want a fluid head that can tilt straight up or down (Fig. 11.10). Not all tripod heads can do this, so be sure to check when reviewing various makes and models. In general, the O'Connor heads can tilt to 90°; the Sachtler and most other manufacturers' heads cannot.

FIGURE 11.6
A well-designed fluid head will pay you dividends for years, long after your present and future cameras are relegated to doorstops.

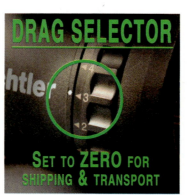

FIGURE 11.7
Incremented drag rings facilitate camera moves by providing a predictable amount of resistance. Some models feature up to seven drag settings for pan and tilt. Lower cost heads may only feature one or two drag positions. Fluid heads with drag dials should always be "zeroed" for shipping to prevent damage.

FIGURE 11.8
Make sure your fluid head's claw ball operates smoothly and has a sufficiently large knob. You'll be leveling the camera many times each day, so you want this operation to be as easy and secure as possible.

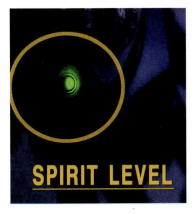

FIGURE 11.10
This O'Connor model can tilt straight down. Not all fluid heads can.

FIGURE 11.9
Some tripod heads offer an illuminated spirit level – a great help when working in low light.

FIGURE 11.11
No! No! No! Never lean your tripod against a wall or post! If it falls, the head can be easily damaged. Most serious damage happens this way!

FIGURE 11.12
With a pro-style ball-leveler and quick-release plate, this head provides good functionality and value. Better described as a "greasy" head than a fluid head, it can become sticky if left too long in one position.

FIGURE 11.13
Horizontal camera movement is called a "pan." Moving vertically is called a "tilt." Every shooter must make it a point to learn his bread and butter. My grandfather in front of his Brooklyn deli in 1937 had to learn his bread and butter, too.

FIGURE 11.14
Dual-stage tripods eliminate the need for carrying multiple pairs of legs.

You may go through many cameras in your lifetime, but you will likely need only one fluid head if you make the right investment. In my almost three decades as a shooter, I've only owned two. The first, a Sachtler 3 + 3 model, was lost at Mount Saint Helens in 1980, a victim of volcanic ash and pulverized granite that penetrated the drag dials and destroyed the fine German action. The second, a replacement 7 + 7, I still use regularly today. That's thirty years of near-continuous service, from tropical rain forests to arctic tundra and everything in-between – not bad for what seemed in 1980 as a ludicrously expensive $1,900 investment. Of course, as things turned out, it was worth that sum many times over. I built my career literally on that one fluid head.

WHAT PRETTY LEGS YOU HAVE

I often hear whistling from onlookers when I work, and I'm almost sure it's my legs. My *tripod* legs happen to be very good looking. They're rugged, versatile, and sexy as hell. You can't buy a pair like them now and mine aren't for sale, so don't e-mail me. The point is I love my legs – and you should fall in love with yours, too.

There are a few features to look for when considering new legs. They should be light in weight yet able to stand up to substantial abuse, whether facing down storm troopers in Eastern Europe or a panicked rhino in Zimbabwe. The leg locks should be secure and simple. Leveling should be routine via a claw-ball and large knob (Fig. 11.8) that can be grabbed, even in winter with heavy mittens. I recommend leg adjusters with inscribed height increments, a useful feature when leveling the camera by eye or with the help of your overworked bleary-eyed assistant.

It's worth having a good relationship with your legs (Fig. 11.15). They support everything you do.

FIGURE 11.15
Key features to look for in a tripod include secure leg locks, incremental leg markings to facilitate level setup, a raised spider that stays clean and can serve as a monitor platform, and a center column that permits easy raising of the camera in tight spaces.

FIGURE 11.16
Be careful of legs (like mine) with hidden pinch points that can crush unsuspecting fingers! Make sure the people you love and work with are duly warned.

FIGURE 11.17
A quick-release plate greatly facilitates mounting and dismounting the camera. You don't want to be fumbling with a 1/4 in. × 20 screw when facing a stampede of angry bison!

HOW TO COUNTERBALANCE THE CAMERA

ASSEMBLE THE CAMERA
Mount the lens, battery, microphone and any other accessories you will be using on the camera.

FIND THE BALANCE POINT (C.G.) OF THE CAMERA
Place the camera on a flat rigid object that's not too heavy, like a clip board. Put a pencil on a smooth table and place the camera and board on the pencil and roll it back and forth until you find the balance point.

ATTACH THE CAMERA MOUNTING PLATE
Fasten the center of the camera mounting plate as close as possible to the balance point of the camera (with lens, battery and accessories installed).

BALANCE THE CAMERA ON THE HEAD
Adjust the slide plate assembly on the head so the indicator notch is over the center of the head (zero mark). Mount the camera to the slide plate. Set the tilt fluid drag lever to zero. Release the platform lock lever. Find the balance point for the camera while the camera is in the level position by sliding the camera back and forth. Re-lock the platform lock lever.

ADJUST THE COUNTERBALANCE
It is very important to make sure the weight of the complete camera configuration is centered on the head. After balancing the camera on the head, tilt the camera forward and back. If the camera continues to drift forward or back when tilted, increase the counterbalance adjustment. If the camera has a spring-back reaction, decrease the counterbalance adjustment. Our infinitely adjustable counterbalance allows you to stop adjusting at whatever feel you like best and quickly readjust for minor changes in weight. The counterbalance is properly adjusted when the camera holds its position when tilted up or down. Now you can adjust the pan and tilt drag settings to your preference.

PROFESSIONAL CAMERA SUPPORT SYSTEMS

FIGURE 11.18
Image courtesy of O'Connor Professional Camera Support Systems. Tripod Setup Guide to counterbalance.

FIGURE 11.19

SEEKING OTHER MEANS OF SUPPORT

Besides the standard legs and fluid head, shooters might also consider baby legs and a *high hat* to achieve a ground-level or low-angle shot. A high hat can also be useful for securing the camera in difficult locations, such as atop a stepladder or car bumper.

With the advent of lightweight camcorders and improved zoom and focus controls, there's no longer any reason to shy away from support options like a jib arm or simple dolly. Many manufacturers have introduced lower-cost versions of their products expressly for the modest HD shooter.

Be wary, however, of less-than-robust gear. Such equipment is unlikely to see much service, as performance is invariably poor owing to a lack of stability. If additional weight is not an issue,

FIGURE 11.20
The Sachtler SOOM combines the functions of a monopod, high hat, standard and baby legs in a single unit.

FIGURE 11.21
This lightweight Microdolly travels in a 13-ft. track and can be set up in less than 2 min.

FIGURE 11.22
When considering a lightweight crane or jib arm, make sure it is sturdy enough to enable smooth takeoffs and landings.

FIGURE 11.24
Camera stabilization systems reduce the need for track and dolly in elaborate setups. Most models require expertise for smooth operation, so be sure to practice your skills before the first day of shooting!

FIGURE 11.23
The heft and precision of a professional dolly enable strict control of the moving frame.

FIGURE 11.25
Ingenious stabilizers like this one support a small camcorder balanced between two ball-bearing grip points. The design allows for a smooth booming effect without the hours of practice usually required for other stabilization systems.

FIGURE 11.26
At times, a shooter may find support at ground level and gain an interesting angle to boot!

FIGURE 11.27
Many shooters over the years have devised their own rigs to support a handheld camera. The great CBS New cameraman Izzy Bleckman used this brace for years.

a more substantial jib arm or dolly is always preferable, as the increased mass provides smoother movement (along with better takeoffs and landings).

HANDHOLDING YOUR CAMERA

If your story demands a handheld camera, there are ways to accomplish the task with a physical support. Some poorly balanced cameras (like the Sony EX models) (Fig. 11.28) are especially difficult to handhold, so a supplemental system should be considered when shooting with these cameras for an extended period of time.

One low-cost option is to extend a friction head and monopod, like the Bogen 680B, from a waist pouch or fanny pack. The system offers improved stability for wedding and event-type applications, albeit controlled pans are difficult to execute using this approach.

A more viable option may be the *EasyRig* (Fig. 11.30) that uses an overhead suspension cable. Some shooters swear by this odd-looking contraption that supports the camera at a range of heights and angles, from ground level to above eyeline. If you're planning a great deal of handheld work, a shoulder-mounted camcorder may

FIGURE 11.28
Some cameras like this one are not well balanced and require a support for extensive handheld work. The addition of accessories, such as a matte box or camera light, can also create an out-of-balance condition.

FIGURE 11.29
Featuring a shock-absorbing column, the inexpensive DVRig Jr can help tame poorly balanced camcorders.

FIGURE 11.30
In this system, an overhead arm suspends the camera conveniently in front of the shooter.

be easier to control; the advantage of a full-size camera being offset by its larger profile and increased conspicuousness in sensitive locations.

MORE POWER TO YOU

The undersized battery that probably came your camera (Fig. 11.31) has been a sore point with shooters for years. Although slowly changing as camera makers see the error of their ways, shooters price shopping for a camera should be sure to budget for an additional power source – a battery with the *highest capacity* available. At this point in time, that battery will most likely be of the lithium-ion type.

Li-ion batteries are, gram for gram, very efficient. Although they rarely last more than 5 years or 500 charging cycles, they're very low maintenance and (unlike NiMH[1]) don't lose much charge sitting in our travel cases or on a shelf waiting for the next call to duty. That's a big advantage for the itinerant shooter; their self-discharge rate is half that of nickel-type batteries.

Li-ion is everywhere these days, in every type of gadget and gizmo. If it beeps, burps, or percolates, it's probably powered by a Li-ion battery. Trouble is, our good friend has an onerous dark side. In 2006, a man in his house trailer went to bed one night and left his cell phone charging. The Li-ion battery in it overheated and exploded, and burned his double-wide to the ground. There was also the case of 1,00,000 batteries recalled in 2008 after several laptop computers

FIGURE 11.31
The undersized battery (top) that ships with many cameras is impractical for useful work. A large high-capacity battery (bottom) is imperative.

FIGURE 11.32
As in other facets of our daily lives, Li-ion batteries dominate professional and consumer video cameras. The ubiquitous Anton Bauer and IDX brand batteries dominate the full-size camcorder market.

---

[1]Nickel metal hydride (NiMH) batteries are safe for air travel and not prone to fire or explosion. NiMH packs of the same physical size are heavier, less able to hold a charge, and only produce about 60% as much power as Li-ion-type batteries. A new generation of NiMH cells is currently in development.

went "thermal," including one in Japan that exploded reportedly in the middle of an electronics technology conference.

A battery can discharge in three ways: in a slow trickle over a period of weeks or months; in a more moderate and controlled way, as in the normal running of a camera; and in a powerful instantaneous release of energy, which may result in an explosion or fire.

Sometimes, a battery may explode due to a manufacturing defect that can produce a short circuit and an incendiary spark. Sometimes the cells are subjected to excessive heat due to overcharging (or over-discharging), or physically impacted in some way. However, once a cell goes "thermal," there is no extinguishing agent in the world that can stop it. As each cell breaks down, it fuels the next

FIGURE 11.33
Li-ion batteries require proper care to forestall a fire or explosion. Never completely run down a Li-ion battery or subject it to excessive shock. Current air transport rules limit the size and number of Li-ion batteries that can be carried on board an aircraft. The carriage of Li-ion batteries is generally prohibited in checked baggage.

SAFE TRAVEL TIPS FOR TRANSPORT OF LI-ION BATTERIES

The TSA guidelines below were in effect as of September 2009. Please refer to the official Transportation Security Administration web site (www.tsa.gov/travelers/airtravel/) for updated information.

Pack spare batteries in carry-on baggage. In the passenger compartment, flight crews can better monitor safety conditions to prevent an incident, and can access fire extinguishers, if an incident does happen.

Keep spare batteries in the original retail packaging, to prevent unintentional activation or short-circuiting.

For loose batteries, place tape across the battery's contacts to isolate terminals. Isolating terminals prevents short-circuiting.

If original packaging is not available, effectively insulate battery terminals by isolating spare batteries from contact with other batteries and metal. Place each battery in its own protective case, plastic bag, or package. Do not permit a loose battery to come in contact with metal objects, such as coins, keys, or jewelry.

Only charge batteries which you are sure are rechargeable! Non-rechargeable batteries are not designed for re-charging, and become hazards if they are placed in a battery charger. NEVER attempt to recharge a battery unless you know it is rechargeable.

If you have already charged a non-rechargeable battery, do NOT bring such a battery on board an aircraft.

Use only chargers designed for your type of batteries. If unsure about compatibility, contact the product manufacturer.

Take steps to prevent crushing, puncturing, or putting a high degree of pressure on the battery, as this can cause an internal short-circuit, resulting in overheating.

FIGURE 11.34

explosion; and given the number and size of camera batteries that some of us pack for travel, a Li fire in one battery could quickly spread to others in the same case – with disastrous consequences if this were to occur aboard an aircraft in flight.

To minimize the potential risk, Li-ion batteries need proper care and feeding. A faulty charger or running a battery down too low can damage and prematurely age the Li-ion cells. As the cells age, their output voltage drops, with a dramatic increase in internal heat as the battery struggles to meet the needs demanded by the load. A fully depleted Li-ion battery produces enormous heat as it is recharged, and must come back up quickly. This is why it is never advisable to run batteries down to a point of total exhaustion.

Rental house batteries may be particularly prone to catastrophic failure because they are worked extremely hard and are more likely to be left on charge for long periods of time. Note that regulated charging systems like those from Anton Bauer closely monitor battery condition. When not in use, Li-ion batteries should be left powered up to these systems in order to ensure optimal battery performance and long life.

SHOOTING IN EXTREME WEATHER

Shooting in high heat and humidity poses its own set of challenges for today's shooters and processor-intensive cameras that produce substantial heat, even under normal conditions. For this reason, HD cameras are designed with large heat sinks to help draw surplus energy away from the lens mount where high temperatures can adversely affect *backfocus*. The heat concentrated around the base of the lens can lead to a noticeable softening of images, especially at wide-angle at full aperture.

Shooting in humid conditions can also lead to moisture potentially penetrating the camera's optics and promoting the growth of a lens-coating eating fungus. My beloved Zeiss 10–100 cine zoom was destroyed in the jungles of Central America by one such fungus; a sad and expensive lesson that has since prompted me to exercise greater care when shooting under such torrid conditions.

Solid-state cameras operating in extreme heat or cold have a compelling advantage over tape models; the cameras devoid of a mechanical transport are impervious to condensation, tape fouling, and clogged heads. Nevertheless, extreme cold can affect the performance and reliability of any camera by drawing down battery capacity, just when the camera needs it most to overcome the greater internal resistance. Very low temperatures can also slow the performance of solid-state memory cards, increasing the risk of dropped frames and other recording anomalies.

Of course, shooting in extreme conditions may be necessary due to story or schedule considerations. Bright sun can be a particular source of frustration owing to the difficulty making out the image on a camera's LCD screen. One solution is a low-cost plastic shade (Fig. 11.35c) that slides over a camera's swing-out viewfinder. Such hoods, and those that attach with Velcro tabs, are available to fit almost every type of camera or monitor.

(a)

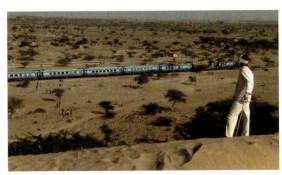

(b)

(c)

FIGURE 11.35
(a,b) Owing to the lack of a mechanical transport, solid-state cameras are well suited for shooting in a range of climatic conditions. An inexpensive hood (c) can be helpful for viewing a camera's LCD in bright sun.

FIGURE 11.36
The Beaufort Sea in winter: shooting at −60°F. While many camcorders will continue to operate at temperatures well below the manufacturers' specified range, the extreme cold may affect performance in subtle ways and shorten the life of a camera's internal components.

FIGURE 11.37
For winter shooting, thin polypropylene gloves offer protection from direct contact with a camera or tripod's metal surfaces, while still preserving the tactile sensitivity necessary to operate a camcorder's tiny controls.

BAD WEATHER ACCOUTREMENT

RAIN COVER

BAD ATTITUDE

STORM JACKET

POLYPROPYLENE GLOVES

GUMSOLE BOOTS

FIGURE 11.38
The resourceful shooter is ready for shooting in all kinds of weather.

(a) (b)

FIGURE 11.39
A camera glove (a) protects against physical impact and imparts a more robust feeling to any camcorder. Look for a design (b) that allows easy access to essential controls. Gloves are available for most camera models and are especially appropriate for expedition-style shooters.

FIGURE 11.40
Camera bags should have a reinforced top panel to protect a mic or sound module. Shooters have to ascertain whether a full-size bag is practical, given their particular travel needs.

FIGURE 11.41
This inflatable airline bag provides protection against overzealous folks violently jamming their copious belongings into a plane's overhead compartments.

FIGURE 11.42
For compact camcorders, I prefer a case that accepts the fully-configured camera with matte box ready to shoot.

CAMERA DUNKED IN SALT WATER!

It happens. It can cause heart palpitations. But what can the shooter do? The important thing is timing. The devastating effect of corrosive sea water is instantly diminished when diluted. So the sooner you get the camera into fresh water the better. Be sure to power the camera down and keep it submerged as you rush it to a repair shop. If the dunking occurs out to sea you can drop the patient into a large pail and cover it with fresh water or liquor. Tasteless American beer, which is so awful for drinking, is perfect for this application.

USE PROPER LANGUAGE

The use of appropriate jargon can help elevate your status as an accomplished video shooter. On a feature set or commercial, efficient communication is critical, as there are too many ways for things to go awry if each member of a crew is yelling or barking orders. Clearly, the director and talent can only do their best and most creative work if loud conversations between the shooter and various support crew are kept to a minimum.

For this reason, I recommend a system of gestures and hand signals. I've indicated a few of my favorites that I use in my camera department.

Feel free to utilize these at any time and you'll gain instant respect from your crew:

- I need an inky with some milky stuff!
- Can you take the curse off that red head?
- How about a tweenie with a cuke?
- What ever happened to the blondie and stinger?

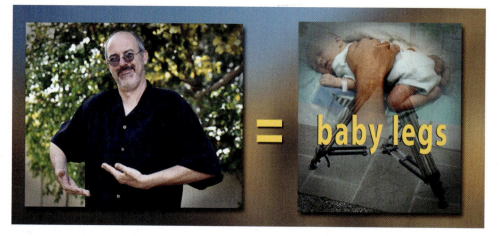

FIGURE 11.43
Bring the baby legs.

FIGURE 11.44
I need the high hat.

FIGURE 11.45
Fetch the French flag.

Translations

- I need a 200-W Fresnel with diffusion.
- I need a piece of light diffusion on a 1,000-W open-face instrument.
- I need a 650-W Fresnel ("between" an Inky and a Baby) with a cookaloris.
- I'm still waiting for that 2,000-W open-face light and extension cord.

THERE IS NO BEST BUTTON!

So, you're encoding your show for DVD in a popular compression program and you're faced with the option: Would you prefer *Good, Better,* or *Best?*

Hmm. I wonder why would anyone settle for Good or Better when you can have Best? Best is definitely better than Better, and Better by definition has to be better than Good. On the other hand, I suppose it's a good thing that Worse is not an option, because Worse is surely worse than Good, but it is better than much worse, and much much better than much much Worse.

All this mental wrangling raises the issue: Can there ever really be a *Best* button? Suppose we had a Best button for the video shooter. We wouldn't need to spend a lifetime learning lighting, composition, framing, and how to maximize texture and perspective. We wouldn't have to learn all the technical razzmatazz, the aesthetic subtleties, and silly names for things. Most importantly of all, we could forego the discipline of *exclude, exclude, exclude!* A Best button would do it all for us. What a glorious concept!

I recall 10 years ago working with *Master Tracks Pro,* a popular sequencing program for quasi-serious musicians. The program offered a *humanize* feature that I hadn't seen before and haven't seen since. Now, I'm a really rotten piano player, and when I see a quarter note I play it precisely as written like a robot. So the program worked splendidly for me. After one of my sessions devoid of feeling, I'd simply add a touch of *humanization* and presto – I'd have an inspired performance!

Of course, the program didn't really produce anything inspired at all; it merely moved my regularly placed quarter notes off the beat by a random amount. This had the effect of transforming my machine-like performance into the work of someone playing badly – an improvement perhaps but hardly the makings of a great musician.

The absurdity of autofocus, autoexposure and autohumanization is akin to the inanity of a Best button. Storytelling in whatever medium – video, music, print or spoken word – cannot be fashioned by autofunction or a generalized algorithm. Compelling video stories must be individually crafted and finessed, for despite their technical nature, they are fundamentally emotional experiences as far from the technology that enables them as one can get.

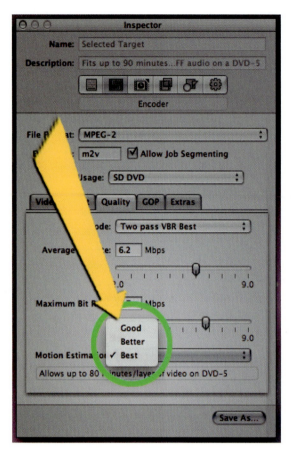

FIGURE 1
Apple Compressor presents the ultimate existentialist choice: Good is admittedly a good option. It's certainly not the Best option, however.

In the mid 1990s, University of Copenhagen researchers[1] monitored the brainwaves of audiences watching the identical content on film and video. The scientists noted that film audiences' brains produced an abundance of *alpha* waves, the kind of signals generated by humans in a relaxed state. The video group by comparison produced many more *beta* waves, the type emitted by the brain when it is stressed or otherwise under intense pressure.

How the brain perceives our video stories is especially critical in the area of 3D. While 3D has gained commercial traction in music videos, IMAX documentaries and animation, long-form dramatic programming has so far resisted the 3D urge. And why is that?

The viewing of 3D can be highly unnatural and even painful to audiences. Like the test subjects in Copenhagen who experienced increased discomfort viewing interlaced video, 3D presents a similar challenge to the processing centers in the brain. The 3D headache is a real and widely recognized phenomenon.

When properly produced, a 3D program does not force the viewer to hold a crossed-eye or splayed-eye position for extended periods of time. Appropriate consideration must be given at all times during a production to the technical craft, including left-right eye alignment, parallax distance, rotation, and scale. The framing of close-ups in 3D is especially critical if a comfortable audience-viewing experience is to be ensured.

RESOLUTION WITHOUT PERFORMANCE

This understanding of how audiences perceive our images is crucial to selecting the right camera for a job. Currently, we are seeing intense pressure on manufacturers to produce cameras with very high-resolution imagers. But is this what we really want or need? Why is more resolution better, especially at the price of good performance and acceptable dynamic range – the two capabilities that *really* matter in a camera system? In all likelihood, your audience is not counting pixels on screen or evaluating you as a master storyteller of resolution refer charts. Hopefully your stories are more interesting than that.

---

[1] "Film Versus Video: What Happens When Motion Pictures are Transferred to Videotape," January 1993 University of Copenhagen.

FIGURE 2
Go ahead. Give yourself a 3D headache. Hold your fingers 2 inches from your nose and concentrate. You get a headache from forcing your eyes to act in an unnatural way, and the brain struggles to fuse the image from both eyes into a single image.

FIGURE 3
Close attention to the technical craft is critical for success-ful 3D programs. This prototype camera from Panasonic holds the promise of simpler, more accessible 3D tools in the future.

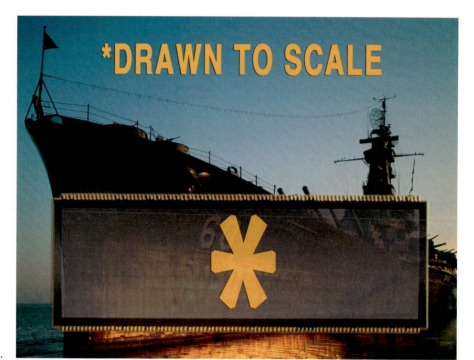

FIGURE 4
Is an imager the size of a battleship really what you want or need? Resolution without performance makes no sense at all.

FIGURE 5
What will the future bring for cameras in a changing landscape?

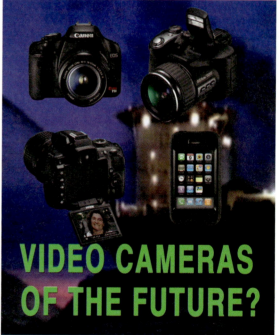

FIGURE 6
What kinds of devices will capture tomorrow's video stories?

OUR PERSONAL BRAND

As the industry of video storytelling drives inexorably Webward, shooters face the challenge now of somehow deriving a viable income from the new marketplace. Content creators of all types are turning to unusual ways to realize financial gain. One major Hollywood record label, for example, has moved on from largely selling CDs and DVDs to licensing ring tones! For the average shooter then, the question becomes how do we find success on the Web, when many folks using the same low-cost cameras and equipment are seemingly content to offer their videos and other creative products for free?

In this daunting new universe, shooters must strive to be recognized for high quality content beyond what the public might expect for free. Developing a personal brand is critical to achieving this goal.

Our personal brand reflects how potential clients, employers and the public as a whole regard us. What image pops up when someone mentions

FIGURE 7
Content is king and so is your brand. You build it. Your audience will come.

FIGURE 8
Stay true to your brand. Your success depends on it.

our name? As shooters are we known for our work photographing beer or birds? Warthogs or bicycles? Can we ski backwards down expert slopes capturing Bode Miller or shoot handheld inside a crowded bar with elegance and grace?

Our personal brand might include signature shots such as extreme close-ups, rapid swish pans, or attention-grabbing compositions.

Producers and networks recognize our brand, what we can offer, and what we're about. Our brand persists and, over time, can add immeasurable value to a project. As a shooter, developing a brand is the single best investment we can make in ourselves. Folks will follow and seek out our brand if they can readily identify what that brand is and have developed a high level of confidence in it.

YOU DON'T NEED MUCH TO TELL A GREAT STORY

It's a dog-eat-digital world out there, and some of us will always be more talented than others in seeing it, framing it, and lighting it. For these folks they can rest easy because there will always be a demand for such specialists at the highest end of the industry. But for the rest of us and for the vast majority of shooters today, the economics of digital media are such that adept use of the camera is just one element in a much greater skill set. To stay relevant and prosperous, today's shooter must understand and embrace the complete odyssey from script and storyboard to display in a digital cinema or streaming over the Web. The process is long and complex, filled with romance, technical challenges and the shifting currents of change, and the shooter who understands it all, the opportunities and perils, will continue to do well wherever the journey may take him.

FIGURE 9
The shooter storyteller is in for quite a ride. Make sure you enjoy it!

Index